AUSTRALIAN COWBOYS ROUGHRIDERS & RODEOS

JENNY HICKS

While every effort has been made to contact the copyrightholders of material contained in this work, in some cases details are missing, illegible or insufficient. The publisher welcomes any information in relation to missing credits or acknowledgements.

Copyright 2002 Jenny Hicks

This book is copyright. Apart from any fair dealing for the purpose of private study, research, criticism or review, as permitted under the Copyright Act of 1968, no part may be reproduced by any process without written permission. Enquiries should be made to the publisher.

First published in Australia in 2000
Reprinted in 2000, 2001 by HarperCollins*Publishers* Pty Limited

Published in 2003 by CQU Press
Distributed by
CQU Press
PO Box 1615, Rockhampton Queensland, 4700
Ph: (07) 4923 2520
Fax: (07) 4923 2525
Email: cqupress@cqu.edu.au
www.outbackbooks.com

National Library of Australia
Cataloguing-in-Publication data:

Hicks, Jenny (Jennifer Ann), 1963 —
Australian Cowboys, Roughriders and Rodeos.

1. Rodeos — Australia — History
2. Rodeos — Australia
1. Title

Cover photographs courtesy of Mike Kenyon — www.kenyonsportsphotos.com.au
Printed and bound in Australia by Griffin Press

ACKNOWLEDGMENTS

There are tens of thousands of Australian roughriders, cowboys and cowgirls who are not mentioned in this book. The rodeo champions who are in the book only became great because they had plenty of tough competition. As there are no icebergs in these parts this book, you might say, is only the tip of the anthill. I hope it inspires others to write their rodeo stories down for posterity.

Thankyous: First and foremost to my family — Diana and Michael Hicks, for showing me the joys in travel and adventure, reading and writing; and together with my sister, Sarah, for their love and wholehearted support of my every endeavour. And, of course, the dog — my mad friend and travelling companion. Likewise my friends (all over the place), who keep the jokes coming, the meals, the drinks, the words of wisdom and reassurance — friends who make life rich.

Thanks to all at Central Queensland University Press for picking up this book and taking it out to the bush where it belongs. CQU Press specialises in outback books - see www.outbackbooks.com. My special thanks to Jane Dorrington who did the new cover design and Mike Kenyon for so generously supplying the cover photos. It has been a pleasure to work together with Old Silvertail, Professor David Myers, the publisher of CQU Press.

Thanks to all the people who rang and wrote to me, who shared their stories, told me of others and pointed me in the right direction. I had a million conversations over cups of tea or beers in homes — grand or shacks — pubs, truck-stops, caravans, at rodeos, on the phone, in hospitals, on street corners and in supermarkets. Everyone, it seems, has a rodeo story; alas, I could not fit them all in one book.

The heart of this book is the interviews I had with about 130 rodeo people, all of whom inspired me in one way or another and most of whom you could write a whole book about. A hundred and thirty is too many people to list. I thank you all for sharing your memories as well as your tables and roofs. I appreciate that it is not easy to trust strangers, especially one armed with a camera and a tape recorder. Thanks for the trust and the good will, especially to those I have quoted. As I travelled around the countryside, most interviewees were quick to offer a bed or a verandah for my swag. These hospitable people include Herb Wharton, the late, great, Wally Mailman and his wife, Jane, Larry Dulhunty, Pat Peters — who spoiled me rotten — Robert McPhee, Jan Seeney, Des (Yogi) and Lyn Steffensen — Taroom was the hardest town to leave. Darcy Twohill, Mike and Robin Kenyon, David Briggs and Bill Gunn, Colin McTaggart and Sharon Hamilton, Bonnie Young and Donna, Vic Gough and Betty, Reece Kennedy, Lionel and Adele and John and Lilian Stanton. I would also like to thank my adopted families out west — the Listers, the Murrays, the Kendalls and the Hitsons.

Writing this book has been a mighty effort, which was bolstered by family and friends. In addition I would like to thank those who shared their knowledge and then through mutual interest kept checking in with encouragement and more information.

They include Darrell Lewis, David Briggs, Eddie Hackman and Bill Wilkinson. Colin McTaggart and John Stanton graciously received the most who/what/when/where/why phone calls. Charlie Webster has stuck by me through rodeo thick and thin for years. Michelle Tonkin, Melissa McCord and Elsie Ritchie have all sagaciously averted author-type hysterics at one time and another.

Thanks to all the people at the helpful historical societies, libraries and rodeo committees and associations. In particular, my gratitude goes to Lang Lang rodeo committee for permission to reproduce material from an early rodeo program; the Diamantina rodeo committee (Winton), who shared their collection of photos; and all at the Australian Pro Rodeo Association's head office in Warwick, for assisting with continual queries and requests. Chris Gladwell at the Australian Stockmen's Hall of Fame head office in Brisbane was extremely helpful, as was Don Tilmouth at R.M Williams's headquarters in Prospect, SA. Thanks also to The Heritage Centre of the Sydney Royal Agricultural Society, The Australian Stockmen's Hall of Fame, the Mitchell and Oxley Libraries and the State Library of Victoria — all for their prompt efficiency as well as permission to reproduce their images. Rosemary Block from the oral history department of the State Library of NSW also gave me some very good advice.

I am indebted to those who trod the trail before me — Mark St Leon, Judy Cannon and Jim Fogarty, for their work in circus history; John Vaughan and Eric Watson, for Country and Western music history; Stan Rowett and Fred Hausler for recording the Marrabel Rodeo story; Bob Morgan, who knew all about the Melbourne RAS; Pat Studdy-Clift, about Miss Kemp; and Richard W. Slatta for his *Cowboy Encyclopedia* — an invaluable (American) reference book. I'd especially like to thank Jack Pollard, who wrote *The Horse Tamer* about Lance Skuthorpe Snr, and Ray McConville, who compiled and published *Thorpe McConville's Wild Australia* — I relied heavily on both books for information on these two great roughriding showmen.

Thankyous to Elsie Ritchie, for helping me with much of the research at the Mitchell Library, and my sister for doing likewise at the State Library of Victoria. My father and Helen Hall also did some library research for me; my mother did a fantastic job typing up most of the transcripts; and Sam Geldens also helped us with that huge task.

I am grateful to those who have generously allowed me to use photographs from their personal collections. Once again, there are too many to mention here. To all the photographers, many of whom are unknown (but appreciated), and especially to Mike Kenyon and Keith Stevens for permission to use their pictures. Also to Robin Yates for permission to reproduce his illustration of John Stanton. Thanks to the authors who allowed me to quote from their books. Ellen Johnson on behalf of her late husband, Don; Jack Scott; Judy Cannon; Mark St Leon; Jack Pollard; Andrea Lemon; Jill Bowen; Jim Lowden; Russel Ward; and R.M.Williams. Also to Rural Press, by whose courtesy the quotes and advertisements of *Hoofs and Horns* magazine appear and to R.M. Williams and Keith Stevens again, for making this magazine such a great record of Australian rodeo history.

CONTENTS

Acknowledgments		iii
Foreword		1
Introduction	Welcome to rodeo	7
Chapter 1	Early days	11
Chapter 2	Travelling buckjump shows	23
Chapter 3	The rope ring and the tent shows	55
Chapter 4	Bushmen's carnivals	93
Chapter 5	The dawn of professionalism	127
Chapter 6	The swinging 60s	161
Chapter 7	Rodeo today	189
Appendix I	Description of modern rodeo events	224
Appendix II	List of Australian champions	226
Endnotes		232
Index		235
Picture credits		241

FOREWORD

AUSTRALIA HAS ALWAYS HAD a great tradition of horsemanship. Our laconic bush stockmen and heroic Light Horsemen of World War I shimmer distantly in the national psyche. The poet horsemen Adam Lindsay Gordon and Harry 'Breaker' Morant and the legendary Man from Snowy River are still household names, along with our champion racehorse trainers, Bart Cummings and the late, great Tommy Smith. Australian horsemen and women have always been at the forefront of international competitions including the most gruelling of them all, the three-day event at the Olympic Games.

But it's a little-known fact that our rodeo competitors are also winning international competitions. At the time of writing, an Australian, Troy Dunn, is the world champion bullrider and another three of our cowboys are in the top 15 of the world standings in their event.[1]

Mention the word 'cowboy' and people the world over immediately think of the American cowboy. Rodeo has long been called 'the all-American' sport'. In Australia we've heard of horsemen and stockmen, but Australian cowboys?

And yet Australian rodeo has a rich and colourful history. The Australian frontier was every bit as dramatic as the American West. It was a vast, rugged, dusty place to be — 'The Outback'. Contemporary Australian rodeo has its roots in circuses, travelling Wild West shows and in cattlemen's carnivals and sports days. It started as entertainment, a bit of a lark, a wager or a challenge for a few extra bob but Australian rodeo has been an officially organised and highly competitive sport for well over 50 years. We are respected members of the World Rodeo Association, a joint venture of the professional associations of the USA, Canada, New Zealand and Australia, and our standard of national competition, particularly the roughstock riding, is second to none. Our cowboys have been winning the major roughriding competitions in North America and Canada for 40 years.

Yet scour the annals of Australian sporting history and you'll find few references to rodeo or rodeo cowboys. There's horse racing, the Olympic teams and polo, but virtually nothing about 'Western' horse events, such as campdrafting, cutting and roughriding. Despite our many international successes the occasional mentions rodeo has in Australian literature tend to be in books about horses and horsemen, bushmen, stockmen, the outback, showmen and Country and Western women, usually in autobiographies or biographies.

Australian rodeo has never been evaluated by social or sporting historians and is rarely regarded as a serious competitive sport by journalists or the urban general public. There is the odd segment on television where, lured by the danger, journalists or media personalities ogle at the costumes and pageantry, marvel at the apparent recklessness and predictably get a good shot of a cowboy getting pummelled by a bull. And apart from our Country and Western and hillbilly singers, Tex Morton, Buddy Williams, Reg Lindsay and Slim Dusty, for example, Australian rodeos and cowboys are scarcely mentioned in popular culture either.

If Australian cowboys are largely ignored in their own country it isn't because they are invisible but because they are 'out there'. They have grown out of 'the bush' — the popular term for rural Australia — where rodeo is still a big part of life. Consequently their evolution from working stockmen and horsebreakers to modern-day athletes has not been noticed by our predominantly urban population, whose knowledge of sport is fed by the network-based sports reports. Other than in sport, horse and stock skills are no longer a part of mainstream culture. Because 80 per cent of Australians are out of touch with the land and its lifestyle, our cowboys and cowgirls are out of sight, out of mind and beyond comprehension.

Not only has Australian rodeo been overlooked as a national pastime, entertainment venture and competition which spans well over a century of Australian history, its development into a multimillion-dollar industry and professional sport has also escaped notice. Rodeo in Australia is the centre of a 200 million dollar a year industry that attracts considerable corporate sponsorship and dishes out hundreds of thousands of dollars in prize money and donations to charity. Rodeos are run nationally by local committees that are coordinated and monitored by a number of rodeo associations which organise insurance for the riders; set standards, rules and regulations; and award annual championship titles. Currently, there are approximately 7000 members competing in anything up to 400 points-award rodeos a year, in front of an estimated million and a half spectators. This does not include the weekly roping jackpots or roughstock-only competitions, like the bullrides, which also number in their hundreds and often pull crowds bigger than rodeos.

~FOREWORD~

Nearly every country town in Australia has a rodeo history. In some the rodeo tradition lives on and has become a part of the community's identity — Warwick boasts 'Australia's most famous rodeo', Mt Isa has 'Australia's biggest rodeo' and Marrabel has its statue of legendary buckjumper, Curio, and their Rodeo Hall of Fame. Tumbarumba, Lang Lang, Kyabram, Mareeba, Tamworth, Winton, Richmond, Rockhampton and Townsville are just a few of our stalwart rodeo towns. And the cities have also had plenty of action. Sydney's Royal Agricultural Society has run its annual rodeo for over 60 years.

Rodeo is a fantastic spectator sport for all the family. To the uninformed it may appear to be a bunch of reckless men and women in flash outfits roping cattle or falling off horses, but it is in fact a complex sport requiring strength, agility, balance, timing and lightning-fast reflexes. Rodeo schools are conducted in each event and like in the United States rodeo is becoming one of the sports at our schools and colleges. A number of Australian cowboys have been given rodeo scholarships to American universities. The bucking stock are no longer wild but are carefully bred; contestants train constantly and, like any professional athletes, the sport dominates their lives.

Our rodeo history is elusive, anecdotal and steeped in folklore, myth and apocryphal tales. Author David Malouf once said, '... history, as we commonly conceive of it, is not what happened, but what gets recorded and told. Most of what happens escapes the telling because it is too common, too repetitious to be worth recording.'[2] Although rodeo has been a form of popular entertainment in Australia since European colonists first arrived with their horses and cattle, exceedingly little has been recorded of rodeo's early days. Perhaps the fact that rodeo has always been a working-man's sport had something to do with that. Early rodeo-type contests were simply an extension of the lives of people who all rode, all day, every day. Those who took part in them were mostly horsebreakers, stockmen, drovers, travelling showmen and professional roughriders whose itinerant lifestyles meant they didn't keep or collect things. Very few had formal educations, or the time to write if they did. And there were no cameras. So we are left with an oral history which is fading fast.

Australian stockmen and women have their counterparts — the cowboy, *vaquero, campista, savanero, charro, gaucho, huaso, llanero* and *paniolo* — living and working in the cattle kingdoms of the United States, Canada, New Zealand, Mexico, Argentina, Brazil, Venezuela, Colombia, Uruguay, Chile, Hawaii and in parts of Europe, China and Africa. All of them have been riding bucking horses for fun or a wager ever since they discovered there were horses that liked to buck. History shows us that wherever there was a large-scale cattle industry, those men and women were generally isolated, with few resources, and they had to invent their own methods, or adapt known methods of horse and cattle management. These were often rough and ready because they worked on a large scale and what they did was physically hard and dangerous. They invented their own sports and entertainment based on what was at hand and what they were good at. Inevitably they developed contests of working skills and inevitably these were also rough, physically hard and dangerous. Regardless of who allegedly invented what, where and when, cattlemen and women everywhere came up with similar methods of work and play in their own time.

This book is about the Australian rodeo experience, but the origins of the sport as we know it today are undoubtedly Spanish-American. When the Spanish colonised New Spain (Mexico) and Florida in the sixteenth century, they brought with them cattle, domesticated horses and animal-husbandry skills. The locals who survived the invasion took to horsemanship like ducks to water and soon enough a race of centaurs was born. Mexicans derived their saddles, bit, their long open reins, the lasso and their mode of mounting in one motion after the style of the northern Europeans, from the Spanish. They in turn had inherited it from the Moors who conquered Spain from northwest Africa in the sixth century.[3]

Horses and cattle gradually spread from the great haciendas of northern Mexico up through Texas and California to the great open spaces of the USA. Long before rodeos started in North America, Mexican equestrian displays and competitions were being held, called *charreadas*. Many of the terms modern cowboys use are corrupted or literal Spanish words — cinch (a girth) from *cincha*, lariat (a rope) from *la reata*, dally (tie your rope) from *dar la vuelta*, meaning take a turn, chaps from *chaparreras*, buckaroo from *vaquero*, ranch from *rancho*, and of course rodeo from *rodear*, which means a gathering place of cattle (a round-up) or to go round. By the 1880s rodeo came to mean a tournament, a competition and/or exhibition of cattlemen's skills. These local competitions on ranches and at cow towns at the end of trail drives included ranchwork skills plus events imported from *vaquero* and *charro* practices in California and Mexico.

The Americans' domination of rodeo stems from their entrepreneurialism, promotional savvy and superior marketing skills. They promoted rodeo to their

~FOREWORD~

considerable ticket-buying public early on and turned it into big business. Rodeo-type contests and tournaments were being held in the USA as early as the 1840s. Spectators were paying to get in by the 1880s, and these bigger and better-promoted rodeos and 'grand cowboy tournaments' were giving cash prizes and trophies.

The Americans reinvented, popularised and marketed their 'Wild West' so successfully that Australians came to favour American myths and icons over their home-grown ones. America has a tradition of enterprise, of people who could make a buck out of anything that moves. In Australia we have often been more inclined to bet on anything that moves and lose our bucks.

In capitalising on their history Americans developed showmanship and exploited nostalgia and romance. Australians found showmanship and self-promotion distasteful and untrustworthy and tended to be cynical or at least irreverent. The accusation 'poser' can still strike horror in the hearts of most Australians. Apart from our bushrangers, diggers and our sporting heroes, we rarely romanticise or glamorise our history. The Americans have a natural gift for mythmaking; we tend to prefer realism. The Australian stockman's character — developed out of isolation, hard work and simple living — was modest. Hence a great proportion of our champion riders were also modest, self-effacing and easygoing. That's why we don't hear much about them. The Americans had none of our problems of cultural cringe; neither did they concern themselves with sticking to the truth about their past if it was going to spoil a good story or a good show.

The American cowboy is one of the world's most enduring heroes and an icon for the American ideals of freedom and independence. The man, the myth and the legend have sold a trillion tickets and captivated our imaginations. He is instantly and universally recognisable in hat, chaps, boots and spurs, as is the entire Western genre, its themes, music and landscapes. All the cowboy's accessories are Western symbols — the lariat, belt buckles, bucking horses, long-horned cattle, horseshoes, cattle brands, chaps, hats, Western saddles, the list goes on. John Wayne, Clint Eastwood and the Marlboro Man have had a lot to do with it but there were hundreds before and after them.

American 'pop culture' aside, the fact remains that most Australians have no idea we have our own cowboys. A whole generation has grown up lacking knowledge of Australian bush heritage and culture and it is precisely during these last 40 years that our stockmen and roughriders have transformed themselves into professional rodeo cowboys and cowgirls, competing in a hard-core international sport.

Australian rodeo cowboys and cowgirls are a fantastic mixture of fact and fiction. As the 'real life' descendants of the traditional Australian stockmen and horsemen they represent our bush heritage cross-bred with the American cowboy. They started out as working horsemen, stockmen and roughriders who competed against each other on the weekend but they were inspired by the showmanship and commercial viability of the American rodeo cowboys. Today they run American-style events in American attire and use American lingo but they have developed the professional skills necessary to give legitimacy. They are true athletes competing in a sport that is expertly run for the entertainment of the crowd. It's Australian stockmen heroics dressed up in American cowboy style.

Rodeo might be a whiz-bang international sport now, and modern Australian cowboys and cowgirls may look like they've stepped straight out of the American west, but that is a recent development in the scheme of things and a superficial one at that. Look beneath the costumes at who they are, what they do and where they came from and you've got more Australian heritage than you can poke a stick at.

INTRODUCTION

Welcome to Rodeo

Usually it seems it's a hot afternoon, with flies for company and hats and sunnies for survival. But rodeo is always a festive affair, whether it kicks off at sunset or goes sixteen hours a day for a couple of days straight. The first thing you notice is the children — everywhere, and running amok. The rodeo grounds bustle with activity, expectation and excitement. A steady stream of people and horses weaves through a jumble of trucks, trailers, caravans, goosenecks, utes and portaloos. Drying washing and electric fences criss-cross the maze, adding to the obstacle course, as do the deceptively lolling cattle dogs chained to the vehicles — they'll take your leg off if you come within reach. Cowboys and cowgirls practise their roping on hay bales, prepare their horses or lug buckets of water and feed. Others lie about, conserving energy. More carloads arrive just in time for the show.

Spectators find a spot and settle in. Some come every year, rain, hail or shine, decked out in their personal Western styles. Old bushies are in R.M.s, plain shirts and Akubras; top-to-toe cowboy kids sport cowboy hats, boots, belt buckles, loud shirts, Wrangler jeans and six-shooters. Families sprawl on blankets, old couples sit patiently in the stands, teenagers check out the talent, best friends do the rounds. The water truck is busy over the dirt tracks and around the arena, trying to settle the dust that is suspended over everything.

It's show time. The brightly painted arena and colourful chute gates are alive with sponsors' banners, flags and bunting. There are stars and stripes, lots of red, white and blue, and Western designs and motifs galore. Florid shirts; big white hats; flashy chaps; silver and gold spangle. Glamorous cowgirls in lipstick and jewellery sit straight-backed as they jig-jog by. Sleek and shiny horses — creaking leather and clinking bits and bridles — heads high, ears pricked forwards, fit to busting and proud to be admired.

It's carnival atmosphere. Sideshows are in full swing — gaudy caravans sell fairy floss and dagwood dogs; tents; tarps; the jumping castle; and dodgem cars. The queue at the baked potato van banks up, enveloped by the waft of sizzling sausages and steak sandwiches, cattle and horse smells. Children rush, parents lag. Stalls of Western clothing crop up beside trucks and under tents. Photographers sell action shots from rodeos gone by.

Over at the secretary's office, entry fees are rolling in, unloaded from wallets dug out of tight jeans — notes counted, names ticked, jokes cracked. What's the news; who rode who; when and where and how; and who's drawn what today?

Gear bags and saddles are dumped. Out come the chaps, boots, spurs, ropes, bandages, support braces, straps, wraps, Dencorub, resin, riggings, protective vests and helmets. Time-event cowboys and cowgirls are adjusting leather and warming up their horses. Round and round they circle, meditatively, swinging ropes and nodding g'days to passers-by.

Back to the ring in front of the chutes. The announcer, judges and chute bosses cluster over names and numbers. Behind, stock contractors are unloading, sifting and sorting; yard workers whistle and shout. Dust spirals everywhere. There's stomping and snorting and bellowing, snickering and whinnying, and the occasional bitchy squeal. Down the other end of the arena milling steers are sorted, run through the crushes and up the race. Horses are readied, ropes coiled and recoiled.

'Testing, testing, one, two, three.' Country music fades in and out amidst the announcements. Cowboys and cowgirls line the top rail around the chutes and time-events boxes. 'Stockyard liars' lurk amongst them and along the bar, which is headquarters, and it's frantic there all day. It's mostly beer and rum, scotch bourbon and cigarettes if you're lucky — but they'll be the first to run out.

Rolling slams of slide gates signal that the horses are in the chutes and action's about to begin. Cowboys lean over the rails expertly adjusting riggings or saddles and flanks, or perch like cockatoos to watch the goings-on. The microphone crackles to life with those ageless words, 'Ladieeeees and Gennelmen'... Grand parade — manes and tails and flags and banners flying — hats off for the national

~INTRODUCTION~

anthem, or a verse or two. Then the announcer's away as the first horse bucks out. He's the ringmaster, holding it all together, hour in hour out for four hours or 40.

The crowd applauds when it should, cheers and yells when it's good. Plenty of experts, old-timers who did it harder with tougher stock, friends and relations of the contestants. The odd city slicker and tourist wanders about, dazed, easy to spot by the pristine Akubra, shorts and sandals and a look of bewildered enchantment. Country classics lilt on the breeze — Willie and Waylon, Slim Dusty, Gina Jeffreys, Garth Brooks, country rock. The bulls get pure rock 'n' roll, AC/DC, and George Thorogood. Switching from one end of the arena to the other it's roughstock, time event, roughstock, time event.

From behind the chutes and time-event boxes comes a bellowing bedlam of dust, sweat and tension. Thudding hooves rumble constantly. Slide gates slam, wooden chute gates and rusty hinges creak, clank, bang. From the yards come snorting, swearing, shouting. Time-event name callers cut through the lot. Psyching up — think, don't think, be calm, be ready — suppressed energy, concentration, adrenalin. Each horse and rider enters, backs and readies, nods and charges out. With a thunder of hooves and a flash and a flurry, each run is over five to ten seconds later. More dust, more applause. Tenths of seconds separate winning and losing. Judges and chute boss huddle further over names, numbers and times. The announcer keeps on talking, and the music keeps on playing.

Centaur-like pick-up men gallop gallantly, horses sweating or waiting patiently. Comedy clowns tell bad jokes about blondes, mothers-in-law and politicians. The crowd eats, drinks, and eats and drinks some more. There's the taste of dust, the touch of sun, wind or rain. Either lying on the grass or trudging through mud, or sitting on a bum-numbing wooden stand, there's that never-ending parade of cowboys and cowgirls on foot and on horseback to watch go by.

Bulls get the crowd's undivided attention. Last event on the program. Worth waiting for. Almost everyone gapes and winces. Children yell at the 'bad old bulls' and teenage girls scream for certain cowboys. Someone gets a pummelling — gasp; delicious horror. Kids swarm the fence to ogle the limp body and jump back quickly as the bull skips by with a glint in his eye and a haughty flick of his tail. Cheers from the crowd as the steamrolled rider drags himself to his feet and staggers, heroic, back behind the chutes.

Rodeo. Every weekend, somewhere in Australia, it'll be happening. It's a brilliant spectacle, a great day out for the family — it'll wear the kids out. Yes, it's tiring, very tiring — long drive to get there, long day or night outside, then head to the roar of the bar for a beer or a rum. Later the band turns it on, then turns it up to be heard over the cacophony or shouting and laughter, rum and beer and beer and rum. Under big hats and party lights, contestants regale each other with the day's dramas as they ride and rope them all again. The dancing gets going, the sensible hit the sack. More beer and rum, and the locals are looking bleary and sometimes falling over and sometimes fighting and arms over shoulders — making a mess of it — till the booze runs out.

1

EARLY DAYS

And Clancy of the Overflow came down to lend a hand,

No better horseman ever held the reins;

For never horse could throw him while the saddle-girths would stand—

He learnt to ride while droving on the plains

The Australian pastoral scene

**YDNEY, 1788: ONLY TWO** of Governor Arthur Phillip's horses survived the first couple of years in the fledgling colony; most of the sheep died or were 'lost'; and his small herd of cattle also disappeared. Neither stolen nor eaten, the cattle had escaped and they went feral. Over the years they could be seen grazing, fat and happy, along the western side of the Nepean River. Their numbers grew as they eluded all efforts to catch them. Their favourite spot was set aside and called the 'Cowpastures' and by 1810 it was estimated there were between 4000 and 5000 of them. About six years later it was officially noticed that the wild cattle herd had suddenly reduced by about three-quarters, and this, it was speculated, was probably due to the establishment of Aires County just down the track.

Aires County was a stretch of fertile bush along the Nepean that Governor Macquarie, who arrived in 1809, had reserved for the granting of land for small farms. Many of the recipients were the emancipists, or freed convicts, known as the 'men of County Wicklow'. They were accomplished cattlemen from the mountain clans of Ireland who had been sent to Australia for their part in the Irish uprisings of 1798 and 1803. Macquarie presumed they would have the necessary skills to make a go of the Nepean runs, and he was right. But they also had the nous to duff the government's wild cattle, which they then branded as their own. And why not? No-one else Macquarie sent out could get past the wild bulls, let alone catch them. It wasn't till 1819 — when Lieutenant John Macarthur employed George Johnston, 'Australia's first truly notable stockman and cattle musterer' — that any 'official' attempt at capturing the cattle was met with any success. It wasn't an entirely auspicious beginning for our cattle industry.[1]

In 1806 brothers John and Gregory Blaxland arrived in the new colony and were granted a block on the Nepean. Over the years they established Sydney's first dairy and opened a butcher's shop, which saw the end of the colony's dependence on salted beef shipped in from England.

However, it quickly became apparent that wool was the premium investment and English companies, based in London and Manchester, bought up millions of acres of land and employed managers to run their properties and stations. The majority of independent pastoralists also made their fortunes in wool, and a huge export market developed. The saying, 'Australia rides on the sheep's back', aptly described the burgeoning economy. Though a lot of people became rich very quickly and the majority of the early pastoralists concentrated on wool the cattlemen's presence was always apparent.

As each new penal settlement was established the cattlemen provided beef for food and hides and fat for leather and tallow. The cattle business may have played second fiddle to the lucrative wool business, but it kept everyone alive and soon developed a smaller but substantial export market of canned and salted meat products. Because most affluent and influential squatters and absentee landowners were primarily wool men, cattlemen often ended up where sheep didn't prosper, or where the dingoes were too thick. Very hard or rough country, very dry country, very steep or snow country — this was cattle country. There were cattle among the sheep of course but the far north and north-west of the continent was, and still is, cattle country.[2]

Rodeo has its roots in the frontier grazing industry and developed as a form of entertainment for cattlemen. Most modern rodeo families and individuals are direct descendants of these outback pioneers. Unlike the sheep men, cattlemen's working skills were dangerous and dramatic enough to entertain the public, and rodeo events were originally competitions based on their work practices. The establishment and development of the Australian cattle industry is the historical and cultural backbone of the sport of rodeo as we know it today and no other sport reflects Australia's bush heritage better.

Our early pastoralists were accustomed to small stock herds on small farms, perhaps 10 or 20 head of cattle with a few dairy cows roaming a few acres, not 10 or 20 thousand cattle roaming the formidable and fenceless bush. Far from the quaint green fields of 'home', *Terra Australis Incognita* was a gigantic wild forest full of strange flora and fauna with an uncertain yet seemingly hostile climate. Within 50 years of white settlement it was teeming with hundreds of thousands of sheep and cattle that had to be managed and moved about.

Into this harsh and unpredictable world the colonists brought with them two familiar and faithful things — the horse and the hound, and together they improvised. Utilising green-hide (untanned leather) and the multi-purpose stringy-bark tree, the bushmen built slab huts and adapted their previously known methods of stock handling. Over the years they developed their own styles of mustering, drafting, branding and droving to suit the prevailing conditions. Methods varied with climate, geography, stock numbers and finances. Stock whips grew out of a normal whip, and were used as a defence weapon as well as a motivational tool. Stock saddles were adapted from the English saddles and the bushmen developed their own style of loose-fitting clothing, including wide-brimmed cabbage-tree hats to keep off the sun. The dogs and horses they brought out evolved, too. Kelpie sheepdogs were developed as a breed in the 1870s and the blue heeler cattle dog was an official breed by the late 1890s.

Horses were their lives

In all colonial experience, in the city, the bush and especially in the frontier pastoral world, the thing most needed after shelter, food and water was a horse. For transport, communication, work, play, whoever they were and whatever they did, the people of early Australia had one thing in common — horses.

In 1795 good mares were imported from the Cape of Good Hope and four years later our first English-bred stallion arrived. From the beginning we were importing horseflesh from the racing communities of England and Ireland. Ireland in particular is noted for its horses and horsebreeding, and so we have always had fine horses, fast horses, spirited horses mixed with strong working horses. Horsemanship and horsebreeding and breaking were integral to life. By 1821 it was estimated the colony had 4564 horses and a small export trade had begun. By 1901 there was some 1 700 000 horses on record,[3] let alone those unaccounted for, and in 1905 we exported over 20 000 horses, primarily to China, India and Japan.

Horseracing was the first and most popular of sports in the colony but racehorses in the bush were for the rich squatters and their nemeses and menaces, the bushrangers. To live any length of time, these bush-dwelling bandits had to have a combination of bush survival skills, the shrewdness to pick the best horses around to borrow or steal and the skill and daring to outride their pursuers. The rest of the bush folk haphazardly bred what horses they needed, depending on their profession. The hardy, versatile, 'big-hearted' breed that evolved was exported and became known around the world as the (New South) Whaler. Much later still, with a lot more thought and thoroughbred blood, we developed the Australian Stockhorse. Nineteenth-century Australian horses astonished early European travellers with their stamina, stock sense, courage and ability to buck rider, saddle, bridle and all straight off over their heads. Like the people who bred and rode them, much has been written of the endurance and adaptability of the Australian horses. The first hundred years is where they had it pummelled into them.

You could judge someone's wealth and position in society not just by their clothes, manner of speech and demeanour, but by their horse. Surveying the horses tied up at a shanty pub, you'd know who was there by the horse or the brand on it, and if not who, then what their business was and whether they were a good judge of horse flesh. This in turn defined their experience and character — not too much different from being able to 'read' the cars, utes and trucks parked outside a bush pub these days.

So if a person's horse was a measure of their wealth, trade or standing in society, because it represented their livelihood, *horsemanship* was a measure of their character as well as their abilities. A person was judged by their horse *and* their horse skills. Horsemanship was a great measure of manhood in general (along with a man's drinking and fighting abilities) but nowhere more so than on cattle stations.

Large cattle stations, particularly in the semi-arid pastoral zones necessarily covered hundreds of thousands even millions of acres and could have 500–600 horses on the books, not to mention the ones not on the books or the brumbies. Such a station might have had three mustering 'camps' based in the bush away from the main homestead and out-stations. The men could stay out there for months for the annual muster, finding the cattle, sifting and sorting them, branding the youngsters and treating the old and ailing. Bullocks were separated and sent to market. Each camp might have 10 stockmen, a cook and a horse tailer. Each stockman was assigned three horses that he rode alternately during the weeks they were mustering; the cook would have his pack horses and/or horses to pull his wagon; and there were spare horses in case of wrecks or horses going lame. Each horse tailer, whose job was to look after them all, may have had to gather 40 or 50 horses every morning. With three camps, that meant 150 horses in active duty throughout the mustering season. Then there were the station's mares, stallions, foals, unbroken horses and rogues, so it's easy to see how a station could have so many horses. This continued to be the case right up until the 1960s, when mechanisation began to change the business.

Bushrangers weren't the only ones who survived by their horsemanship — stockmen did, too. A stockman needed a horse that was sure-footed, able to negotiate trees, scrub and hidden gullies chasing cattle at a flat gallop. The horse had to last all day long and half the night, if that's the way the muster was going; it needed to be able to find its way home if the rider got lost or had a buster, to be easy to catch, hobble and saddle and preferably not kick or bite. A horse needed good stock sense, to read cattle and act without being asked to. It needed to know when to get out of the way (bull charging) and when to stand its ground (holding a beast off camp) and when to accelerate (when its rider is throwing a beast). Stockhorses needed to be calm and steady and not spook the cattle by leaping at the breeze and most of all plod along with no surprises for its snoozing rider on the way back to the camp or home.

A rich man may have had a horse for every occasion, work and play, but the battlers probably had the one or two horses that did everything. There were horses everywhere, and everyone rode. Rich and poor alike, every bush child could ride almost before they could walk, they had to if they wanted to go beyond the back gate. In the bush in those early days reliable dogs, clever stockhorses and fast racehorses were a currency over and above money.

In parts of the country like the Snowy Mountains, all along the Great Divide, and in the wilds of the north and west, brumbies were caught, broken and traded. On the smaller properties of Victoria and the Hunter and the New England areas of New South Wales, time and care was taken with the breeding and breaking of horses. But in the inland and north — the pastoral zones, the general scope of things was enormous and horses were broken in, 10, 20 or 30 at a time, in a week. Professional and generally itinerant horsebreakers got paid per head, so it was in their interests to make a fast job of it. The horses were generally broken in at an older age, say five or six, so that they were already strong enough to withstand the gruelling work that was required of them, but that made them harder to tame and more powerful in their resistance. The horses were then ready to work but were often left in the horse paddock until the next mustering season, when they had to be 'tuned up'. Educating and re-educating station horses was constant and it was pretty rough and ready, resulting in pretty rough and ready stockhorses. Consequently, horses off these big stations were a lot wilder and more intractable than most. These were also the best bucking horses in the country, and arguably in the world.

It was always the case that some horses simply never complied. If these horses liked to buck, that is they preferred to communicate their objections by bucking rather than slamming, crushing or savaging you, they would live. Rogue horses were simply shot. No-one put up with difficult or dangerous horses; they were tools of the trade, a livelihood but also dispensable. The horses that loved to buck were nicknamed 'buckjumpers'. They were kept for special occasions and if they could unseat the best of the riders in their neighbourhood then their names spread like wildfire among the stations and the challenge was laid open to all. When the travelling buckjump shows and bushmen's carnivals became popular, every station had at least one rogue buckjumper they brought in for the competition or gave or sold to the showmen or their carnival committee. In our rodeo history, the most notorious and longest-surviving professional buckjumpers were big-hearted, recalcitrant station-bred horses from the backblocks.

Work hard, play harder

Professional horsebreakers were everywhere and it was a highly respected trade. Although it was a job most bushmen could do, not all of them had the time, so they employed professionals, usually once a year, and these men went from station to station breaking in horses as needed. Some people have a special way or understanding with animals and some were just brutal and cruel; each had their own particular method.

Whereas a station hand may have been required to fix the fences and the bore pump, the stockmen and ringers specialised in stockwork, on horseback, rather than regular station tasks. Stockmen or ringers worked with the cattle on the station. The drovers, working as independent contractors, specialised in moving the cattle from A to B. American cowboys were both stockmen and drovers rolled into one. However, the term cowboy in Australia was literally the person on the station who milked the cows, chopped the firewood and carried heavy things for the Mrs. They were either very old or very young or completely hopeless — low-life compared to the horsebreakers, drovers and stockmen.

Contrary to popular belief, not every stockman or ringer was able to 'ride anything with hair on'. Most could ride well, day in, day out; most could stay on

— it was always a long walk home — but it takes an inherent gift to be a truly great horseman. Those who had a special talent for riding or taming the difficult, unbroken or 'rough' horses were called roughriders. Roughriding was a job, whether you were horsebreaking or having to ride the camp's roughest horses daily — it was for work. But it was also a lot of fun for the young and the reckless and an irresistible challenge to young men who were good at it.

In the spirit of one-upmanship that produced 'the gun', (best or fastest), stockmen would always compete to ride the roughest horse. Author and poet, Herb Wharton remembered when he was a ringer and they'd bring in the fresh horses to get ready for the muster, 'there'd nearly be a punch-up over who's going to ride the bad ones'. There was constant competition all day every day, which also got the jobs done faster. This competitiveness and the challenge of setting yardsticks for a day's work was human nature but also a sort of frontier goal-setting. Men measured themselves against each other; who could shear the most sheep, dig the most post holes, lay the most railway sleepers, cut the most fenceposts, brand the most calves, run or ride the fastest, jump the highest or ride the meanest rogue horse in the district. This was not for money, but for manhood — to earn the reputation as the best.

Roughriding was always a way of proving yourself. In his introduction to the book *The Stockman*, ex-ringer and artist, the late Hugh Sawrey recounted the day he arrived at Babbiloora Station in Queensland. He immediately backed himself for ten bob to ride the district outlaw (buckjumper), which he did, and in so doing proved himself to all the other stockmen who were there — in a couple of minutes flat.[4] Newcomers — new chums — were always fair game and roughriding was also an initiation of sorts.

Gordon Beetham, ex-ringer and roughrider, remembers:

Some of those places had hundreds of horses on them and if you couldn't ride, there was no job for you. It was always the first question when you got there, 'Can you ride?' And if you were dumb enough to say 'yes', well, that was the worst mistake you ever made in your life. Because, sure enough, there would be some rogue buckjumper among them that they kept for such occasions, and he'd be the one they'd fetch for you.

'Can you ride?' was one of many ways of quickly sizing up a person's character and experience in the bush. So what *did* you say when the sly challenge came and you could ride but weren't fool enough to say it? 'I dunno, but I'll have a go,' was the vague enough answer to that curly question, Beetham reckons.

And of course money did come into it. The contest was always there. Horsebreaking requires the skill of riding a horse that does not yet understand or agree that it is to be ridden, and so the challenge between man and beast is set. Add to that a little one-upmanship, and we have man against man and man against beast — a few bob here and there thrown in for good measure and we have a proper (and entertaining) competition. Impromptu buckjumping competitions were often held on stations to reward the ringers after a long week eating dust in the yards; a mob of horses might be run in to test their skills. Or if the boss had a great buckjumper he would send out challenges far and wide to anyone who could ride his notorious outlaw and he'd often back his gun roughrider against incoming men.

One such challenge near Warwick, Queensland, in the 1850s was recorded by and unknown observer. Working as a horsebreaker for George Leslie on Canning Downs Station was a young man called Rory McLeod. Leslie was so impressed with McLeod's abilities with horses that he boasted about it. R.C. Haley, a squatter from the Brisbane Valley and Burnett districts, heard about it and wagered that his horsebreaker, a Mexican, could outride Rory McLeod — 'any day you like'. Leslie accepted the challenge, a bet for £50 a side, which was about a year's wages for an average man in those times. The competition was held at Canning Downs Station, and the chosen horse was their 'very wild and savage grey sired by the mankiller Vagrant'. News of the wager spread and it became the social event of the year. The Mexican was thrown and then McLeod rode second:

> *The grey's blood was up now. He used every trick he knew and had tried and invented a few more, but he just couldn't shift the leech on his back. He sunfished, spun, changed gait, propped, sucked back, jarred, but it was no use.*[5]

The victorious McLeod was then given the grey as a present by a delighted George Leslie.

People would come from miles around to see a man ride a rogue if they knew his reputation was 'unthrowable' and conversely to see a horse buck if it had a reputation for being 'unrideable'. Roughriding for a wager took place all over the country, in cities and towns as well as in the bush. Cities had lively horse scenes and horsemen always gathered at the horse sales where unbroken or rough horses were ridden. In Melbourne, from as early as the 1850s, the horsemen; breakers, jockeys, trainers, hunters, show riders and stockmen used to congregate at a livery stables called Kirk's Bazaar. Situated between Kinnear's, the saddlers, and Pearson, Rowe and Smith, the stock and station agents, it was where any visiting horseman and bushman was sure to find men of like mind and spirit. The legendary Lance Skuthorpe Snr was to give his first city exhibitions of a roughriding there in approximately 1901, but a visiting Irishman named Cuthbert Fetherstonhaugh recorded that he watched two ladies ride buckjumpers simultaneously in downtown Penola, South Australia, for a wager in 1860.

By the 1880s public roughriding competitions, horse and bullock competitions and bullock-throwing exhibitions were definitely taking place in Victoria and presumably elsewhere because they were written up in the newspapers. Legendary Victorian horseman Tom Lloyd Snr entered a competition in the early 80s at Wangaratta. It was a roughriding competition between eight men and a big black horse called Morrison. Tom was the only man to ride the horse, which bucked among the crowd and over a child in a pram. Luckily no-one was hurt, and 'the judges' unanimous verdict was that Lloyd was the "Australian Champion".' Soon afterwards he rode in another challenge match, this time against 'one of Victoria's best horsemen', Jim Bullock, for £100.[6] 'Australian champions' were a dime a dozen until 1945 because they were crowd drawers, and until then there was no official body to dispute the claim.

It takes a quiet confidence in one's own skill and a respect and understanding of a horse's nature to be a great horseman. Over the years in this country there have been hundreds of legendary horsemen and women — the special ones — but far fewer than that have also had the heart to regularly and seemingly with ease, go up against the great outlaws, as unrideable buckjumpers were known. The horses and horsemen who later took their skills into the sporting and entertainment arenas were still called buckjumpers and roughriders, just as their counterparts in America, the working cowboys who took their profession into the rodeo arenas, were still called cowboys.

Wherever in the world there was a large cattle industry, the natural progression of rodeo events from the working cattlemen's everyday skills to the show ring happened more or less simultaneously during the late nineteenth century. In Australia, around the 1880s and 1890s, roughriding had become such a popular spectacle that it began to grow in two separate but intricately entwined directions. The first was as a weekend sport for horsemen and women from stations and properties. It became a competition or exhibition in a day's worth of horse sports at a carnival, gymkhana, sports day or annual agricultural show. Years later, when the country was more populated and transportation had further developed, these stockmen's events became highly contested and eventually evolved into rodeos.

Secondly, and more importantly at the time, roughriding exhibitions and competitions became popular entertainment in towns and cities when they went on the road with travelling circuses, Wild West shows, and buckjump shows. Roughriders were seasonally employed to give daily exhibitions of bucking horses in a small rope ring and the showmen would call for challengers to come out of the audience to ride their buckjumpers. These travelling shows brought Wild and Western bush entertainment into the cities, and the showmanship of professional entertainers to the bush.

Although they were two separate worlds — one a part-time hobby and sport, the other professional itinerant entertainment — they developed at the same time, side by side, and often bumped into each other. Graziers, their families and the townsfolk would often set up committees to run their annual sports days or agricultural shows and later bushmen's carnivals, usually in aid of a community project or charity. The travelling shows were run by professional 'proprietors', originally out of the circus community but increasingly the business attracted all sorts, including young men 'off the land'. But it was the same pool of talent riding the horses in both arenas and the same events being contested. It was common for the buckjumpers to be traded, lent or borrowed between the two groups and their shows often happened at the same time and place.

Regardless of whether the events took place in tents or paddocks, it was the same challenge between man or woman and bucking horse — a test of endurance, tenacity, skill and wits. It basically came down to how much money was up for grabs and how far roughriders had to travel to get there. The professional travelling buckjump riders would, if in the area, compete in local agricultural shows and bushmen's carnivals and later rodeos, just as the working stockmen/ringers/horsebreakers could never resist the challenge put out by travelling buckjump shows. They would back either themselves or one of their horses for a challenge, and many joined the shows for a week or a season or perhaps for years before returning to their steady jobs. It was the same game in two different guises, the main difference being that for one it was weekend sport, for the other it became their life.

'A Buckjumper', 1873

'The Buckjumper Collared' – England v Australia, 1880

An 1897 photographic compilation

Clockwise from top left: Jim Bullock, Roy Morrison, 'Jigger' Lavell and Mulga Jack, 1904

Ashton's Circus at Clermont, Queensland, 1873

Mr Martini

Cowboys from Wirths' 'Wild West Show', 1890

'Miss Kemp'
(Elizabeth Jesse Hunt)

Professor Kemp

Lance Skuthorpe Snr

'Wild Australia' at the Wirths Olympia, Sydney, c.1926

Harry Farber

Jack Morrissey

Billy Waite

Thorpe McConville

Miss Cleopatra and Miss Bonita, 1911

Joe Atkinson souvenir postcard, early 1930s

Notes and Personalities.
From "Who's Who in Wild Australia."

RIDING BUCKJUMPERS.—Some of the best riders and buck jumpers in the world are to be seen in the arena. The animals are ridden under the fairest conditions, without bit, and in many cases without halters on their heads. The men ride in polo saddles without knee pads. The fun is fast and furious, and for a bit of Wild Australian life cannot be beaten.

MISS MARION WAITE, the Lady Stockwhip Cracker Champion of Australia, is a clever artist. She uses whips from eight to thirty-eight feet in length with the utmost ease and does astonishing things, three in each hand being cracked simultaneously. She usually finishes a very clever exhibition by cracking four whips at once, holding the lot in her right hand.

MISS CLEOPATRA gives a thrilling exhibition of what can be done with snakes and crocodiles. The latter weird creatures are supposed to be untameable. She has been handling snakes since eleven years of age, and this is not without its risks. "Cleo," as she is known, has been bitten three times with poisonous snakes. On one occasion, when she was performing with a snake weighing 30lbs., the monster made a savage attack on her and repeatedly bit her face. She will carry the marks to her grave.

MISS BONITA is the Champion Lady Rifle Shot of Australia and South Africa (single bullets only). With unerring aim she shoots discs from off her sister's head. Little Bonita finishes up her marvellous exhibition of rifle shooting by shooting her own name out in discs suspended on a blackboard—thirty shots in thirty seconds.

MISS NEAVE is a daring wild bullock rider. Is a niece of Mr. Alfred Neave, the Managing Director of Wild Australia, who has spent 15 years overlanding stock in Australia, and who got the Wild Australia Troupe of Bush Artistes and horses together.

MISS HYLAND—Australia's Champion Lady Horsebreaker—undertakes to break-in and ride any unbroken colt in two hours—that is, she will catch and teach him to lead, mouth him, pick up all four feet, and ride him. When at home she breaks in all her father's horses; has her own race-horses, which she trains and rides herself. She has won eleven races out of eleven starts with one favourite of hers. She drives ten in hand as easily as the average gentleman drives a pair. She gives daily exhibitions of rough-riding or buck-jumpers, and shows what can be done in the way of horse training.

BILLY WAITE (the Champion Rough Rider and Whip Cracker of Australia), born and bred on his father's Cattle Station in Queensland, was reared in the saddle. At an age small boys go to school Billy was in a school of a different sort, learning bushmanship on the Cattle Camps and droving mobs of "fats" hundreds of miles to market. Billy has probably ridden more bad horses in Australia than any other man. At Bownes, in Queensland, on one ocassion he rode 450 colts in two-and-a-half days, putting up a record by riding 250 the first day. He had six men catching and saddling for him. Billy gives exhibitions in buck-jump riding, etc.

JACK MORRISSEY is a native of Grafton, New South Wales, born and bred in the Australian Bush, having spent the earlier part of his life in the ranges where the wild Bush horses roam. Jack is clever with the stockwhip, rifle, lasso, and is a first-class horseman; having won the Rough Riding Competition at the Sydney Stadium promoted by Philip Lytton in 1909 in honour of the visit of the American Fleet to Sydney. In the final Morrissey defeated Bert Fletcher holder of the Championship. Jack is a good all-round athlete and he usually finishes his clever turn of lassoing and rope spinning by a running high jump over his mare, which stands about 16 hands high.

Excerpt from 'Wild Australia' program

Left to right: 'Rocky Ned', Thorpe McConville Jnr, Doug Turner and 'Swannee', 1937

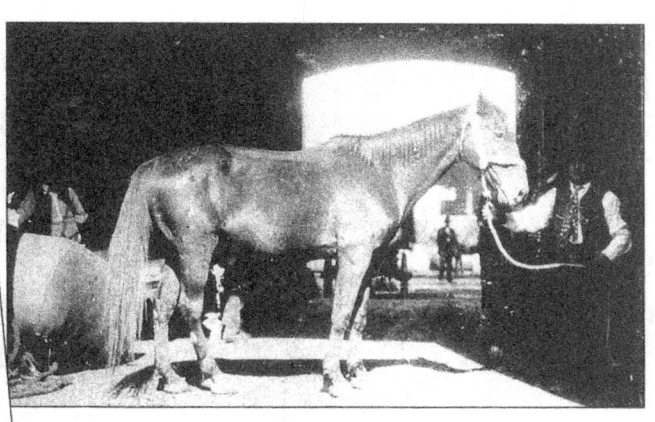

'Bobs', 1911

Billy Jonas getting on bullock, 1911

Left to right: Art Creasy, Jack Watson, Violet Skuthorpe Jnr, Lance Skuthorpe Jnr and Ron McPhee, 1938

Thorpe McConville and his truck, c. 1934

Jack Hay's travelling buckjump show, late 1930s

Setting up a tent show, 1940s

Thorpe McConville's roughriders. *L–R:* Ernie Gordon, (rope spinner) Jack Tracey, Tom Lloyd, Leo Lloyd, Thorpe McConville Jnr, Jack Agnew and Jumbo Foster

Lance Skuthorpe Jnr and Tex Morton, 1940s

Jack Clarris buckjumping in his father's show during World War II

Flank rope in use at Bill Clarris' buckjump show, Taroom

Violet Skuthorpe Jnr, 1940s. Top left is her brother, Lance.

2

TRAVELLING BUCKJUMP SHOWS

A is Australia — 'Orsetralia, you know;

There was wit in the wisdom that christened her so.

B is the Buckjumper, I may suppose you

Have heard of the creature that jumps up and throws you

WILD AUSTRALIA

Riding a Famous Australian Buck-Jumper.

Defining spirit

WHEN EDWARD HARGREAVES DISCOVERED gold near Bathurst, New South Wales, in June of 1851, people came from all over the world to try their luck, notably the British, Irish, Americans, Europeans and Chinese. The Australian population trebled in a decade. Gold was also discovered in Victoria during the 1850s. In 1853 gold temporarily surpassed wool as Australia's major export. The gold rushes dominated Australian life in the south-east for many years and gold continued to be discovered in the rest of Australia through the 1860s, 70s and 80s. The various rushes opened up new regions around the country and if the graziers were not already there, they soon were, to feed everyone at highly inflated prices.

The 40 years following the first gold rushes proved a period of strong economic growth that saw the settlement of the Australian interior and advances in transportation and communication. The city and the bush grew closer together and Australians became more educated and affluent. Australia was maturing and a pool of home-grown political activists, artists and writers were stirring the pot. The 1890s saw a wave of nationalism in Australia inspired by the nation's centenary in 1888. The new century and the Federation of States (1901) were looming; we were on the brink of becoming a nation. Australians became conscious of themselves and began to reflect on who they were and to be proud of it.

According to historian Russel Ward, 'the frontier tended to promote nationalism [and] the sentiment of nationalism tended to make men ... romanticize the frontier.

During the last century both the United States and Australia were both new countries seeking, unconsciously in part, for national self consciousness and cohesion.'[1] The artists and writers of the times helped to define Australia's identity both spiritually and politically through art, culture and myth-making.

This burgeoning nationalism was reflected in the arts and literature by an evolving Australian style and spirit. Tom Roberts, Arthur Streeton and Charles Conder were the leading figures in the Heidelberg School — painting natural impressions of the Australian character and landscape. In literature, Rolf Boldrewood and Marcus Clarke were writing novels capturing life in Australia. Henry Kendall first published his Australian landscape poems in 1862 and Adam Lindsay Gordon's *Bush Ballads and Galloping Rhymes* came out in 1870. But the heavyweights, those who really popularised the bush, came later. Henry Lawson's first poem, 'Song of the Republic' (1887), and his first story, 'His Father's Mate' (1888), were published in *The Bulletin*, and in the following two years A.B. 'Banjo' Paterson's, 'Clancy of the Overflow' and 'The Man From Snowy River' also appeared there. Joseph Furphy (who called himself 'half bushman, half bookworm'), Steele Rudd, Harry 'the (horse) Breaker' Morant, the brilliant Barcroft Boake and the Scot, Will Ogilvie, all wrote of the bush and its people, because, without exception, they had lived and/or worked among them. It was once said of Lawson, arguably our greatest bush writer and poet, that 'everything he wrote he lived'.

A myriad of writers and poets were being published in radical and nationalist journals that knocked authority, including *The Stockwhip*, *The Bulletin*, *The Queensland Worker*, and later *The Lone Hand*, as well as the more mainstream publications. Many of these writers came from doomed small selections so they were familiar with the life of the battlers of the bush as well as the adventurous lifestyle of stockmen. They espoused the various blessings of the bush and its people and were anti-establishmentarian, pro-union and pro-republic.

In the latter part of the nineteenth century, Australian nationalism took a definite form in the class struggle between the landless majority and the land-monopolising squatters. The nomadic tribe of pastoral workers had had enough of the squatters' social and economic system of 'patriarchal despotism'.[2] They held large strikes, culminating in the Queensland Shearers' Strike of 1891, to protest pastoralists' attempts to employ non-union and therefore cheaper labour. This activisim led to the birth of the Australian Labor Party.

By the end of the nineteenth century Australia already had a predominantly urban population whose economic realities and cultural sensibilities leant towards middle-class liberalism. But its ethos was fundamentally 'pioneering' and working class. The bushman, in particular the stockman, became a national icon in the 1890s and his idealised image, character, language, costume, skills, values and attitudes were intrinsically that of the itinerant pastoral worker. Perhaps the bushman, a highly romanticised free spirit, was simply an escape from city life, but certainly for many years his image and character had strong representation in Australian culture.

Let's get this show on the road

Circus entertainment had been a European tradition for centuries. Circuses travelled the world, an anomalous tribe that made fortunes, went bust, amalgamated, split up and picked up acts and animals as they went. European, English and American circus troupes travelled around North America, Europe and 'the Empire' — Canada, India, South Africa, the 'Far East' and, after the gold rushes, Australia and New Zealand.

Tasmanian publican Robert Radford launched his Equestrian Circus on 27 December 1847 at the Horse and Jockey Hotel in Launceston. This is generally thought of as Australia's first. It seems there were quite a few errant equestrians and acrobats who had ended up in Van Diemen's Land and his show was a resounding success. Australia's first travelling circus families, the Burtons and the Ashtons, both hit the road in the 1850s.

Because of the gold rushes, Australia's population was widely spread and wherever gold was discovered, these intrepid showmen and women were never far behind. They went wherever there were people — if not a goldfield or town, then a station when the shearers were there, or they stopped and did a show for the outback railway workers. Trundling along in covered wagons, they travelled thousands of miles along rough bush tracks, swimming rivers, getting bogged, bush-bashing through the scrub, lowering the wagons by rope down cliff faces and encountering tribes of Aborigines and bushrangers along the way.

Pulling up outside town, they'd spruce up a bit before the bandwagon would take the lead and strike up a tune to announce their arrival. Throngs of children and dogs would rush out from everywhere, yelling and barking with excitement, and accompany the circus wagons up the main street. They performed under calico tents lit by carbide lamps and these early circuses dazzled the small towns with their colourful costumes and spectacle.

It was great family entertainment, full of high drama, daring and dangerous feats, music and laughter. There were gymnasts, acrobats, clowns, contortionists, Houdini acts, trapeze artists, tumblers, bicycle acts, singers, performing dogs and ponies and, of course, the bareback equestrian acts with their somersaults and leaps through rings of fire.

The circuses brought music and culture to the people in the bush — for many it was the first time they had heard classical music — but they also swapped news and information and relieved the monotony of isolation. 'The range of entertainment [on the road] was quite extraordinary. There were travelling drama companies, light opera companies, vaudeville tent shows, comedy companies, minstrel troupes, magicians, phrenologists, magic lantern shows, wandering bands of musicians, marionette shows, boxing troupes, merry-go-rounds, travelling menageries and carnivals', and the list goes on.[3]

Australian circuses were basically family concerns, with family members making up the main core of the performers. The St Leons, Wirths, Fitzgeralds, Perrys, Lennons Gills and Eronis were all on the road by the turn of the century, but competition was stiff with the overseas shows, who were made up of professional artists from all over the world.

In a meticulously researched history of Australia's longest-surviving circus family, the Ashtons, *Take a Drum and Beat It,* Judy Cannon describes the man who was one of our first travelling showmen:

A man schooled in the tradition of English circus and of nineteenth-century hard times, James Henry Ashton was a first-class equestrian with the vision and passion of an entrepreneur ... A man of compassion and generosity, but always spiced with a dash of roguery ... a man of entertainment, of fun, of puff, exhortation and exaggeration. He was an equestrian whose talents genuinely astounded audiences accustomed to ride themselves, always ready with a joke ... he combined an innate generosity with a shrewd instinct for enticing and holding audiences. He became part of the bush way of life ... Ashton's generosity to local causes when society was establishing itself was at times more abundant than sensible, but his largesse brought him overwhelming affection, lasting reputation and good old-fashioned publicity. His entrepreneurial spirit was forever egged on by the love of the show, a shrinking purse, an expanding family and the next hill.[4]

Not all travelling showmen were as likeable as Ashton but generally they had the same qualities and embodied the passion and spirit of entrepreneurial adventurers. Some were more rogue than larrikin; some more crim than rogue; and many of them were overly fond of alcohol. But living on the road means facing constant challenges, amusement and mishap — especially so in the turbulent years around the turn of the century. Surviving on your wits is nothing if not character-building, and all the showmen were great characters with big personalities.

Influences from abroad

In America the entrepreneurial adventurers were also hard at work. In the early 1880s the Wild West shows were starting to take form. The leading exponent was William F. 'Buffalo Bill' Cody. In 1882 his 'Old Glory Blowout' in Nebraska attracted 1000 contestants. From that time on, in brilliant collaboration with the sharpshooter Annie Oakley, Cody presented cowboy skills as popular entertainment and added all sorts of other death-defying drama. His Wild West spectaculars sold flamboyant 're-enactments' of frontier life to American and European audiences from 1883 to 1913 until he went bankrupt, and he later died, completely broke, in 1917. Like most natural-born showmen, Cody 'spent his money lavishly, foolishly and generously' and he liked to drink.[5]

Cody was the original and the best 'frontier' myth-maker. He glamorised truth into fiction, and the urban masses fell in love with the idea of the Wild West. He paved the way for the hundreds of entrepreneurial showmen who followed in his footsteps, re-inventing, mythologising and exploiting the Wild West and its cowboys and putting rodeo competitions in the public eye.

Self-styled doctor William Frank Carver, was one of them. Probably invited as part of Australia's centenary celebrations, in 1888 Doc Carver brought out a team of American cowboys for a buckjumping competition against Australian roughriders. The horseman Gus Powell was asked by the organisers, the National Agricultural Society of Victoria, to put together an Australian team. It included Allan Selman, Dick Powell and W. Henderson. The first round was held at the Friendly Societies' grounds in Melbourne and ended in a draw; the second round was in Sydney and the Australians hit the lead; the final contest was back in Melbourne:

> *During this contest Gus really showed 'the stuff that he was made of'. Whilst his horse bucked for 28 seconds, Gus took a cigar from his pocket, struck a match on his leather trousers and lit the cigar. This feat won him the 'Championship of the*

World' — or so it was claimed at the time. Each of the Australians received 100 pounds and a medal.[6]

Carver went back to the United States but returned two years later with his Wild West Show, opening in Adelaide in December 1890 before touring the east coast.

When 'Wild West' fever took off in the USA, the international circus community immediately saw the potential and jumped on the proverbial bandwagon. The first Australians to do so were the Wirth Brothers.

Johannes Wirth arrived from Germany in 1855 to join the search for gold. He didn't find any and eventually joined Ashton's Circus instead. Later he worked with Ridgway's Circus before deciding to buy a second-hand Cobb and Co coach and start his own. In 1878 together with his family, including sons, John, Harry, Philip and George, he toured New South Wales and Queensland, playing at the agricultural shows. Wirths were an instant success and were soon travelling internationally, touring non-stop for 83 years. Of the four brothers, Philip Wirth was the great horsetrainer and always chose top-class horses and equestrian performers from all over the world.

In 1890, Harry Wirth went to the USA and was 'spellbound' with the size and scope of 'Barnum and Baileys Three-Ring Circus Hippodrome and Wild West Show'. The Wirths decided to add the American West acts to their program and Harry signed up two well-known Wild West showmen, Captain Jack Sutton and Broncho George. There were also a number of American cowboys and trick-riders, including the Arkansas Kid and Cowboy George, American Indians and Mexican vaqueros, including the one and surely only 'Ralph the Mexican'! The outfit arrived in Auckland on 13 September 1890, where as Philip Wirth later reminisced:

> *...crowds lined the pier to watch the arrival of the steamer. It was the fashion in Auckland at this time for the men to wear cowboy hats, and when our friends on the steamer saw so many of the people on the wharf wearing them, they remarked that there seemed to be more cowboys in Auckland than in Texas.*[7]

When Wirth Brothers' Circus Hippodrome and Wild West Show opened in Auckland on 9 October 1890, Harry Wirth claimed they were the first Wild West show to appear in Australasia. But a 'Great Californian Circus and Wild Bronco Horses' show was touring Australia in September 1889 and the English circus, Harmston's, who mainly toured the Far East, had Harmston's Wild West Hippodrome and Circus touring Australia in February 1890.[8]

On 15 December 1890, Wirths' Circus and Wild West Show arrived in Adelaide. When they heard another Wild West show was in the harbour, the brothers rowed over in the harbourmaster's boat to find sharpshooter and showman, Doc Carver wondering what to do. He had arrived in Adelaide straight from a successful tour of Europe with Buffalo Bill Cody. Astonished to find Wirths' posters already plastered all over town, he had decided not to continue. They joined forces. Dr Carver top-billed for Wirths before he went on to Melbourne and Wirths went to Brisbane; they would later share billing in Sydney.

Wirths' Wild West Show was a three-hour spectacular with 25 acts and plenty of simulated American frontier chaos, including bucking bronco exhibition rides. Among the acts on their 1890–91 tour program were: Virginia Reel, the equestrian performer; an Indian war dance; the emigrant wagon — 'dangers and hardships of pioneers'; the hanging of a horse thief; a lassoing exhibition by the cowboys; exciting attack by the Indians on the famous Deadwood Coach; cowboy's sports, for example, trick-riding displays like leaning down off a galloping horse to pick up a coin from the dust. There was the chase for a bride, the Pony Express Exciting Congress of Nations Race, which was 'between a Mexican, a cowboy, and an Indian', an attack (by Indians) on a hunter's cabin and of course the bucking horses exhibition — 'by cowboys and Mexicans'.

Wirths continued touring until the Australian banks crashed in 1893. In August of that year they left from Perth on a seven-year world tour, travelling to England, South America, Malaysia, India, South Africa and New Zealand. Broncho George decided to stay and probably bought Wirths' horses and Wild West gear because from at least August 1893 to 1909 he toured Australia as Broncho George's Wild West Show.[9]

During the early 1890s Australia was inundated with local and international 'Wild West' shows that must have been tripping over each other as they toured up and down the east coast of Australia. They came from all around the globe. Texas Jack was an American showman who had had his own show both in South Africa and Australia before he joined forces with Harmston's for their Australian tour. Harmston's top-billed him alongside 'Arizona Charlie' Meadows, another American 'frontier' celebrity. Australian gold prospector turned circus proprietor, Darcy Hyland was touring as 'Professor Hyland — Wild Horse Tamer and Bullock Rider' assisted by his versatile and extremely talented daughters. Looper and Brown's 'Wild West Show with Great Globe Circus' were here and Australian 'horseman extraordinaire', Mick Fenton had his show, 'Fenton and Fillis — Grand American Cowboy Entertainment'.[10]

These were the first of multitudes of Australian and/or American Wild West shows and showmen who continued to tour Australia in various shapes and forms for the next 70-odd years. Different acts and personalities under various guises mixed it with our circuses and show performers, influencing and competing against each other. American and Canadian talent agencies orchestrated a free flow of talent between Canada, the USA, New Zealand, Australia, Europe, India and South Africa with men and women 'Western' performers on their books. Cowboys and American Indians, Australian stockmen, Mexican vaqueros and later Russian Cossacks were supplied to circuses and Wild West show entrepreneurs, as horse tamers and trainers, dog trainers, rosin-back riders (who do acrobatics on bareback horses as they canter round the ring — like in the circus), musicians, singers and dancers, bronc and steer riders, trick riders and ropers, sharpshooters and whipcrackers. Individual acts and whole troupes were generally employed on two-year contracts.

It was all about big spectacle — chariot races cowboys and Indians fighting it out in American-style frontier drama. Indians burning stagecoaches and pioneer homes and cowboys charging in to the rescue. The Mexicans excelled with ropes and gave displays of trickroping, ropespinning and throwing wild steers. The American Indians were the experts with bows and arrows, and knife and tomahawk throwing and the Australians were the star whipcrackers. All gave exhibitions in buckjumping (bronco riding) and the showmen often promoted buckjumping contests between American cowboys and Australian roughriders. They also ran contests between the Australians and their skill of throwing and tying a bullock versus the cowboys and their Spanish/American method of roping it.

The nineteenth-century American Wild West showmen's influence on the Australian circus families was long-lived. The Australian public clamoured for the bucking horses because it was a challenge that was intrinsic to our culture — our bushmen and horsemen were national icons and we have always loved horse sports. After the turn of the century, the Lennons, Ashtons, Spillmans, Eronis, Gills and Holdens were just some of the Australian circuses that began to use buckjumping to augment their shows. Multi-talented family members would be trapeze artists, acrobats and gymnasts doubling as clowns and often the band members as well. Performing dogs and ponies and rosin-back riding had been around for years, but add a couple of buckjumpers and roughriders and good takings at the door were assured. This was especially important during the depression years of the 1890s and 1930s when the circuses couldn't afford to pay performers' wages. Buckjumpers were cheap if not free and the riders could be challenged out of the crowd.

Bucking up the takings

Buckjumping challenges were also a way of milking more money out of the small bush towns. The bucking horses were often of 'local' interest as local rogue horses were brought in to test the roughriders. The challenges of unrideable horses and of course the prize money lured the riders in, which in turn lured all their mates and female admirers to watch. For the circuses buckjumping was a novelty, but out in the bush it was a test of manhood. The further into cattle country they went, the bigger the crowds.

Judy Cannon says in her book, *Take a Drum and Beat It* that, 'local newspapers published the names and numbers of seconds winners [who] managed to stay on. What bets were placed on whom was anybody's guess, but police sometimes had to cart out unconscious challengers.' She quotes Doug Ashton, who says his grandfather and father used buckjumpers as a ploy, especially in little country towns:

Dad said the first night would be a circus, and that night they'd pick somebody in the audience that could ride, because most people in those days were good horsemen and buckjump riders. Dad used to carry a team of buckjumpers. So he'd throw out a challenge; who would ride the buckjumper the next night? So that night (the second night), it would be circus and buckjumping. Then they'd pick a fight with some of the locals in the audience, and they wouldn't have the fight that night but they'd have the fight the third night. Then they'd have more riders in the audience. So the third night they'd have circus, buckjumping with the locals, and a couple of fights. That used to bring the same people back into the tent in a small town three times. Fortunately, the circus men were fit.[11]

The 1890s Depression was drastic. Hundreds of thousands of men hit the road hustling up work where they could. Young dispossessed men from the bush were among them and more than a few joined circuses and travelling shows as horse trainers, roughriders and entertainers — they were naturals, and they were fed. The cities, especially Sydney, were always ready for new entertainment, particularly during hard times, and by now audiences were primed to the hilt with romantic tales of the bushmen and stockmen from our poets and writers. It was easy for the enterprising to bring these fashionable folk heroes into town and show them off. Buckjumping was exciting and dangerous and horses were still very much a part of life in the cities. The showmen organised exhibitions of 'spectacular daring' and challenges with the urban horsebreakers and horsemen. Capitalising on the bushman and stockman mystique, the showmanship of an enterprising few glamorised and popularised the roughriding and whipcracking skills of a whole generation.

These professional showmen of the 1880s and 1890s, the American entrepreneurs and the Australian showmen who emulated them, introduced Australian audiences to the idea of 'cowboys' and 'bucking broncos' as 'get your tickets at the door' popular entertainment. Nevertheless, 'bronco busting' was just one feature of a show, an addition to a variety of 'circus' and/or Wild West attractions.

Another type of Australian travelling showman soon emerged, one who specialised in buckjumping. Over the years there had been numerous 'professors' of horsemanship, horse tamers and breakers and trainers who gave exhibitions of their skill and passed around the hat. Professor Hyland and his daughters had been 'taming' horses as the main act in their show for a decade — taming generally meant getting an unbroken horse to lead and pick up its feet and accept a rider in a few minutes flat. Professor Montgomery was another great horsetamer who worked with the various circuses. But buckjumping is not about taming and training, it's about being untamed and revelling in it. It was not until the turn of the century that there was the emergence of the much more grassroots entertainment — the Australian buckjump shows.

Skuthorpe, Martini and Kemp

The three most colourful and successful instigators of the Australian buckjump shows were Lance Skuthorpe, Martini and Professor Paddy Kemp.

Lance Skuthorpe (1870–1958) is generally considered to be the first Australian to run buckjumping as the main act of the show. According to Jack Pollard, who wrote Skuthorpe's biography *The Rough Rider,* Skuthorpe's father, Jim, was a selector and manager on many different stations before he eventually lost his struggle with the banks and the droughts in the early 1890s and became a drover. Too ambitious for life as a drover, Lance joined the thousands of others looking for work during the Depression years. He drew on his many bushmen's talents to make a living. He was also an extraordinary all-round sportsman and backed himself to beat anyone who was game at hop, step and jump, sprinting, high-jumping, fighting and riding. He used his gift as an orator, reciting the poems of Adam Lindsay Gordon and Barcroft Boake outside pubs and on street corners, then passing around his hat. He got work breaking and gentling horses, and word spread that he 'seemed to cast a spell over wild animals'.[12] Skuthorpe was giving exhibitions as a 'professor' of horse-taming around Mount Gambier and the speed with which he mastered them caused even the most astute horsemen to suspect he was fraudulent. But he was not. Skuthorpe once claimed that in seven minutes he had ridden seven horses that had not had a man on their back before. As Jack Pollard puts it, he was 'more an exhibition rider than a full-time horse-breaker, intent on avoiding the punishing, frugal life horse-breakers led'.[13]

Skuthorpe realised that the harder the horse was to master the more the assembled crowd liked it and when he passed the hat around he found that the wilder the ride the heavier the hat.

In 1896 Skuthorpe performed his first great publicity stunt. In front of a huge crowd, including the celebrated pastoralist, Sir Sidney Kidman, he re-enacted Adam Lindsay Gordon's 1860 legendary feat at 'Gordon's Leap'. He backed himself for £200 and repeated Gordon's death-defying act, jumping a borrowed horse called Wallace over a six-foot fence onto a six-foot ledge — the precipice of a 300-foot chasm above the Blue Lake near Mount Gambier. He was on his way to becoming a legend.

Skuthorpe stayed on the road, taming or riding wild horses. He wrote a pamphlet preaching gentleness as the key to horsetaming, which he sold to his customers. For all the folklore that envelopes our rodeo history, it is undisputed that Skuthorpe had what his son once called a 'magical' way with horses and what others have said was his ability to mesmerise them. He could always pull a crowd.

In 1900 Wirths Circus returned from their overseas trip and employed Skuthorpe as an act — riding buckjumpers in their lion's cage. He and Wallace were also exhibited as a sideshow attraction where people paid a shilling to view them as 'The Heroes of Gordon's Leap' and to hear his theories on horsemanship.

After Skuthorpe left Wirths in about 1901, he wandered around Victoria looking for his next meal ticket and soon found it in Snips. A nondescript looking grey, not much more than a pony, Snips had a spectacular king buck where he 'bucked within a buck', executed while all four feet were off the ground.[14] Skuthorpe bought him for £7 and took him to Melbourne, where he started charging people to watch him ride Snips in the yard of Kirk's Bazaar. The word spread. Challengers came from everywhere and soon the overflow of spectators ran out into the street. Snips threw them all, and bucked him out of debt.[15] Skuthorpe, knowing about the king buck within a buck, rode him nightly with aplomb, 'vaulting neatly from the saddle' before the horse was spent.[16] Ever publicity-wise, Skuthorpe would parade Snips about Melbourne in the back of a horse-drawn wagon and it wasn't long before he bought more buckjumpers and moved to bigger premises at the Cyclorama. Eventually Skuthorpe sensed the show had run its course — he was running out of challengers — and he sold Snips for £700 to another showman. Skuthorpe spent the money living it up in Melbourne before heading back to the bush. This was a pattern he continued throughout his life, making a fortune, blowing it all and then starting again from scratch.

Snips went on to have a long and distinguished career as a buckjumper, that is, if it was the same horse — the showmen often used the same names to capitalise on notoriety. Skuthorpe was bucking him again on a tour of western New South Wales in 1906.[17] Sadly, in 1911, en route to England as part of Alf Neaves' 'Wild Australia', Snips broke a leg and had to be put down.[18]

During the Australian Federation celebrations in 1901, Lance had another great publicity break when he was invited to give an exhibition buckjump ride for the Duke of York (who became King George V), who was here to open our first Australian parliament. From then on Skuthorpe would publicise that his show was 'Under Vice-Regal Patronage'.

His one-time star rider and later manager, Lem Partridge, talked about his years working with the mercurial but lovable Skuthorpe as being 'full of laughter and heart-break':

> ...we were rich one day and broke the next. Lance was the product of an era which can never come again. If he had been born a few centuries earlier, he would have sailed down the Spanish Main with a cutlass between his teeth.[19]

Martin Breheny, better known as 'Martini', was born to Irish migrants in the 1860s in the gold town of Adelong in the Snowy Mountains but the family eventually settled in Sydney. He is alleged to have chosen his show name Martini after the Martini–Henry rifle,[20] but it is more likely to have come from the fact that he was a circus performer who worked with Italian and French gymnasts for a few years. The first evidence of Martini as a showman is on a bill of fare with 'Harmston's American and Continental Cirque' during their 1890–91 tour of Australia.

He is billed as 'A surprise – Martini, Baretta, and Gilbarto on the Triple Horizontal Bars'. Among the usual circus acts billed in Harmston's show that season were 'P.G. Harmston — the Great Horseman of the Universe' doing 'thrilling and sensational somersaults on bareback horses'; 'Black Eagle — the horse of knowledge' and 'the Educated Pig'. Later that year Harmston's became a Wild West Hippodrome and Circus. Black Eagle and the pig were dropped but Gilbarto and Martini remained, and the tour now boasted Mexican Bill, Texas Jack and Arizona Charlie, all three successful Wild West celebrities.

Martini may well have gone back to India with Harmston's and then joined Abel and Klaer's Circus there because he was with their show, again giving exhibitions on the horizontal bars, when they arrived in Australia from India and toured in 1894. But Abel and Klaer's Circus went broke and when Harry Wirth bought them out Martini was no longer with them. He probably stayed with circuses but the details are unclear. Sometime over the next six years he would have crossed paths with Lance Skuthorpe. Jack Pollard, in his book *The Roughrider*, says that Martini worked for Skuthorpe at one time but that he left and set up his own show in opposition. The first recorded mention of 'Martini's Roughriders' is at Mackay, Queensland, on 16 December 1902.[21]

The key to a successful buckjump show was having a famous buckjumper. Apart from Skuthorpe himself, it was the buckjumpers the showmen promoted, not the riders. Martini's first star buckjumper was Dargin's Grey, bred by Arthur Dargin on the Hawkesbury. Like Snips, Dargin's Grey went on to become a legend. He had a relatively short but well-publicised career until he met with some sort of accident around 1904. Martini gave him a spell before bringing him back on tour in 1906 as 'the legend that was'.[22]

Unlike Skuthorpe, Martini was not a horseman or a roughrider, simply the proprietor of the show. Martini spent his first couple of years mainly touring Queensland and it was at Cloncurry that he picked up a special duo — the roughrider Billy Waite and Bobs, the unrideable chestnut — they became two of the greatest stars of their day. Due no doubt to Martini's promotional savvy, Dargin's Grey and Bobs were Australia's most famous buckjumpers until the 1920s, when Rocky Ned hit the trail. Bobs, in particular, was quoted by the roughriders of the era as being the outlaw buckjumper to beat, and all three horses are still legends today.

The exact origins of John Patrick Daly, also known as Jack Daly, Professor Paddy Kemp and, on occasion, Professor Montgomery (after the celebrated horse-tamer), are unknown, although an individual of that name was born in 1877 in New South Wales. Professor Paddy Kemp shared his contemporaries' great knack for getting and holding people's attention. Like Martini he would have perfected his showmen's skills during his time with circuses and specifically Fitzgerald's Circus. He was a renowned horseman but promoted himself as a horsebreaker and tamer rather than as a buckjump rider. He was an excellent ringmaster, too. Kemp also designed saddles, which he entered in competitions at the agricultural shows he toured with his buckjump show. The popular Kemp saddles were made by a Mr Urquhart in Bondi and sold by Walker's and Stevenson, a saddlery in George Street, Sydney.

The mischievous and somewhat mysterious Daly was arrested in Melbourne in May 1906. The articles that appeared in the newspapers throw some light on this otherwise elusive character. The *Western Argus* of 15 May 1906 described his arrest on charges of larceny and horse-stealing and told of his hair-raising escapes from the law over an eight-year period, including jumping from a train running at 40 miles an hour. Another time, when a policeman went to a boarding house with a warrant for his arrest:

> *... with calm unconcern, {Daly} walked out at the back door, round to the front, and mounting the constable's horse rode off, with a wave of his hat. Constable Glennon, securing a horse from the farmer, took a short cut, intercepted Daly, and covered him with a revolver. Daly, who was a superb horseman, sent his horse straight at a wire fence, and though he got over it, he severely injured his ankle through the horse coming down with him. The constable locked him up. The prisoner feigned madness and was sent to Kenmore Lunatic Asylum, from which he escaped in a week.*

Professor Paddy Kemp's buckjump show travelled extensively from 1903–1906, then from 1914 on and off until the late 20s. There are a series of disappearances and reappearances, obviously connected to his dance with the law, until 1934 when a catalogue selling his saddles referred to him as the 'late' Professor Kemp.

He was quite a character. Jack Pollard describes Jack Daly:

> *a swashbuckling spruiker with tree-trunk arms ... {he} had shoulder-length hair and a long, scraggly beard, and he would stride through dusty bush streets*

declaiming poetry, oozing saccharine sentiment, smacking his vast chest, an incorrigible brawler as wild as a rampaging buffalo.[23]

Lance Skuthorpe said that Kemp's poetry readings were better than his own, certainly more dramatic, but that Kemp could not match him with the horses. He claimed Kemp was a scruffer not a tamer. But later in his career Kemp was well known for his horse-gentling skills; he apparently used some secret 'scent' to quieten the horses — chloroform perhaps.

Kemp, it seems, was a consummate rogue, but like many rogues, he was a likeable one. He put on a free show for prostitutes at one time, because he felt sorry for them. He always did well by having a woman, usually a 'Miss Kemp', as part of his team to ride buckjumpers and bullocks. The first verifiable appearance of 'Professor Kemp' and his buckjump show is in Mackay, Queensland, in June 1903. He was at the time on the run from the Victorian police, who knew him as Daly or Montgomery.

These three men had all been in and around circuses and itinerant showmen throughout the 1890s, learning the tricks of the entertainment trade from the experts. They probably worked together on numerous occasions and the supposed animosity played out in the challenges between them in the papers was for publicity. All of them pulled huge audiences wherever they went and they travelled the length and breadth of the country. In the cities, thousands of people would pay to get in and there were hundreds in the outback towns. It was highly lucrative.

Sometime before 1910, Skuthorpe's show made £1400 in one night at Richmond, Queensland, and £1700 another time not long after at the Brisbane Exhibition. It was the first time Australian roughriders — the horsebreakers, stockmen and drovers — performed in their own show. Roughriding ventured out of the stations and stock camps and into the limelight.

The key feature of the Australian buckjump shows was the unrideable horse as drawcard. 'Unrideable' buckjumpers pitched against 'unthrowable' roughriders *was* the show. And apart from Skuthorpe and to a lesser extent Kemp, it was not the talented men and women riders that were the 'stars' of the shows — but the horses. These small independent outfits were in direct competition with the large flamboyant American productions. They scoffed at the American razzamatazz, the phoney re-enactments of burning stagecoaches and pioneer homes, promoted themselves as 'authentically Australian' and went for dramatised realism — with artistic licence, of course. Skuthorpe, in particular, was a stickler for Australian authenticity:

> *He adhered to outback realism in the staging of every act until it became a fetish, and always he went to the outback searching for ideas. He introduced bullock roasts, cattle throwing and tying contests ... and insisted that his staff wear bush clothes even in the biggest cities.*[24]

Skuthorpe lugged around cumbersome piles of gear to provide his own 'authentic' posts and rails and created backdrops of eucalyptus trees and branches. Even Martini, who was not a born and bred bushman and who augmented his buckjump show with circus acts and other entertainment, took pains to advertise his Australianness:

> *The management wishes the public to understand that this is not a Wild West, Deadwood Dick, or Broncho Bill Show, and there are no alleged Wild Men with long hair and big hats such as have been gulling the Australian Public for some years past.*[25]

Drawing a house

But perhaps the quintessentially Australian aspect of our travelling buckjump shows is the amusing fact that they operated chiefly on betting. Exhibitions were given by the show's employed roughriders and of course the key to the show was challenging the nightly crowd — volunteers out of the audience or by prearrangement could win ten or twenty pounds if they could stay on a horse for a certain length of time. Via the newspapers, showmen threw out challenges around Australia for roughriders to come in and have a go. The showmen promoted themselves by backing their star horses in a challenge to all and sundry (except their employees) to ride them under certain conditions, and the roughriders would then back themselves (or find someone else to) in the contest against the showman's horse. It was all about a wager. Most showmen had a continual open challenge for the star roughriders of the day to back themselves against their gun horse. It was generally £100, though Skuthorpe had £1000 on Firefly in the 20s and Martini backed Bobs against Skuthorpe for £1000 in 1906. Skuthorpe, being an excellent rider, was his own star and had a continual open-ended challenge to the world that he would back himself to ride anything against anyone.

A lot of times it was rigged for publicity and the money 'had a string on it', but generally it was fair dinkum and for the most part the horses won. 'Gs' were sometimes planted in the audience. If no-one else came forwards, these prearranged riders, often members of their own or another professional outfit, ensured that the audience would get to see some action. Exhibitions were given every night but the crowd was mainly there to see the competitions between their local men and the showmen's horses or their local horses and the showmen's roughriders. The show's managers doubled as bookies and no doubt the wagers that flew between showmen and roughriders were nothing compared to what was going on in the crowd. The buckjump shows were extremely popular in the towns and cities of Australia, which were full of game horsemen, rogue horses and gamblers.

As practically everyone in the country rode horses, buckjumping was something everyone could relate to and have an opinion about. For the most part competitions took place in small roped rings, 30–40 feet in diameter, softened with sawdust, with stringer seating and carbide lamps, surrounded by calico or hessian side walls to prevent onlookers. In time some of the shows expanded and went under canvas. Because the rings were small people were packed in close to the action, which heightened the tension and drama.

The showmen were always on the lookout for buckjumpers and advertised for people to bring in those with promise. If they bucked well, the showmen bought them. Once it dawned that the job involved walking all over Australia between gigs, some buckjumpers stopped bucking; not all horses enjoyed being in the spotlight either. If a horse did enjoy its new career and was good at it then it was set — corn-fed, groomed, fussed over and worked a maximum of 15 minutes a week. It sure beat being a stockhorse and over the years there have been many horses who bucked professionally for 10 or 20 years or more. The great buckjumpers were not just legendary for their spirit in the ring, but also because they settled into the lifestyle of living on the road. They had the stamina and heart to travel and buck consistently and victoriously, sometimes up to three times a day.

Roughriders who came in to challenge were also offered a job if they were good. Naturally the showmen didn't want their horses beaten — the good riders were put on the payroll quickly and therefore were not allowed to ride the horse out. They stayed for a week, a month or a season and got to see Australia while they were at it. The secret to longevity as a professional roughrider was threefold — staying on till the whistle; vaulting off and out of the tiny ring stylishly, without getting your head kicked in; and being able to live rough and work like a trojan. Young men and women would join up and ride with the shows for the freedom, travel and adventure. Like the circuses, they also provided a family for those who had none. For youngsters who loved horses it was enjoyable, exciting and provided a way of earning a crust.

Exhibition rides were only ever for six to eight bucks maximum. The boss would signal by word or whistle when he wanted his riders to jump off, before the horse tired or stopped bucking. It was and still is important to let the horse think it was the victor and not break its spirit. Horses are proud. The duration of challenge rides varied depending on the horse, the rider and the deal. A showman would challenge local heroes to ride his 'outlaw' for anything from 10 seconds to 2 minutes or to a standstill — meaning till it stopped bucking. Riding a buckjumper till it gave up was rare in professional buckjump shows and only happened with horses or riders without reputations or where there was very big money and professional reputations at stake. Once a bucking horse knew it had been beaten, it would frequently 'never be the same again' — neither would its reputation as an unrideable outlaw, and therefore its commercial viability.

Among the great Australian roughriders who were often seen in the showmen's rope rings in the years before World War I were Lance Skuthorpe and his gun riders, Queensland Harry, Rolly Doctor and Galloping Jones; Martini's men, Billy Jonas and Billy Waite; and the feisty Miss Kemp, who rode for all of them at one time or another. Then there were Mulga Jack; Thorpe McConville; Tom Lloyd's son, Ned; Bert Fletcher; the Dempsey brothers, Jack and Arthur from Narrandera; Jigger Lavell; Ben Bridge; Joe White; Billy Carver; Charley Armstrong — Melba's first husband; Snowy Baldwin; George Hoskins; and all the Jacks — Morrissey, Hehir, Atkins, Pendergast, Noble, and Jacky Jacky.

Rough riding, rough living

The Australian stockman's skill of whipcracking was the most popular act between the bucking horses. Skuthorpe and Kemp tamed horses. Skuthorpe could rope anything that moved. Martini invented 'Fun in the Stockyard' — ponies, mules and donkeys would be let out into the ring and all the kids from the audience could jump in, try to ride them and generally run amok with the help of the clowns. Martini and Kemp had performing dogs who could jump through hoops and hop about on their hind legs, and ponies who tapped the time of day with their hooves or pointed to the prettiest girl in the crowd. Boxing was also touted about — Harry Seymour toured with Martini for some time and Skuthorpe, naturally, backed himself to fight anyone who dared and breathed.

Skuthorpe and Kemp both recited Australian bush poetry and told tallish stories during the breaks. They all drew on their circus backgrounds, Martini in particular, used various circus and vaudeville performers, including Miss Mena Val, who cracked whips and did bicycle aerial wire acts, Bonita the sharpshooter and her sister, Cleo the snake charmer. But it was the buckjumpers and roughriders that people came to see.

Apart from Martini and later Mrs Martini, Kemp and Skuthorpe, some of the other buckjump shows from that era belonged to roughriders who wanted to be their own boss — 'Snowy Baldwin's Buckjumpers'; Jack Morrisey with his 'Great Buckjumping Show';[26] Frank McFarlane with his 'vicious outlaw', Frisco; the Spillman Brothers; and Jack Williams. Some had it all covered, for example 'Phillip's Buckjumping, Athletic and Novelty Circus'. The Americans were still about — Broncho George until at least 1909 — and in 1908 Bud Atkinson brought his 'American Circus and Wild West Show' to Australia. He returned in 1912–13 bringing champion ropespinner, Tex McLeod. Wirths continued their Wild West entertainment; Will Rogers toured for them in 1903 billed as the Cherokee Kid and in 1912 they promoted 'Captain Rose's Wild West Show'. The Tullipans, Cuzcos and Ashtons all had a circus and buckjumping show on the road.

Many of the smaller buckjump shows stayed in and around their home territory, say Victoria or central Queensland, or the Hunter and New England districts, but the bigger outfits travelled more extensively and the main agricultural and circus show circuit went from Adelaide to Cairns and everywhere in between, with occasional jaunts across to Tasmania and Western Australia. Apart from the cities, the buckjump shows were most popular in the bush towns of cattle country, which were full of fearless horsemen, great buckjumpers and expert crowds. Whenever they were near the mission stations Aboriginal boys would come in and have a go and get a job if they were 'sticky' enough. This era was the only time Aboriginal roughriders were more often than not the stars of the professional arena.

Moving from town to town was slow and laborious. They travelled on horseback with pack-saddles and bullock- or mule-drawn wagons along rough bush tracks, cut up badly by other travellers and teamsters. When it rained everything stopped. They generally averaged 20–30 miles a day, it used to take six weeks to get from Sydney to Brisbane. The bucking stock, mules and ponies were driven along behind by the horse tailers, either the children or a roughrider. Horses were picked up from all over the country and dropped off in someone's paddock when they stopped bucking.

Getting around was also dangerous and the showmen needed to be ingenious as Jack Pollard's account reveals:

They forded rivers in Northern Queensland, with the Skuthorpe children sitting in the waggon banging kerosene tins to frighten away crocodiles. They cut down trees and lashed them to the back of the waggon to brake it on very steep hills, when ordinary brakes would not hold. They fought to control their waggon team when snakes frightened them and they shaped to stampede.

They bogged in sand going through a dry creek. Mrs Skuthorpe took her children and sat them down beside a lime tree, and went back to the creek to help. They crossed rivers in flood with empty fuel drums acting as buoys.[27]

The showmen tried to keep out of each other's way. Most had an advance agent who plotted the route according to seasons and where the other showmen were. They avoided drought-stricken areas because the stock needed grass — star buckjumpers were hand-fed but the rest grazed as they travelled. The agents then travelled ahead in a horse and sulky. They booked the grounds, arranged paddocks and feed for the stock, pasted handbills and posters up all over town and placed advertisements and challenges in the local papers.

The southern showmen took 'winter quarters' (a break) at someone's property for a few months when it was too cold to show outside, during this time they worked at whatever they could.

From the beginning there were women roughriders — buckjumping relies on skill and balance, not brute strength. Kate Kelly, sister of Ned, is alleged to have escaped the publicity surrounding her family after Ned was hung, finding anonymity in a Wild West show in the 1880s. Miss Kemp was adopted into the circus community before riding bullocks and horses in all the buckjump shows from around 1905 on and off to the mid–1920s. Ettie Edwards was roughriding and trick-riding in the tent shows pre-World War I, and Violet Skuthorpe rode bucking bullocks in her husband's show from 1911.

It was a pretty rough and amoral world. If a woman was not partnered with a man then folklore has it that every 'good girl' who travelled the show circuit slept with a pistol under her pillow. Jack Pollard's description of Skuthorpe's extended family tells why:

> *He always employed a nucleus of experienced bushmen. But Lance rarely turned down someone seeking a job ... Frequently they were boys who had run away from boys' homes or prison terms; but such was Lance's faith in the therapeutic qualities of the bush, he always thought he could handle the most dangerous men. 'The runaways usually dropped out once the going got tough,' he said ... {There were} card-sharps or confidence men, who would remain with the show until they reached the race meeting they wanted to get to. There were knife-throwers and gunmen and jugglers and acrobats ... Lance let them come along while they did not interfere with his show.*[28]

There were plenty of women who worked alongside their men both in and out of the arena. Wives often kept the books and ran the business as well as organising behind the scenes and keeping everyone fed, clean and healthy. They depended a lot on the Indian/Afghan hawkers and the Chinese merchants for supplies; meat was usually plentiful, but vegetables, cloth, pannikins, saucepans, utensils, cutlery and so forth were not. Women did the cooking and washing, droving and driving, fixing, mending and bandaging, and they brought up the kids. None of this was any mean feat considering they were living out of a dusty wagon, exposed to the elements and continually on the move. They cooked on an open fire, washed in cut-down kerosene tins, creeks and rivers, slept in tents or under the wagon and then often, at the end of the day, donned a glamorous outfit and rode in the show. No-one stole the show like a woman on a buckjumper or a bullock, especially in the practically womanless west.

1906, an eventful year

The first of Australia's two most famous buckjumping competitions took place in 1906. Martini set up in the grounds of Christchurch School on Pitt Street, opposite the entrance of the new Central Railway Station. He had a record run of 22 weeks with 4000 in the audience each night. There was whipcracking with Saltbush Bill, buckjumping exhibitions and competitions and 'Fun in the Stockyard'. But Martini's drawcard was always the fiery bay gelding, Bobs.

Bobs was bred by a Mr Sawtell of Byramine Station, near Cloncurry, Queensland. He had thrown all the local challengers when Martini arrived with his show in 1904 and after seeing Bobs in action, Martini bought him for £4/10. By the time Martini and his show reached Sydney Bobs was still unridden, despite some 800 attempts.

Early in 1906 *The Referee* printed a number of interviews with the top professional roughriders of the day: 'Bobs, of course, is the champion among buckers ... I don't think there is [a] man living that could keep on him. He is the only horse I could never manage,' ventured Jack Dempsey. Billy Waite added:

> *By the time I was on him three quarters of a minute I was leg weary and sick and I lost my seat and Bobs. It was the roughest ride I ever struck in an English saddle. Bobs is a tough 'un. I've ridden some warm mokes in West Australia, but they soon give in. With Bobs the longer you stick to him, the worse he gets.*

There was a standing open challenge to ride Bobs and Martini backed him for anything up to £100. The basic wage for an unskilled worker was little more than £2 a week so it paid to have a go.

Bobs lured 'Jigger' Lavell, 'champion' of Victoria, and Jack Pendergast, 'champion' of New South Wales, to Sydney and defeated them both. As early as January a Mr Evans from Queensland had publicly offered to back Martini's archrival, Lance Skuthorpe, to ride Bobs but in the interests of good publicity, Lance dragged it out until 21 March. He had to get down to Sydney from Queensland first — he and his 'Boys from the Bush' had just finished a show with Kemp's Buckjumpers — and he figured he might as well bring his whole kit and caboodle with him. On 7 February *The Referee* announced that Lance had dropped into the office with a Mr R. Clark and deposited £25 for a match for £100 for 28 February, conditions 'now being discussed'. It is believed that someone, possibly a racehorse owner by the name of Cassells, offered Skuthorpe £1000 if he could ride Bobs. Martini had apparently been bragging that even 'the great Lance Skuthorpe' couldn't ride Bobs, but whether he put his money where his mouth was is unknown.

Once they were both in Sydney, Martini and Skuthorpe were calling for challengers from around the country to come in and ride their horses. Bobs was a bigger drawcard than anything Skuthorpe had except himself. Skuthorpe had to do something to take away the glory from his opponent, or to give fantastic publicity to both of them ... He'd have to ride Bobs. The advert finally appeared on 14 March that Martini's Buckjumping Show would present:

> *Billy Waite v. Skuthorpe, Saturday March 17th. 3 horses each. Waite will ride Skuthorpe's three horses in a hunting saddle without kneepads. Skuthorpe to ride Martini's three horses in stock saddle with 3 inch kneepads — including Bobs!*[29]

It was the match of the universe. Skuthorpe, even at 36 years of age, was considered to be Australia's best buckjump rider, the professional roughrider Billy

Waite was considered to be the only other man at the time in his class, and Bobs to date was unridden.

There were three postponements before the competition finally took place on St Patrick's Day. It was allegedly held in an auditorium below street level at Rawson Place in Sydney.[30] There were more than 3000 people squeezed in, including the Governor, Sir Henry Rawson:

> *Waite, at 23 and about thirteen stone, is in the heyday of life, and as active as a panther, a gift that he is never disposed to hide under a bushel as he disdains to crawl through the slip-rails and jumps from the ground into the saddle on a bucking horse. He is as clever as a fox terrier, a first-class horseman.*[31]

There was much discussion and disagreement about saddles. Eventually Lance and one of Martini's men caught a cab to a saddlers in George Street where they picked out a saddle they both agreed to, took the cab back and continued with further arguments, debates and negotiations. 'The crowd in the popular parts began to get violent', said the *Evening News*, and a couple of men hopped into the ring, evidently wanting to fight, but they were bundled out. Finally the competition got under way around midnight. Waite went first and rode all three of Skuthorpe's horses — one of which was called Dargin's Grey, 'named after the most famous buckjumper of all' — without any trouble. And then, finally, Martini led Bobs into the ring.

After all the yelling, whistling and carrying on the crowd 'hushed and edged forward' as Lance bowed extravagantly and vaulted on. Bobs bucked the second he hit the saddle and Skuthorpe rode him ... to a standstill:

> *The crowd's wailing, screeching near-hysteria quietened now as it realized Bobs would not dislodge Skuthorpe; and as the last bucks ebbed away, Skuthorpe dropped his eyes sadly ...*[32]

It was something a buckjump showman would never like to do, ride a buckjumper — the buckjumper — to the finish. But those were the conditions; it was worth a lot; and it was business. The crowd of course cheered and clapped like crazy but Skuthorpe then forfeited the rest of the competition to Waite. He had ridden Bobs and didn't want to continue the contest as he didn't trust the judges and he had done what he came to do. He also might have been a tad shaken; Bobs was a very tough horse to ride.

There is strong suspicion among showmen that it was a put-up show, that the £1000 had a string on it. Maybe it *was* all for publicity. In any event it worked, as that particular ride out of a million rides is the one that escaped obscurity. And Martini and Skuthorpe both drew huge crowds to their shows ever after.

Hopelessly tempted by the phenomenal success of Martini and Skuthorpe in the big southern cities, Professor Kemp decided to risk venturing out of Queensland. In May 1906, he was gamely showing in Melbourne when he was recognised and arrested for his earlier horse theft. The *Western Argus* reported: 'The accused, who is 6 ft, 3 in. in his stockings, presented a picturesque appearance in court.' He was remanded on bail at £1000 and, while defending the allegations against him, Kemp's Buckjumpers enjoyed a successful run at Fitzgerald's circus building under the careful supervision of Mr Castles, his business manager, and Miss Kemp, his leading lady. *The Referee* records that on the first night of Professor Kemp's buckjumping exhibition, 'The place was densely crowded, partly because the people dearly love a horse show that is good, and partly because of the publicity that had been conferred upon the "Professor" by his arrest by the police.'

The week after that Professor Kemp 'temporarily retired, owing to legal complications' but the show was kept going by Miss Kemp, well known for her efficiency and organisation, whether it was leading the buckjumping troupe or later, hiding out with her cattle-duffing gang. Snowy Baldwin and Miss Kemp did the roughriding, the latter with a 'dazzling succession of flying bucks', Charlie Hassett gave a stockwhip performance and there was a lasso act and performing dogs. But 'the crowd wanted bucking, and more bucking; they hungered for horse and the more it capered and pawed and kicked the more the for-the-time-being critter was appreciated'. The shows were 'calculated to please all lovers of horseflesh', and the crowds were 'immense' every night.[33] After that season finished Martini was having a break, during which time (Billy) Waite's Buckjumping Show went on the road. Baldwin's Buckjumpers also started touring. Snowy Baldwin probably bought out Kemp's show and hit the road while Kemp was doing his time in jail. Miss Kemp, who had performed with Skuthorpe and Kemp for years, must have then gone to join Martini because she supposedly became his wife, or took his name at least, before he died the following year.

Buckjump shows were constantly dealing with accidents and tragedies of all types, and the performers were not the only ones who copped it. In Armidale on 2 July 1907, on the afternoon before his show was set to start, Martini was picking up sawdust for the ring from the local sawmill. A train went by and its piercing whistle scared his horses. Martini was thrown from the wagon and sustained internal injuries. He died in the early hours of the following morning at the Royal Hotel.

Mrs Jane Martini, as Miss Kemp was now known, again picked up the reins and continued gallantly on with the show through to the end of 1910. She still had Bobs, and she had Joe White as her gun roughrider. She used *The Referee* to good effect for publicity. Each week under the heading 'Those Buckjumpers' or 'Those Buckjumpers Again' and 'More about Buckjumpers' she took part in long-running arguments and challenges with Lance Skuthorpe, Snowy Baldwin and various other buckjump showmen and roughriders. As each one made claim to a legendary ride, someone else would write in and debunk it.

The letters argued about challenges made and broken, times, conditions and handicaps, types and sizes of saddles and kneepads, and whether or not a long flank or a short one should be applied. To quote Mrs Martini:

I will back Joe White to ride Skuthorpe's Snips in a hunting saddle with a loin cord tied on. What I do bar is a long flank rope, as what the horse can't do, he {Skuthorpe} will, by holding the other end, to get the man off.[34]

She had a point. Skuthorpe, who generally challenged nationally, backing his horses or himself for big dollars, was careful to always include that the use of the 'long flank rope' was part of the deal, for example:

FIREFLY The greatest buckjumper the world has ever seen — This is the opinion of Lance Skuthorpe, the man who has ridden buckjumpers all his life and has never been thrown. Can be backed to throw any man in the world for £1000 out of a poley saddle, no spurs, with long flank rope.[35]

There is no way Skuthorpe could afford to risk paying anyone £1000 for anything. He was an expert horseman and rope man, and it's simple to yank a horse out of rhythm with a long flank. It's said he could even throw a half-hitch around a roughrider's boot and send him flying. They probably all did it, which might explain why there were so many unrideable horses. It's a controversial subject as the remaining buckjump showmen and women completely deny this sort of thing ever happened and yet the remaining roughriders who worked for them say it happened a lot.

Not all showmen used long flank ropes; some used short ones, but the long ones were easier to retrieve. They were about 30 feet long and made of rope (unlike the fleece-lined leather straps of today) and after each ride, as soon as the rope man let go, it would loosen and be kicked off. No-one had to chase the bucking horse around the ring to get the flank rope off it.

Buckjumping was, after all, the showmen's livelihood. They may not have meddled with the locals coming in and riding horses for a few pounds here and there, but if they were offering really big money it would have been very tempting. Skuthorpe's Snips and Queenslander and Martini's Dargin's Grey and Bobs were all exceptional bucking horses, but no horse is unrideable and they all have bad days. A thousand pounds is a lot to lose if your star horse isn't in the mood for it or isn't feeling 100 per cent.

Roughrider Dan Edwards rode for the Gills after World War I through the 1920s and then Tom Handley's buckjump show in the late 20s and early 30s. Dan says unlike the boxing tents, buckjump shows were never rigged, but when it came to the local riders and challengers, everything was done to unseat them. A long flank rope could be used to turn the horses, especially when they were up high in the air and a rider may have lost his seat for a split second — a quick tug and he'd never get back into the saddle. 'A good roping man,' according to Dan, 'can make a horse do anything and that went on all the time.'

Although these early buckjump shows were advertised and written up in sporting newspapers like Sydney's *The Referee*, which dedicated a couple of pages each to cricket, football, horseracing, boxing, athletics, rowing, swimming and so on, they were in the entertainment section on the back page with the theatre, circus and vaudeville news. The buckjump proprietors also advertised and eulogised in entertainment papers, such as *Stagelands* and *The Showman*. These published chatty letters written by showmen and theatrical types from all parts of Australia, indeed the world, letting each other and their fans know where they were and what they were doing. The buckjump shows remained a grand mixture of sport and entertainment right through to the late 1950s.

Wild Australia entertains England

By 1910 the pastoral industry had recovered from the calamitous effects of depression and prolonged droughts and was prospering with increased demand for local beef. The buckjumping shows also continued to prosper, and we went international.

Australia was invited to contribute to the 'Pageant of the Empire' celebrations for the coronation of King George V. An accomplished horseman and showman called Alf Neave of Bullfinch, Western Australia, gathered a troupe of the finest roughriders, circus performers and equestrian acts from around the country. He purchased Mrs Martini's buckjumping show, riders, horses and performers and also Phillip Lytton's show, 'The Australian Buckjumpers', that was touring India at the time, starring Billy Waite and Snips. In March 1911 they sailed for England under the banner of 'Wild Australia' and they opened the Pageant of Empire at London's Crystal Palace during the first week in May 1911. King George and Queen Mary were reported to have enjoyed the show on several occasions and even commanded private performances for themselves.

'Wild Australia' was billed as a representation of a stockyard on an Australian cattle station in what was called 'Never Never country'. It depicted scenes 'from the everyday life of boys and girls who spent their lives in the saddle'. The cattle were Scottish (the Australian cattle being barred for quarantine reasons), and the show was a great success. Apparently the whole of England was on holiday for a week and capacity crowds of 5000 filled two or three sessions a day in London. Wild Australia then toured the country.

The showmen/roughriders, 'rigged out in the orthodox Queensland outfit of skin-tight white riding breeches, concertina leggings, white shirts and brown felt hats',[36] included Billy Waite and Billy Jonas (both had been Martini's star roughriders), Jack Morrissey, Jack Hawkins, Thorpe McConville, Ned Lloyd, Billy Lea, Jack Atkins, Mick Terry and Ernest Winning. '"Wild Australia" is a perfect feast of buckjumping,' a newspaper gushed, 'and while Billy Waite or Ned Lloyd or Thorpe McConville or any other of the bush lads is "up" the spectator gets more thrills in 20 seconds than he probably experienced in the preceeding 20 years.'[37]

'Wild Australia' offered a prize of £500, open to three representatives of each of the crack cavalry regiments of England and the continent, for a roughriding contest using the Australian horses. Among these were Bobs, Grey Echo and Bumper the bucking mule. Bobs was the big challenge and £50 was offered to any man who could ride him for 30 seconds in a poley saddle with no kneepads or stirrups and no bridle, only a neck rein, leaving the horse's head free — Australian roughriding conditions — no-one succeeded.[38]

In addition to the buckjumpers and roughriders, Miss Agnes Hyland (of Hyland's Vice Regal Circus, Professor Hyland's daughter), Australia's champion horsebreaker, gave exhibitions of horsebreaking (taming and riding) and also rode buckjumpers. Miss Neave, niece of Alf, rode bullocks bareback. 'The infamous buckjumper' Grey Echo was ridden daily as an exhibition by Billy Waite, who also demonstrated whipcracking using stockwhips and bullock whips, including the longest stockwhip in the world — 60 feet long and weighing 26 pounds. The rest of Martini's show was there too — the Dreshler Sisters, Cleo with her snakes and crocs and Miss Bonita; Australia's champion rifle shot, Miss Marion Waite; and Jack Morrissey also cracked whips. 'Fun in the Stockyard' entertained the children.

Australian versions of American Wild West show acts and skits included: the round-up; lassoing; 'The Horse Thief', realistically illustrating the fate meted out to one; an exciting kangaroo chase by Australian Aborigines; double bank riding — 'how new chums are taught to ride in the bush'; the 'Commonwealth contrast', the largest camel in Australia next to the smallest horse; demonstrations of log chopping and sheep shearing; and the grand finale, 'The Kelly Gang', a skit depicting Ned Kelly's last stand at the pub in Glenrowan, which was extra ghoulish considering that Ned Lloyd, Ned Kelly's nephew, was one of the buckjump riders in the show.

After six months the show finished and the troupe dispersed. Jack Morrissey and Thorpe McConville both found work in the USA — Morrissey with Buffalo Bill Cody's outfit and Thorpe with the 101 Ranch Wild West Show. Ned Lloyd and Agnes Hyland allegedly went to the USA and joined the mighty Hagenbach-Wallace Circus. Folklore says Billy Waite also went to the USA and died there soon afterwards — what became of Waite is a mystery, as is the fate of Bobs.[39]

However, these were not the first Australian roughriders to work and compete in the USA. There is the wonderful, but unsubstantiated, story of an Australian fellow named Daly — he may or may not have been our Professor Kemp — who went over with a shipment of horses and met former bushranger Frank Gardner in San Francisco. By then a prosperous hotelier, Gardner organised a series of roughriding contests against the Californian cowboys and backed the young Australian for £100. Daly 'emerged triumphant, much to the amazement of the West Coast champions, who had imagined themselves pre-eminent in the art of "bronco-busting".'[40]

Andy Middleton, a roughrider from Victoria, was reputedly three times World Champion Roughrider at competitions 'probably' held in San Francisco before World War I.[41] And John Rogers, a roughrider from near Roma, Queensland, claimed he was the Champion Buckjump Rider of Australia and the United States in about 1912.[42]

The outdoor showmen — whether they were circus or buckjumping people or any of the various eccentric entertainers that wandered the country — were all extremely adaptable and enterprising. They would change their names and appropriate each other's names — and especially each other's horse's names — to capitalise on fame. They often joined forces or imitated each other's shows and acts, all of which makes it virtually impossible to get to the bottom of this anomalous, amorphous tribe and renders the truth elusive.

Some buckjump shows came and went in weeks or months; some lasted years and they varied tremendously in size and scope. Few of the travelling buckjump showmen were in the business for any great length of time. They came and went depending on the seasons and seasonal work available. The smaller shows only really scratched out a living and lasted a few weeks or a season. The Skuthorpes managed longer than a season and were on the road practically non-stop until the mid–1950s; Lance Snr died in 1958. The Lennons and Ashtons are all still in the business after a century of outdoor showmanship, as are the Gills, a circus and rodeo family with a venerable history. These showmen were related both literally and figuratively, by blood, sweat and tears, a love of horses and horsemanship, animals in general and a gift for training them. They all trod the same long trails and survived off their remarkable talents and skills.

The American Wild West shows, circuses and buckjump shows put a whole new angle on the roughriding business. Our already popular horsemen — the horsebreakers and stockmen whose trade it was — moved out of the poetry anthology and into the limelight. They became an entertaining spectacle celebrating a great contest, the battle between man and beast. Other stockmen and bushmen's skills such as whipcracking, bullock riding, bullock throwing and tying, which the likes of Gordon and Lawson had eulogised, were exhibited and capitalised upon — they recited Gordon and Lawson while they were doing it!

The Australian buckjump shows were very different from the faked glamour of the American outfits.

Ours were raw competitions under the incandescent carbide lights where horsemen and bushmen could choose to watch or to have a go. There must have been a great sense of camaraderie in the midst of the grunts, squeals, shouts and cheers. In the cities it suddenly seemed the 'bush' was in town, in all its hyped-up, sawdusty drama. Literally thousands packed in around the ring; to watch the dashing, horsemen and the 'outlaw' buckjumpers pitch their skills and determination against each other and thrilled the crowds with daring and danger. In the bush towns the crowds loved watching 'their own'.

For the showmen and for the roughriders who went with them, buckjumping became a profession and a way of life. It was the 'head on down the road' — 'free as the breeze' — 'do as you please' kind of lifestyle that 'cowboys', according to their mythology, are supposed to have.

3

THE ROPE RING AND THE TENT SHOWS

Texas Jack, you are amusin'. By Lord Harry, how I laughed
When I seen yer rig and saddle with its bulwarks fore-and-aft;
Holy smoke! In such a saddle how the dickens can yer fall?
Why, I seen a gal ride bareback with no bridle on at all!

Wild Australia

PROGRAMME
OF THE
Thrilling and :::
Realistic Spectacle
OF
LIFE ON
THE CATTLE PLAINS
AND
IN THE BUSH.

EXHIBITIONS TWICE DAILY
At 3 & 8.
Doors open at 2.30 and 7.30.

ADMISSION:
Reserved Seats 5/- 4/- 3/- 2/-
Other Parts 6d. & 1/-
Children under 12 Half price except 6d. parts

A family affair

THE MANY BUCKJUMP SHOWS ranged from fly-by-nighters who ran in some brumbies and threw up hessian side walls stitched together from chaff bags, through to large circus and Wild West shows with 50-foot rings and a canvas canopy which at least sheltered the audience. And, if they prospered, they graduated to the huge extravaganzas put on under a proper big top circus tent, as did the likes of Thorpe McConville, the Skuthorpes and the Gills.

But most of the travelling buckjump shows fell somewhere in the middle. They had canvas side walls, sawdust floors, three strands of rope making up a ring and stringer (collapsible) seats; at night they were lit by carbide lights. Between the buckjumpers they had acts like whipcracking, performing dogs and ponies. The circus-based families added tumblers, gymnastics, acrobatics and equestrian performers. Many towns had a buckjump show at their sports days or carnivals to raise money for community causes and the shows never travelled anywhere at all.

Often the smaller buckjump shows followed the agricultural show circuit, sideshowing alongside the boxing tents. It was quite lucrative as the bushmen, cattlemen, stockmen and horsemen would already be in town so there were always men to accept their challenges and an enthusiastic audience to watch them. Good crowds were also guaranteed at other bush carnivals and in cities during show week or over the Christmas break. If they were members of the Showmen's Guild, buckjump showmen could set up on the side of the showground or in sideshow alley. Some smaller line-up shows — so-called because the roughriders, or the boxers as the case may be, lined up on the board out front and spruikers yelled their spiel to the crowd — stuck entirely to the agricultural show as sideshow business. Others, like the Gills and Skuthorpes, took their small turnouts to agricultural shows, but when they had bigger shows they'd travel independently. If a showman was not a member of the guild, they would set up elsewhere in town on a vacant block or paddock, often with other carnival shows. Sometimes there was a buckjump show at the showground doing morning and afternoon sessions and after the showground activities had finished for the day — there were no lights on the showgrounds back then — another buckjump show would gear up elsewhere in town to do the Saturday night. Sundays were always a day off. However, most buckjump shows, were independent and, favouring larger regional centres and cattle country, they went where they pleased and stayed as long as they could pull a crowd.

During World War I most of the travelling shows and circuses stopped. Just under 40 per cent of men and boys between the ages of 18 and 44 joined up. Most of the horsemen from the bush were drawn to the Light Horse divisions and the roughriders were recruited for the remount units, which specialised in horsebreaking and training. A few showmen continued on — the Eronis, Wirths, St Leons, Colleanos and Ashtons all toured during the war with reduced versions of their circus and buckjump shows. Professor Kemp's buckjump show appeared sporadically from 1914 until his death sometime in the late 20s or early 30s. A Miss Kemp had a show on the road in 1915 and the same (or another) Miss Kemp was showing in south-east Queensland in the 1920s. Whether this is the Miss Kemp also known as Jane Martini is not known. An 'Australian Buckjumping Show' starring roughrider Mulga Jack and the horse Queen Snips did a season at the Hippodrome at Wirth's Park in Melbourne in March 1917. The following year, same time, same place, the 'Australian Buckjumping and Wild West Show' was on with Jack West as manager and 40 head of 'unbeaten outlaws', including 'Demon, the man-eating horse' and a young Jack Hehir riding the buckjumpers.

According to Jack Pollard, when war was declared, Lance Skuthorpe was showing at the Brisbane Exhibition Ground. He'd bought a visiting American show called 'Joy Town', which included the great buckjumper, Queenslander. He charged a shilling a head, admitted those who were broke with an IOU then went broke himself. He tried to enlist but was rejected because of his partial deafness so he broke-in horses for the army instead. But before long Skuthorpe was back travelling with his buckjump show.[1]

By the time the war ended in 1918, the official death toll had reached ten million. Some 331 814 Australian men enlisted, 65 per cent were wounded and 56 639 killed, the highest rate of injury and death of any nation fighting for the British. Two out of every three Australians who went to the war either died as a result or were incapacitated in some way. An influenza epidemic, thought to have been brought back with the returning soldiers, killed another 11 989 people and didn't abate until 1920. It was a sorrowful time; every family in Australia was grieving. It was the job of our intrepid entertainers to cheer everybody up.

On 31 December 1918, the town of Coraki in New South Wales opened their local paper to this advertisement:

Hullo people. We are Ashton's Great Wild West Show. That genial gloom dispeller is here, broader, happier and more infectious than ever. And what's the reason? Why, because that bounding bunch of Buckjumping Horses and Steers, those devil may care riders commence their screaming joy ride of thrilling fun, and hair raising sensations that all Australians love. Because it's the cleanest, most sensational, and the Safest Show that has ever been in Australia, and because you can bring your wife and children without running any risk of getting hurt and sit and enjoy the old National Sport of Australia and America.[2]

Apart from a fertile imagination and entrepreneurial flair, showmen and their families had to have fortitude to survive life on the road, athleticism to survive life in the ring, and most importantly someone had to have the gift of the gab. The shows hinged on it, not only to negotiate and hustle for daily needs in different towns all over the country, but they had to be able to draw the crowds and entertain them.

As a ringmaster Lance Skuthorpe was a gifted orator and raconteur but apparently he had nothing on Professor Kemp, who would beat his chest and roar and bellow for effect. Tex Morton was legendary for 'sucking them in', as was Jack Gill, another larger than life character. Dramatic licence and theatrical exaggeration were part of daily life. The best of the showmen had the charisma to carry it all off with aplomb.

According to his nephew, John McConville, 'Thorpe McConville could talk under water, it's a McConville trait'. This was probably why, apart from business acumen, McConville's 'Wild Australia' became the biggest and most successful show of its time.

Thomas Thorpe McConville was born in 1890 in Tarago, New South Wales. He was the eldest of five children and his father was a railway stationmaster. As a child Thorpe had been blinded in one eye in an accident but it didn't affect his balance any more than Lance Skuthorpe's deafness affected his. Thorpe rode his pony to and from school and, inspired by Martini's buckjumping show, started organising buckjumping competitions with his pony at lunchtimes. When he left school he went to work breaking and dealing in horses for an uncle and soon had earnt a name as a horseman and roughrider.

In 1911 McConville was selected to ride in England with Alf Neave's 'Wild Australia' show. Then he went to America and signed up with the '101 Ranch Wild West Show'. The vision of Colonel Joe Miller, it employed more than 500 people and was reputedly the biggest Wild West show in the world at the time. Famous American cowboys with the show at this time were Tom Mix, Hoot Gibson, Tex McLeod and Bill Pickett, who invented bulldogging.

McConville was billed as the 'Australian cowboy' and the Americans thought his white shirt and breeches and concertina leggings looked like long underwear. All jokes ceased when he continually outrode their 'broncs' with grace and style in his tiny Australian saddle without stirrups. He eventually dyed his breeches.

When McConville returned to Australia in 1913 his father, by now a wealthy publican, bought him the Gillenbah Hotel in Narrandera. He operated it throughout the war as his blind eye made him unfit for service. To raise money for the war effort McConville ran buckjump shows in Narrandera — he and the other local heroes, the fabulous Dempsey Brothers, were the roughriders.

He married Alice New and they had a son, Douglas. Tragically Alice died after an operation in 1919, and in 1920 McConville sold the pub, handed the care of Douglas over to his in-laws, and headed for Sydney with a string of buckjumpers and the men to ride them. One of these young roughriders was Allan McPhee, also from Narrandera, who became a top all-round horseman and enjoyed a successful career in Australia and America in the 1920s in both buckjumping and high-jumping.

'Thorpe McConville's Wild Australia' set up in Hyde Park, where the entrance to St James Station is now. McConville was ringmaster; the horses were fit and shiny; and the men dressed in impeccable whites. It was good clean family entertainment, the public loved it, and he packed them in for eight weeks. Over the next 30 years Thorpe McConville's Wild Australia just got bigger and better.

Thorpe McConville always encouraged local talent. In Sydney he found 16-year-old lady roughrider Dorrie Phillips. She and her brother, Fred, joined 'Wild Australia' in 1922 and rode for McConville for the next seven years. Among his other notable discoveries were Jack Delahunt and 'Snowy' Thompson, who later represented Australia at Wembley, England in 1924. Snowy then formed his own show, which lasted until at least 1933. He took to riding his buckjumpers in a straitjacket for something a bit different.

During these early years 'Wild Australia' took place inside canvas side walls with no cover overhead. It wasn't long before McConville had a canopy over the seating to protect the audience from the rain but it was 1938 before he went under the big top. Throughout the 20s he stayed south, mainly around the Riverina District and Victoria, with infrequent trips to South Australia. He did annual shows in Melbourne and Adelaide and occasionally Sydney.

Thorpe McConville always thought big. In 1922, inspired by the Wirths, he had a special train built for Wild Australia. The show included buckjumping, surcingle riding and bullock riding. There was goat racing and donkey rides for the children plus the ever popular 'Fun in the Stockyard'. Saltbush Bill, the famous Aboriginal whipcracker, was one of his regulars and when in 1922 he included the strongman act, the Romas, they proved so popular that McConville began to employ all sorts of acts — lasso and rope experts, clowns and performing dogs. He hired the talented Jack Morrissey as a whipcracker, sharpshooter and ropespinner for a season or two until Morrissey started his own show in 1926.

McConville's roughriders included Billy Dodd, Gordon Cleeland, Fred Young, Harry Cook and Dorrie Phillips. Harold Lockwood, a champion cowboy ropespinner and lasso expert, also appeared. By 1922 he had about 60 head of horses, donkeys, mules and bucking bullocks. McConville built up a good string of horses — Touch and Go, Bouncer, Cayenne, Lone Hand, Blackboy, Rocket, Homewood, Grey Echo, Lightning and his star horse, Warrigal, the grey, remained unridden until the day he died. Snowy Thompson claimed Warrigal was the toughest horse he'd ever been tossed off.

Warrigal was later replaced by the big-hearted bucking pony, Young Warrigal, whose trick was to spin. He was one of those rare buckjumpers that could turn on a 'trey bit' (threepence). The standard challenge was £10 to anyone who could stay on a minute in a hunting saddle.

A rodeo dynasty

If one family could encapsulate the history of rodeo in Australia, it would have to be the Gill family. They can claim 125 years and five generations of showmen and roughriders. The Gill family emigrated from Scotland. Stanley Gill was born in Australia in 1885 and joined Denners' Circus as a cornet player in 1906, working the race meetings in New South Wales and Queensland. Jack Denner's daughter, Violet, was a talented trapeze artist. She married Stan Gill and they formed their own outfit, Gills' Circus, in 1917.

Stan and Violet had seven children, Pearl, Alice, Stan Jnr, Violet 'Tibby', Jack, Victor and Doyle. The three daughters and their mother were 'The Gill Sisters' but all seven children performed in their show — as trapeze artists, wire walkers, tumblers, rosin-back riders and clowns with balancing acts — and they had performing dogs and monkeys.

Although Stan Gill didn't ride, he was shrewd enough to capitalise on the buckjumpers' popularity and after World War I the family was on the road as 'Gill Brothers' Circus and Rodeo'. They had a very good buckjumper called Pitch and Toss during the 1920s, and Stan employed roughriders such as Dan Edwards until his sons were old enough to ride the buckjumpers in the early 1930s.

Jack, Stan and Doyle all became great roughriders, both in the rope rings and later in the rodeo arenas in the late 1930s. Violet Jnr married one of the visiting American cowboys and returned with him to the USA, whereupon they toured with Tom Mix. Victor didn't ride the rough ones much; he specialised in rosin-back riding and tumbling.

Around the ridges

Apart from those already mentioned there were many other buckjump showmen on the road in the 1920s and 30s. Jack Morrissey, a roughrider and whipcracker who also went to England with McConville as part of Wild Australia before spending time in the USA, had a buckjump show pre-World War I and, after a season or two with McConville in the early 20s, had his own show again in 1926. Tom Handley, a World War I veteran, was touring New South Wales before 1927 and he retired from the road in late 1934. Jack Williams had a buckjump show in New South Wales in the 20s and Sam Fuller and Galloping Jones, both ex-Skuthorpe riders, were touring in Queensland by the late 20s. The Galloper's show was short-lived but Fuller kept going to World War II and after the war he supplied buckjumpers to western Queensland rodeo committees such as Longreach and Winton. Jack Hehir, from Victoria, toured his show around Queensland, New South Wales and Victoria during the 20s, 30s and early 40s. Mick Fenton and daughters were about — Fenton had been a 'champion' buckjump rider and had ridden for Wirths' Wild West Show in the 1890s. In 1934 Philip Wirth considered Fenton 'the best rider Australia has ever produced'. Lipton's show featured lady roughrider, Ettie Edwards, and Buttson's and Jim Fisher's shows both toured in the 30s. Harry Farber and the Ireland family were covering Western Australia at that time.

Apart from the showmen themselves, most of whom were roughriders, other well-known professional roughriders during the 1920s included Mulga Jack, Mulga Fred, Colin McLeod, Allan McPhee, Vic Cowan, Mick Cowan, Curley Bell, Bob Brewster, Dan Edwards, Hilton McTaggart and Jack Stanton.

The Americans maintained a presence — Captain Greenhaig's Wild West Circus and Buckjumpers and Kid Carter's American Wild West Show both toured Australia during the 20s.

The Australian circus families kept up their buckjumping shows — notably St Leons' Circus and Rodeo, the Ashtons' Wild West Show and the Emery Brothers' Combined Circus and Buckjumping with their 'Notorious Australian Outlaw Buckjumpers'. Lennons' Circus and Buckjump show split three ways in 1927 and the family scattered to the circus winds.

In 1923 The Lennon Brothers Travelling Circus and Buckjump Show bought a horse called Rocky Ned, who went on to be the greatest buckjumper Australia has ever had. When the show split in 1927, old Mrs Lennon sold the horse to Tom Handley, who had a buckjump show, and it was during his years with Tom (1927–34) that Rocky Ned became *the* legend. Ned is spoken of in hallowed tones as 'a great old horse', 'a tame horse', 'an old fella', 'the quietest bloke' and 'there was no vice with the horse till he got in the ring'. Ned would never let them down. 'The four-legged fury', as he became known, was a very steep-kicking horse and extraordinarily fast. But his greatest advantage became longevity. 'He was smart.' 'He knew every trick in the book.' 'He's had that many victories, as soon as he felt you move he was gone.' 'He was the easiest horse to part company with that I have ever met.'

There has never been another horse to match Rocky Ned. He pelted professional roughriders in anything up to 36 challenges a week for nearly

20 years. For all the claims and counter-claims as to who might have ridden him, six men's names keep reappearing — Harry McPhee, Jack Stanton, Billy Timmins (twice), Hilton McTaggart (twice), Ben Singleton and Gordon Attwater — all while Ned bucked for Handley. Attwater's is the only undisputed claim. He rode Ned in Handley's tent for a minute at Grafton showgrounds in 1929.

There were some, the circus families in particular, who showed all over the country, making epic trips across the Nullarbor and the Top End, and covering the length and breadth of the east coast. But most showmen stuck to a certain area. Travel was difficult, particularly in the 20s as most still travelled by horse- or mule-drawn wagons with the horse tailers droving the rest of the stock behind them. The Gill family, for instance, trundled around New South Wales in horse-drawn vans with eight mules hauling a big wagonette full of seating, canvas and all the other paraphernalia. Their string of horses and steers brought up the rear with the horse tailers — children or roughriders such as Dan Edwards.

Dan Edwards was one of nine children, his parents were struggling share dairy farmers in Newcastle, New South Wales. He was 16 when he joined Gill Brothers' Circus and Rodeo in 1918: 'It was ten bob a week and your tucker, not much but better than nothing.' They were following the agricultural shows at this stage. Violet and her daughters were doing most of the circus acts between the rides. They used calico side walls six or eight feet high to stop the dust and the onlookers, a small three-rope ring and sawdust floors, with no canopy at all. If it rained, Dan remembers:

The cockies would pull the side walls out and get underneath the side walls and we'd be riding in the rain, slipping and sliding ... it was chaos all right ... you washed your clothes in the river, each man for himself. We'd be working until late at night. Say the show finished at 11.00, we'd have to pull the show down if we were going to move on, a one-day show I'm talking about, pull the tent down, pack it all up, have a cuppa tea and go to bed. Next morning at 5 or 6 o'clock ... away you'd go again.

In town or on the road they camped each night in swags under a tree or a wagon, pulling canvas under and over themselves if it rained. It was camp-oven fare on an open fire. Dan:

The food was very rough — you'd have a stew and a bit of curry, all that sort of thing, and plenty of bread and butter. {But} if you weren't there when the bread and butter hit the table, you'd miss out ... No, things were tough, I dunno why a man used to like it.

The buckjumpers were blindfolded and either held (lugged) or tied to a snubbing post while they were saddled and mounted in the ring. When the rider was ready they would just nod their head for the blindfold to be whipped off and the horse to be released — with a 'right-o' voice signal the horse would leap into action before they could release the tie or snap hook. A nod is still used today when the cowboy is ready for the chute gate to open.

Riding conditions were hard. The equipment consisted of Kemp's roughriding poley saddles or exercise saddles — with no crupper. A chest rein was fastened to the girth and came up between the horse's forelegs for the rider to hold on to, so they had no control over the horse's head. There were no stirrups and you rode one-handed; balance was the name of the game. The surcingle or bareback rides and bullock rides were still two-handed at this stage — a leather surcingle with hand-holds was used, or simply a rope. Spurs were optional; some riders never used them but others wouldn't get on without them. Often riders tucked their spurs into the string girth to help them stay on.

Showmanship was the bottom line. Spruiking and lairising is what got the audience in at the agricultural shows, and the ringmaster could made or break the show. Whether it be from the boards in front of the hessian in a dusty bush town or centre stage under the spotlight before thousands of city slickers, the showman had to adapt and pull it off. Every show was bigger and better than life itself and certainly wilder and more exciting. They were billed in the most dramatic and sensational terms — 'spectacular' and 'dangerous' with 'man-eating outlaws' that, despite 500 attempts, had never been ridden and 'champion' roughriders that had, of course, never been thrown. There was a great sense of humour in all they did and it was a case of 'anything goes' when it came to drawing a crowd.

Amidst the general hotchpotch and hubbub of the sideshows and before the era of microphones, yelling ruled the day. Unperturbed by the cacophony of 'Sideshow attractions, sideshow attractions; right over folks, right over', next to the boxing tent with its banging drums and dramatic roars of 'Who'll take a glove?! Who'll take a glove?!', Dan Edwards would reach deep for his biggest, most resonant and reverberating voice and spruik for Tom Handley:

> *Hurryeee Hurryeee Hurryeeeeee! If you'd care to go! Thrills and spills of the all Australian outback life in realityeeeee! Fun fast and furyeeeee! No waiting, no delayeeee! And the funny clowns will make you laugh laugh lauggghhhh! Till the shirt runs up your back like a window blind!*

He'd introduce the other roughriders and talk up the various exploits of Handley's hellfire horses before bellowing out whatever the challenge may have been for the day. It worked. He packed them in for six shows a day.

Australian shows — American-style

In the evolution of Australian rodeo 1924 proved to be an interesting year. A high-profile international rodeo competition was to take place in Wembley, England, so a number of open roughriding competitions were held to select the Australian representatives. Enthusiasm petered out when the promoter wouldn't pay the Australians' passage — because no-one could afford to go. Arthur 'Snowy' Thompson was selected at the last minute and sent to represent Australia by *The Referee*. This event, the controversy that surrounded its preselection competitions, and the fact that Snowy Thompson never had a chance of winning at Wembley stirred up a lot of interest among cattlemen, horsemen and the Australian public. It helped roughriding to shake off its vaudeville and circus roots and raised its profile as a *sport* — one for which we needed proper championships. For example, at one of the Wembley preselection competitions a crowd of 30 000 had watched Vic Cowan win the buckjumping at Jubilee Oval in Adelaide, but when it was subsequently publicised that Cowan was the 'Commonwealth Champion' no-one agreed. Arguments raged in the sporting papers, and most said that if *anyone* was going to be called the Commonwealth Champion, it should be Ned Lloyd.

Snowy Thompson came home with plenty of good stories about how the American showmen had cheated and stood over him at Wembley. But now the Australian horsemen's rough riding abilities needed proving. Thorpe McConville took advantage of the media attention and decided to determine once and for all who were the best Australian roughriders. He promoted a series of rodeos (between 1924 and 1926) that he called Australia's first 'Commonwealth Rough Riding Championships'.

At Wirths Olympia in Melbourne, during show week in September 1924, McConville ran a 'Mammoth Show where the Australian Championships for Roughriding will be settled'. He invited the champion cowboys from Wembley, and Tex McLeod, who was here ropespinning on the Tivoli Circuit. The Australians included Snowy Thompson, Curley Bell, W.J. Johnson, Harry Simmes, Bob Brewster, Ted Kenney and Bert Smith. The buckjumping was won by Vic Cowan ahead of Billy Dodd. They then took the train to Sydney for McConville's 'Interstate Buckjump Riding — Championship of Australia' which he advertised as a 'Mammoth Australian Rodeo'.

This also appears to be the first time McConville had put on a 'rodeo'. It might well be the first time any Australian had used the term 'rodeo' as for many years the showmen called any sort of rodeo-type affair (i.e. any that took place outside their rope rings or tents) a 'paddock show'.

The event took place over three days at the Sydney sportsground. There were two sessions a day, nominations were free and prizes, first to fifth, were £100, £50, £25, £15 and £10 — huge for the times. Ever the professional, McConville even wrote a rule book for the event, probably another first. The buckjump riders had to contest in a poley saddle, which was commonly known as a Kemp after our mad professor. It was, he said, an improvement on the ordinary 'Park' or 'hunting saddle', as it had larger pads and was built to give the rider a better grip, but it was not as easy as a stock saddle, which had big knee and thigh pads. All competitors were to ride with a halter and reins. No whips were allowed and no 'holts' (holding onto the mane or saddle). Spurs were allowed but rowels had to be filed off. There were also competitions in the ladies' buckjump, steer riding, bareback buckjumping, a wild horse race, and a chariot race. There was bulldogging, lassoing, whipcracking and woodchopping. Entertainers were on hand throwing boomerangs, cracking whips and spinning ropes and there were various other novelty events to thrill the crowd. It was a proper American-style rodeo.

Seventy-five roughriders nominated, but the drawcard, Snowy Thompson, declined as he was busy setting up his own buckjumping show. Jack Watson, who had ridden for Skuthorpe, won the buckjumping, and was awarded a handsome trophy and the £100. Tom Handley, Vic Cowan, Billy Dodd and W. Hock all placed. After the show McConville signed up Jack Watson and Allan McPhee and toured through New South Wales and Victoria.

In September 1925 McConville opened the new grounds for the Royal Agricultural and Horticultural Society of South Australia with another big 'rodeo' and Buckjumping Championship in Adelaide. This one was won by his rider, Alan McPhee, who also won the bareback (surcingle) competition. Snowy Carr came second and Billy Dodd third. All three men continued on to Melbourne to ride with 'Wild Australia' for their annual season at Wirths

Olympia during show week in late September. The write-up in the Melbourne weekly, *The Hawklet*, which was dedicated to 'Sport and Stage' and occasionally 'Sensation, Sport and Drama', records that nearly 5000 people flocked to the Olympia on Saturday night to see the spectacle: 'Certainly many hundreds were turned away, unable to get accommodation.' A newspaper journalist marvelled that lady roughrider Dorrie Phillips '... could ride Pegasus to the stars, if that equine inspirer could be produced for her in the flesh. To see her handle a bucking outlaw is a sight that Satan would applaud.'[3] All the flappers from Melbourne's show ring and hunting fields had turned out en masse to see Miss Phillips ride.

Coincidentally, at that time, just down the road at the Motordrome, Lance Skuthorpe was supplying the stock for Melbourne Carnivals Pty Ltd, who were also promoting a big 'rodeo'. There was seating for 6000 people and £300 pounds prize money. Roughriders were expected from all over Australia. *The Hawklet* explained that McConville's 'Wild Australia' at Wirth's Olympia had invited all the State Champions to ride against one another for 'The honoured and coveted title of Australian Champion'. By the following week, in the same paper, Skuthorpe had dropped 'Melbourne Carnivals' and was using his name to advertise the show at the Motordrome as another 'Australian Championship Rodeo'. Two Australian Championships going on in the same city during the same week. Lucky Melbourne.

Both entrepreneurs had successful shows and both also had new star buckjumpers. Skuthorpe had Firefly, whose chief trick was his shoulder buck and who by this stage had thrown over 600 men. He bucked for Skuey (as Skuthorpe was affectionately known) for the rest of the 20s. In Skuthorpe's words: 'He gets up very high in the air, sometimes 5 or 6 feet between the ground and his hoofs and it appears as though he meant to go forward but he goes back while in the air. When he lands on the ground his shoulder almost touches the soil.'[4] McConville had Swannee, who had thrown 74 of the 75 riders in three days at the Sydney Championships the previous year. Swannee was with McConville from 1923 to 1943. This 'notorious outlaw', according to the man who promoted him, was unconquered: 'Every nerve in his body tingled when he was brought into the ring ... he never let me down.'

After *The Hawklet* had been covering Skuthorpe's and McConville's shows for weeks, it announced that 'Buckjumping is no doubt a National Sport, and we are very pleased to note the great strides it has made in the last 12 months.' Skuey charged off to Adelaide and put on another Australian Buckjumping Championship on Boxing Day.

The incomparable Skuthorpes

During 1926–27, the Skuthorpe family worked their show through the Victorian country towns then headed on down to Adelaide. The motley crew included Lance and his wife Violet and the three children — Madge (born in 1913), Lance Jnr (born in 1915) and Violet Jnr (born in 1919) — 14 riders, a cook and scores of hangers on. Lem Partridge and his brother Colin handled the roughriding. They had 136 horses, five buffalos, eight mules and three donkeys, and managed 30 miles a day.

They arrived in Adelaide broke and Lance put the bite on Sir Sidney Kidman for money to publicise the show. Opening day at Jubilee Oval saw 14 000 people turn up and the money flowed in. After the season they lived it up in Adelaide for six weeks until they'd spent all the profits and then moved on to Port Pirie and Broken Hill.

After that the seemingly indefatigable Mrs Skuthorpe decided that enough was enough and they bought a house at Riverstone, outside Sydney, so the children could go to school. Skuthorpe leased his show to another showman and started a brick business. The business went bust when the Depression hit, so he took at job at the meatworks. Although he was over 60 years of age, it was the first time Skuthorpe had had a regular job. On the weekends they still did the odd show on the outskirts of Sydney.

There was always something a little regal about the Skuthorpes, which reinforced the rumour that the first Skuthorpe in Australia was the illegitimate son of the Duke of Sutherland! Apart from the fact that it was difficult to get your wages out of him, by all accounts Old Lance Skuthorpe was a 'great man'. His physical prowess was legendary — he could jump over a saddled horse in one graceful leap. He was a good dancer, writer and illustrator. He was always well dressed and, always the debonair showman, wore lots of jewellery. Because of his deafness — it was a hereditary affliction — he compensated by becoming a storyteller. Both Lance Snr and Lance Jnr carried themselves with an air of authority that made those who knew them wonder if perhaps the Duke of Sutherland's genes were indeed alive and well.

Apparently Lance Snr was scared off investing money by witnessing his father's crushing losses in the 1890s. The Skuthorpes used to go from broke to rich and back again with infamous regularity. When Tex Morton became famous in the late 1930s he often made a packet and would extravagantly blow it all. Showmen by their very nature were free spirits; few if any ever saved. They worked their guts out and if they made a killing in a town they either gave it away to some charity, paid off debts from months gone by or bought fancy clothes, bigger tents and partied hard.

The consummate showman

Thorpe McConville was altogether different. Whereas most of his peers rarely thought beyond their current season, his pub dealings were lucrative (he bought and sold pubs in various country towns, including Albury, Thurgoona and Merriwagga) and he carefully consolidated after the early success of his show. He was game enough to think big and had the business acumen to pull it off.

The most tangible difference between McConville and the other buckjump showmen is that Wild Australia was never a sideshow. His shows were always big self-contained numbers, completely independent of the agricultural shows, except when he used their grounds to put on a championship buckjumping competition or when he was invited to put on a rodeo for an agricultural show — in the main arena. Even during the tough Depression years McConville's show was *the* show. He always promoted himself as being a class above the rest and some considered him to be a bit of a snob. Most of the other buckjump showmen did some shows in sideshow alley, which was a good money-spinner as it only required a small outfit and there was a ready-made market.

Over and above any pretensions he may have had, Thorpe McConville was a first-class horseman, roughrider and showman and he had had a lot of experience in buckjump and Wild West shows and rodeos in the USA and in Australia before he created his own. While many of the other buckjump shows were trundling around the countryside financially winging it and surviving on their wits, Thorpe was straight and honest — he never had to leave town in the middle of the night to avoid bailiffs. His was good, wholesome family entertainment without bawdy acts or sexual innuendos.

McConville and his wife stayed in the best pubs and hotels — while the rest of his team stayed in tents — and the whole troupe travelled by train. His riders were renowned for their spotless appearance, crisp white shirts, jodhpurs and bow ties, polished-to-gleaming boots and well-groomed horses. Thorpe didn't appear to go in for gambling either. He generally preferred straight challenges and competitions with prize money for time ridden.

Taking the rough with the smooth

Being outdoor showmen they were at the mercy of the weather, not only in the arena but constantly. Droughts worsened the perennial problem of finding feed. Dan Edwards recalls the trials and tribulations of working through a drought with Tom Handley:

The reason I remember the drought is that I was the horse tailer ... Now, I'd have 30 horses and my job was to find grass for them. Didn't matter where I found it. And if you're travelling behind 10 000 sheep and they're travelling around looking for grass, too, imagine! I used to hate sheep ... I'd have to open someone's gate and get in there and see if there was feed. Tom Handley and I had an understanding, he used to sack me. I'd put the horses in someone's paddock, I'd be up before daylight or I might even stop out there with them, sleep with them, you know and then bring them in. These blokes of course, they'd come in to the show: 'Your horses have been in my paddock!' Tom would call me up: 'Where did you put those horses?' And so and so and so, 'I didn't tell you to put them in there, God almighty, don't you ever listen?! — Pack your ports and go.' The understanding was I'd be waiting down under the culvert, I'd have my port and my swag, I'd get down there and when the wagon come along I'd just throw it up and get on. The cocky would go home satisfied and everyone was happy.

In 1929 the Wall Street stock market crash plunged the western world into a five-year depression. The decline of commodity prices crippled the Australian economy, unemployment soared and along with everyone else the pastoral industry was reduced to despair. Many graziers were forced to walk off their land; the station employees had left long before them. In the cities it was worse; hundreds and thousands were homeless and families were living beside road or camped in the bush. Shanty villages developed along rivers and creeks on the outskirts of towns and cities, and everyone grew their own food.

In the 1920s only the rich had cars and without motor transport the unemployed took to the roads on foot or on horseback. Jumping trains became an art form. Just as in the 1890s, there were thousands of Australians on the dole —

five shillings — lugging their swags from town to town, living from rations to rations. A lot of properties and stations fed them, a lot didn't. Unemployed 'swagmen', or swaggies as they were known, have become popular folk heroes represented in Australia's unofficial national anthem, 'Waltzing Matilda'. The Great Depression has tended to obscure the fact that the 1920s were by no means a prosperous decade for most workers, anyway. Contrary to the song's lyrics, there wasn't much that was jolly about it at all.

Once again the social and economic chaos was a perfect breeding ground for the itinerant buckjump shows. They didn't cost much to put on — horses were free and horsemen were hungry — and it didn't cost much for the public to get in. For the bushmen and horsemen without job prospects, life with a buckjump show was a means of existence.

There were always plenty of men who'd ride for a feed and the circus and buckjump families had barely faltered. In the early 1930s buckjump shows sprang up all over the place as out-of-work roughriders started their own outfits. There was Jack Hay, a 'big tough fella who also cracked whips', Snowy Baker from at least 1929–34, and George Hong, an Irishman from northern New South Wales who had a feature horse, Barcoo. Piebald Moore was better known as a high-jump rider but he had buckjumpers in the 30s, as did Johnny Shield. Jack Stanton, who was one of Australia's champion roughriders at the time, got together with his brother, Bill,[5] and Tommy Woods 'Stirrup Iron Mick' to form their own show. Most of these men stayed in New South Wales. Queenslanders were also being entertained by Joe Atkinson, that state's best and most respected 'champion roughrider', who lasted the decade until war started again in 1939. Ken Huntley, who like Joe Atkinson learned the game riding for Skuthorpe before starting his own show, lasted from at least 1930 through to 41 when he went to Sydney and showed there during the war. Ken's brother, George Huntley, also had a buckjump show at one point. Famous roughriders Curley Bell and Harry Tullipan had buckjump shows in north Queensland throughout the 30s, possibly longer. Alec Wall used to have a show out the back of his Malbon pub in Queensland's far west. Colin Russell, the Fletchers and Roy Pigeon also worked that back country. Noel George, originally a Queenslander, took his high-jump horses, hunters and buckjump show around Western Australia through to the late 1950s. Jones' Buckjumping Show joined the others in Western Australia, and the Judd Brothers, sheep drovers from around the

Riverina district, always carried a roll of hessian and ropes and would throw together a show in each town as they went. Some of the better-known roughriders who rode for them were 'Bushman Bill' Francis, who rode bullocks back to front for the crowd, Bill Mendis, 'Queensland Bill', who rode for Skuthorpe Snr for a long time, Colin Bell, Tommy Kelly, Harry and Ron McPhee (no relation to Allan), Tom and Leo Lloyd (Ned's half-brothers) and Frank McFarlane, who had plenty of different buckjump shows after World War II.

The lifestyle of the buckjump showmen was pretty rough and tough but living outdoors in the fresh air, and with hard work and plenty of exercise, they were certainly fit and healthy. It was rare for anyone, including the children, to get sick. Accidents were the problem and over the years there were many, both inside and outside the ring.

Dolly Lennon is the matriarch of the Lennon family, who have been in the Australian circus business for over 100 years. With her husband, Mick, and four children, she toured first with Thorpe McConville then with their own buckjump show in the late 1930s and 40s. Dolly happily describes her life on the road as 'very, very primitive'. But as she also pointed out, life at home in the backblocks was scarcely any different:

This, you might say, is almost true. We had a very luxurious lifestyle, very elegant; we slept in tents. We had a beautiful green grass carpet under our feet, until it became dusty. But, anyway, you'd listen to the rain pitta pattering down as you were cuddled up in bed, pitta pattering down on the canvas only a few feet above your head. In the morning you'd step out of bed ankle-deep in water. If you were lucky you'd just catch your shoes as they were floating out of the tent ... We had good beds and everything and we cooked on an open fire ... We always had a fire as well to heat up a bucket of water for a bath ... I had the baby's bath, but we also had big galvanised iron tubs ... they were good tubs and they'd last a few years ... you could even sit them on the fire to get it hot ... I made sure before I went into the ring each night I had my bath. And being in a tent, too, you had to make sure you put the candle on the other side of you because it could throw your shadow onto the white wall — anybody walking by could have a picture show.

Mick and Dolly's tent, the home where they slept and bathed, was about 12 foot by 12 foot. There was another tent where everyone ate. As there were no refrigerators, all the produce had to be bought fresh every day. They used petrol irons and Dolly hated them:

... because I could never light them. I wasn't game to. And the petrol flame would trickle down into the iron and burn, you see, otherwise you'd just have to have a flat iron stood up against the fire ... It would go black but you'd rub it on a cloth first, ironed things inside out if you could. I hated that, of course, but then I hated ironing ... Everything was ironed. When we were out on our own I cooked for half a dozen people probably and hated it ... We used camp ovens and pans, roasts, stews and things like that.

Music!

There was another reason for the proliferation of buckjump shows in the 1930s. The Depression years were the catalyst for a worldwide resurgence in cowboy popularity. Hollywood had been successfully exporting their cowboy heroes ever since Buffalo Bill and Annie Oakley starred in short vignettes in the early 1890s. In 1921 a record 854 Westerns were released and by 1926 they comprised 26 per cent of Hollywood feature films. Through a decade of silent-movie Westerns, Australians came to know and love Western actors, such as William S. Hart, and cowboy stars like Ken Maynard, Hoot Gibson, Buck Jones, Tim McCoy and Tom Mix. The advent of the 'talkies' in the late 1920s brought us Gene Autrey and Roy Rogers, and the 1930s saw the first films of the great Western actors, John Wayne and Gary Cooper.[6] These celluloid characters epitomised 'individualism, masculinity, righteousness, and personal triumph over hardship'.[7] The cowboy was a hero for all, galloping across the screen, saving the day, and saving us from reality for an hour or so.

Grassroots Country and Western music, hillbilly music and yodelling also soared in popularity in the early 1930s. The lyrics focused on the gulf between the establishment and the unemployed and dispossessed who roamed their respective countries in large numbers. Rural America was a dustbowl and their songs related feelings and experiences with simple melodies and simple instruments. The down-and-out-and-wandering themes were a product of the misery and poverty that prevailed.

Although Australian teamsters, drovers and selectors had long been singing their own songs and ballads, no-one ever wrote them down and most were forgotten. When American country music records started arriving here in the late 1920s they seemed tailor-made for our own struggling farmers. The American country music industry went commercial during the 1930s and many memorable stars arose. Before long, Country and Western cowboys started appearing around the globe singing in every conceivable language.

The Gill brothers were quick to see the potential. Beginning in the mid–1930s with Buddy Fahey they always included a 'hillbilly' singer in their shows. In 1937 their rodeo included the new singing sensation, Tex Morton. He was an instant hit so the following year Tex Morton's Rodeo Show was born with Tex, Sister Dorrie and the Roughriders' Band providing half an hour of country music, followed by whipcracking, ropespinning and Tex's popular sharpshooting act. But the core of the show was the 'rodeo' provided by the remarkable Gill brothers.

From around 1937 Tex Morton had various travelling shows on and off in Australia and New Zealand, often collaborating with the Gills and the Skuthorpes. Buddy Williams sang with Ken Huntley's show in the early forties and later the Gills. He went on to run his own shows with various buckjump men behind him, including the Gills and later Doug and Walker Williamson.

Because of their collaboration with the buckjump showmen, Australia's Country and Western singers are about the only artists to celebrate our roughriders. Tex Morton was born in New Zealand but is regarded as the father of Australian Country music. His 'Rough riders' were Australia's first Country and Western band. Tex's classic rodeo songs did much to promote his own show, including his three famous buckjumper songs — 'Rocky Ned' (1939), 'Aristocrat' (1940) and 'Mandrake' (1941). The latter two were about his star horses. Tex Morton virtually finished his recording career in 1941 at 24 years of age, after producing 87 tracks in five years, but he continued as a showman, hypnotist and later as an actor. After the war Buddy Williams recorded such rodeo classics as the 'Warwick Rodeo', 'Chain Lightning', 'The Outlaw', 'Australia's Kitty Gill' (he travelled extensively with Stan and Kitty Gill's show), 'Rocky Round-up', 'Les Dingo', 'The Mad Sam Fuller', and 'A Cowboy's Life is Good Enough for Me'. A host of other Country and Western singers have followed. Those who have penned classic rodeo songs include Reg Lindsay, Tex Ritter, Rick and Thel Carey, Slim Dusty, Smoky Dawson, Sam Costa, Reg Poole, Tom McIvor, Brian Young, Ted Egan and now the likes of Steve Gibson in the 1990s.

Back to the show

Life on the road is addictive; travelling gets into the blood; and by 1931 Lance Skuthorpe Snr couldn't sit still any longer. He rallied the family and got the buckjump show back on the road. The horse and wagon era was over. The Skuthorpes now travelled by train. Firefly and Big Queenslander were his gun horses and from then on 16-year-old Lance Jnr became more involved in the show. He convinced his father to swap the cumbersome and costly 'authentic' wooden arena fencing for the showman's poles, pegs and ropes.

The elder Lance gentled the horses, wielded the flank rope and did the spruiking to lure in the crowd. Lance Jnr rode the horses, along with the likes of Jack Stanton and Mulga Bill. Like his father, Lance Jnr was a gifted roughrider. He'd had plenty of experience, being the horse tailer with a sack for a saddle for most of his young life:

'If my son is not the greatest roughrider who ever lived, and I honestly think he is, said old Lance, *'then he is the most graceful man who ever mounted a horse.'*[8]

Because of the resurgence in cowboy popularity, extravaganza circus and Wild West shows started appearing in the 1930s — huge outfits. Circus and buckjump showmen once again joined forces, this time under the big top. In 1932 Mawson and Skuthorpe's Rodeo and Circus took over Wentworth Park in Sydney, the Gills had an American rodeo and Wild West circus in 1936, Cody Brothers' Circus and Rodeo was around in 1937, as were Galloways' Wild West Show, and Tex Morton's Rodeo and Circus (with the Gill Brothers behind him) in 1938. Holden's Circus and Worleys and the Ausling Brothers — all circus families — had their own variations. After the war Tex Morton toured with the whole of Ashtons behind him. There were Country and Western singers and yodellers, acrobats, gymnasts, high-wire acts, clowns, comedians, trick-riding, bicycle acts, performing dogs and ponies, rosin-back riding, buckjumping, whipcracking, sharpshooting, knifethrowing, bullock riding, you name it.

From 1935 the Sydney Royal Agricultural Society (RAS) began inviting American cowboys to give exhibitions at their shows. Many stayed and toured with the showmen for a season. The cowboys' popularity during their appearances around the countryside and their continued involvement with the Sydney RAS Easter Show for the next five years helped to solidify the Australian public's love affair with the Wild West.

The flamboyant American cowboys and cowgirls, their style and their acts were adopted by most of the circus and buckjump shows. There continued to be a steady stream of circus and Western performers travelling around the world and the constant exchange of people and ideas once again influenced Australian showmanship. In the late 30s we began to develop our own rodeo culture, and this time it spread beyond the showmen's arenas.

Unlike his peers, Thorpe McConville kept his roughriders in the traditional Australian jodphurs and ties. During the 1930s McConville's team travelled to just about every town in New South Wales and Victoria. There were jaunts to South Australia but Queensland was not an option because of the problem of spraying for ticks at the border. When they were not travelling by train, the horses and bullocks were driven from town to town and the equipment was hauled in wagons until 1933 when Thorpe bought two brand new Chevrolet trucks.

McConville's son from his first marriage, Doug McConville, began riding professionally for his father under the name of Thorpe McConville Junior in 1934. The big name roughriders who came and went with Wild Australia during the Depression were Allan McPhee, Jim Darwin, Norm King, Jim Kennedy, Dave Blair, Tom and Leo Lloyd, Mulga Jack, 'Bushman' Bill Harris, Ernie Maloney, Cecil Pearce, Billy Reynolds, Harry Clollard, H. Collins, Paddy McGrath, 'Jumbo' Foster, Jack Agnew and Jack Tracey, who gave nightly exhibitions buckjumping blindfolded with both hands free.

It was a circus/buckjump/Wild West show — Thorpe had all bases covered. There were troupes of acrobats, wire-walkers, trapeze artists, ropers, tumblers, performing animals, high-climbing and diving dogs and clowns. His stock numbers varied but he rarely had less than 40 head of buckjumpers, ponies, mules, donkeys and bucking bullocks. Thorpe's second wife, Violet Potter, took the tickets at the door, did the books and paid the wages.

Bullock riding was an audience favourite, along with 'Fun in the Stockyard'. The 'Wild Bullock Chariot Ride' was new — a surcingle was placed around the (tame) bullock and a chariot was then attached to a turn buckle on the top of the surcingle. The bullock could charge about in any direction, including back towards the chariot. But buckjumping exhibitions were the climax of every show.

In October 1934, Australia's leading roughriders and buckjump showmen and women converged on Melbourne for Australian promoter, Stuart McColl's ill-fated Victorian Centenary Stampede. Jack Hay, Tom Handley, Thorpe McConville, Ken and George Huntley, Joe Atkinson, and all the Skuthorpes and Gills were there. They brought with them professional roughriders and buckjumpers, including a shipment of 150 horses from Queensland. Most of the showmen and women were also going to compete. There were 74 roughriders invited from all over Australia including Vic Cowan, Charlie Edmunds, Mulga Fred, Bill Hilton, Vic Hazlett, Jack 'Jimbo' Hawkins, Leo Lloyd, Roy Oram, Sam Jensen, Owen and Penny

Perrett, and the Finch brothers from South Australia. The promoter, Stuart McColl, had also assembled an impressive bunch of cowboys from the USA, Canada and Mexico. Yakima Canutt, Pete Knight, Smoky Snyder, Johnnie Schneider, Clay Carr, Ned Winneger, Steve Clemento, George Marciel and Alice Greenough were among them — all champions. They managed a spectacular opening parade but the 'Stampede' was never contested because it was rained out.

When the Stampede folded, Tom Handley sold up and Thorpe McConville bought his string of buckjumpers, including Rocky Ned, who at 27 years of age was still Australia's most famous buckjumper. Rocky Ned bucked for Thorpe McConville from 1934 to 1940 and during this time, despite his age, was unridden.

McColl put the show on the road to try and recoup his losses, and he showed with the Gills' stock in towns on the way to and surrounding Sydney. But the crowds were not big enough to cover his investments. McColl, his cast and crew went broke. This meant there was a number of American and Canadian cowboys and Russian Cossacks who suddenly needed a job. Some went home but George Marciel, Ned Winneger, Alice Greenough and Mr and Mrs Johnnie Schneider went to stay with Tom Handley at his pub in Muswellbrook as they and the Cossacks and the American Indians were contracted to perform at the Sydney RAS Easter Show in April 1935.

During his 1935–36 tour, McConville signed up two of the American cowboys to give roping and bulldogging exhibitions and two Russian Cossacks who gave daring displays on horseback, including vaulting from side to side at full gallop and finishing with a somersault on the horses back with a sabre held between their teeth!

During the 1930s McConville's other buckjumpers included the notorious Swannee, Mickey the Mouse, The Ghost, The Snake, Tom Thumb and Cyclone. The prize was generally £10 to stay on his top buckers for ten seconds; £5 for lesser mounts; and ten shillings for others. They also had bucking donkeys and mules, two heavy bucking bullocks which were, like the horses, saddled with a light poley saddle — no stirrups — and flanked.

By 1936 McConville was transporting Wild Australia entirely by truck, so the show moved faster from town to town, more performances per week were possible and the jumps (trips) between towns were longer. Smaller towns began to miss out as McConville concentrated on the larger towns. The circus acts remained a big part of his show. Members of the multi-talented circus families, the Holdens, Lennons and St Leons, each joined for a season or two. The Fredo Troupe, the Shipway Twins, the Delavanties, Joan Armitage, Ossie Delroy the juggler and trick bicycle rider and Buddy Williams, the Yodelling Jackeroo, all did stints with Thorpe. Thorpe McConville Jnr was giving exhibitions of ropespinning as well as doing his roughriding, and there were always the whipcrackers, trick ponies and clever dogs.

When Mick Lennon did a season with McConville in 1938, buckjump riders were getting £5 a week — $10 a week — bought their own clothes out of that — white shirts and riding breeches. Tent hands were getting 25 shillings a week — $2.50 —and their keep and a tent to sleep in. This was as good as it got. They were charging two or three shillings at the gate to get in.

The buckjump and Wild West shows were family entertainment — everyone came to watch, not only the stockmen and horsemen. The audience covered a broad spectrum of classes because everyone loved 'cowboys' and because the challenge between man and horse is a great spectacle. In a lot of towns it was the only entertainment they got. Dolly Lennon says the young people were mad about buckjumping: 'It was their greatest sport, really ... Once, when a show would go to town they'd all ask, "What's your main buckjumper? You got any buckjumpers? Who's your best rider?" It drew people from everywhere.'

In the late 1930s Thorpe McConville's 'best riders' included Jack Agnew, Ted Lane, Doug Turner, Paddy McGrath, Claude Johnson, Alf Murray, Roy Douglas, Jack Delahunt and Jack Charlton. During the early years of the war he employed Billy Travers, Neville Bamblett, Dave Woods, Vernon Peters, Mick Lennon, Alan Cook, Mick Crisp and Billy Bargo.

Bargo combined roughriding, whipcracking and ropespinning with a career as a singer-guitarist. He toured with the Gills, the Skuthorpes, Tex Morton and Thorpe McConville. Between seasons he competed in rodeos around Queensland, and often performed a few tunes as well. He won the buckjumping and the roping at the prestigious Warwick rodeo in 1941, which at the time made him an 'Australian Champion'.

In the winter of 1940 Wild Australia did its first trip to Queensland. Rocky Ned had an accident and lost an eye. He was 35. He lived out his retirement just outside Narrandera, on the banks of the Murrumbidgee River.

At different stages over the years the Gills joined forces with the St Leons, Ashtons, Sole Brothers and the Skuthorpes. Life on the road was lonely and dangerous, especially in the wagon days, and if two outfits were in the same town they often showed together then hooked up for the next leg. Being from a circus family, Jack, Stan and Doyle Gill were naturally athletic and game. With plenty of practice in their father's rope ring the brothers became excellent roughriders. Jack Gill, who was born in 1918, was performing on horseback with his sister by the time he was eight. He had his first buckjump ride at 12, won the steer riding championship of northwest New South Wales at 14 and went on to become the New South Wales and South Australian bareback champion. An extraordinary whipcracker, Jack could strike a match with a whip at 14 feet and crack a 70-foot bullock whip. He also became one of the best spruikers in the business. The Gill Brothers were among the instigators in the burgeoning 'rodeo' scene in the late 1930s and early 1949s — as was, of course, Lance Skuthorpe.

Lance was between Jack and Stan Gill in age and there developed a great rivalry between Jack and Lance in terms of roughriding. Jack, 'they say', was the better rider (could ride the really rough ones) while young Lance was the 'prettier' (neat and stylish). Both Jack and Stan were fairly wild boys and, at times, had notorious reputations. But Lance Skuthorpe Jnr was no angel either, and stories about all three abound. Jack's son, Happy, tentatively agrees:

They were hard, tough men and a bit wild — they had to be. But they were disciplined wild men. The way they dressed in those days, they had to be able to fight. With their chaps and so on, this country hadn't seen any of that, it wasn't unusual for them to be called Mexicans. But those three men did more for the rodeo styles we are enjoying now that anyone — no-one came within cooee — and Lance Skuthorpe, whilst he was a lair, was also the best all-round athlete of the lot. Dad told me that time and time again.

Madge Skuthorpe never pursued a career in showbusiness but in the early 1930s Violet Jnr was riding buckjumpers behind her father's back. When Jack Stanton joined the show he volunteered to teach her properly. Young Lance eventually pressured his father into letting Violet ride in the ring, perfectly aware that a lady roughrider was always terrific for business. Violet became a gifted roughrider, whipcracker and ropespinner and quickly became a star. In 1938 she and her brother were invited by Colonel Tim McCoy to America. McCoy's Wild West show, 'Roughriders of the World', had a staff of 500 and it was recognised as the biggest show of its kind in the world. Accompanied by their mother, Lance (19) and Violet (15) performed as roughriders along with three other marvellous Australian talents, Jack Watson (Queensland Jack), Ron McPhee and Art Creasy. They gave exhibitions of ropespinning, sharpshooting and whipcracking and roughriding. Once again the Americans were astounded at our tiny flat saddles. A New York paper referred to Lance as the 'lithe, India rubber cowboy from down under', and the journalists loved Violet:

> *This pretty girl from Australia is a match for any fiend in the shape of a horse ... With elegant ability she sat animals whose wild eyed ferocity drew gasps of horror from the watchers. She is a regular Boadicea for courage.* [9]

Legend has it that not one of the Australian team was thrown during their six-month tour.

When they returned, Lance Jnr took over as front man with the family's buckjump show and turned it into a smaller, more commercial, more American outfit. It became 'The Skuthorpes' Wild West Show' and they went sideshowing with it. It was cheap, light to transport, and a good money-spinner. In the late 1930s and early 40s there would not have been a person in Australia that did not know the names Lance and Violet Skuthorpe.

Lance, like his father, was a bit of a renaissance man. He had his father's physical prowess — he was a great roughrider, an amazing athlete, and he could fight 'like a threshing machine'. He had good taste, wore the best of suits, and liked the finer things in life. He was well-read and creative. Lance wrote and performed songs, played the banjo and the piano, and worked in radio with his close friend, singer and songwriter Tex Morton. They often combined shows and toured together in the 40s. Both men were intelligent, talented, good-looking and trouble. Tex drank too much, Lance gambled, and both had a weakness for women. When 'Sex' Morton and 'Pants' Skuthorpe were in town, it was time to lock up your daughters. Teenage girls used to follow the buckjump shows from town to town, 'groupies' they'd be called now or 'buckle bunnies'. Dickie Skinner, who rode for the Skuthorpes throughout the forties remembers the 'Charlie Wheelers' (Sheilas) as they used to call them: 'We used to have to climb trees to get away from them!'

Violet Skuthorpe Jnr was not unremarkable either. Roughrider Beryl Riley (now Beryl Chick) remembers her as 'absolutely beautiful; a really lovely person and she was a person that radiated ... there was a real glow'. Violet was 100 per cent a professional performer. She started her career as a five-year-old riding into the ring on a pony to open the Skuthorpes' show. She was riding buckjumpers by the mid–1930s. Violet was Australia's first and foremost lady roughriding star. After the American tour she was always billed as 'The World's Champion Lady

Buckjump Rider' even though she was only a teenager and never rode in open competitions. Her father refused to allow her to, fearing she'd draw a horse that didn't buck, and hence she wouldn't win. This would ruin the 'champion' reputation that her career was built around. She was their main drawcard — their meal ticket. He was right but he didn't stop her brother. Lance Jnr didn't often ride in open competitions for the same reason and because the prize money was rarely enough to risk life and limb, he mainly entered in the big, prestigious rodeos, such as the Melbourne Stampede, Warwick and Sydney.

In 1940 Stan Gill Jnr married Kitty West. The Wests were well-known circus people and they'd known the Gills for years. Kitty had spent her life riding in her parents' ring and, as she put it, she 'wanted the action'. They were up north showing in opposition to the Skuthorpes, who had Violet as their drawcard, when Kitty got her chance. 'They stuck me on one morning when my husband was away,' and the rest is history. Next to Violet, Kitty became the most famous lady roughrider in the country. She was known as the 'Queen of the Cowgirls' and had fans all over Australia. She rode with Tex Morton and was also the star of her husband's show. Unlike Violet, Kitty also competed in rodeos when she got the chance. She was a natural, a great roughrider — a champion. Kitty's brothers, Phillip and Johnny West, also used to ride and perform circus acts in the Gill Brothers shows. According to Phillip, when Kitty came into the ring in her sexy black outfit on her buckjumper, The Black Devil, the men in the audience 'used to go berserk'.

Jack Gill's wife, Gladys, was also an outstanding roughrider — in an era when many women rode buckjumpers. Gladys was also the star of her husband's travelling show and became a champion in the rodeo arena. Among her numerous victories she was the first lady roughrider to win two Australian titles back to back, at Warwick in 1946 and Kyabram in 1947.

Sydneysider Doug Ramsay joined the Skuthorpes in Kempsey in 1939. He toured with them up to Cairns from April to September. Doug rode in glamorous American cowboy outfits in an American saddle and was billed as 'Slim Ramsay from Tombstone, Arizona, who rides buckjumpers American-style for your special entertainment'. They followed the agricultural shows with six or eight buckjumpers, of which Aristocrat and Baxter's Bay were the stars.

In 1939 the sideshows were a smorgasbord of attractions, Doug Ramsay remembers:

> *Sideshow alley was more of a freak show ... 'Ubangi' the little dwarf lady from the Congo jungle, the Pin-Headed Chinaman ... the Headless Lady and the Bodiless Lady ... The Fat Lady, She's fat fat faat faaat faaaght! When she walks the earth tremblllllesss! When she lies down there's an EARTHQUAKE!' I heard that so many times it's been stuck in my head for years.*

Old Lance and Mrs Skuthorpe travelled with them until they retired from the road during the war. Lance Snr looked after the horses and the long flank rope and his wife did the books. Lance Jnr did the spruiking and gave exhibitions on their star horse, Aristocrat. Violet Jnr gave whipcracking and ropespinning exhibitions from atop her patient horse, Rainbow, in the centre of the ring. She often gave exhibitions riding Baxter's Bay with a neck rein but in a 'big' stock saddle, with stirrups tied underneath. There were two other roughriders with the show during this time, Jack Chalkley and Billy Bargo, who was well on his way to becoming a star himself. Other riders came and went and there were no extra hands.

It was always a dangerous business. Doug remembers one particularly close call he had while with the Skuthorpes:

> *Old Lance was on the scene all right. He nearly killed me one night. They used the long flank rope and we didn't ride with stirrups in the show. Old Lance somehow put a half hitch around my boot and spur and pulled with the flank. And I went out backwards and I hit the ground backwards and of course it also pulled the horse backwards. The horse came back and sat on me and then jumped up and started to go round the ring again with me dragging around behind with my foot caught in this damn rope. Young Lance stepped in with great risk to his self-preservation and pulled my boot off ...*

That was the first time Lance Jnr saved him but not the last. Lance was actually well known for leaping into action to save riders in trouble, both in the big ring and small.

There was no insurance. As Dolly Lennon put it, if someone was hurt in the ring, 'it was their bad luck'. Show proprietors would comfort the injured and do the best they could to help out with doctor's expenses, but that was about it. Dolly heard of three men who were killed in the rope rings in the late 30s alone, but considering the hundred of thousands of bad busters over the years, not too many lost their lives. Exploding carbide lights and dinky old trucks on treacherous roads were more of a problem.

Skuthorpe Snr, like all showmen, would never allow his horses to be ridden out by his employees. He would simply call 'right' when he wanted them off. Four or five bucks, that's all — the horses had to think they had won. If any of the riders were ever hurt, they had to leave the arena themselves regardless of injury. 'If you want to die, do it outside,' he'd say. To show pain in the arena is not good for show business. Even in the rodeo arena today, an injured rider will (provided they can move) always stagger out of the ring and out of sight before they collapse.

Changing times

On Sunday 3 September 1939 Robert Menzies, our newly elected prime minister, announced that Australia was at war. When Japan attacked Pearl Harbor in December 1941, and Singapore fell in February 1942 Australia came into the firing line, and the showmen shut down.

Doug Ramsay was working with Joe Atkinson in north Queensland at the time. Joe was in the militia and he was called up immediately. Doug joined the Light Horse and later volunteered for a 'very special secret commando unit', the North Australia Observer Unit (NAOU), and was sent to the Northern Territory to patrol the coastline from Normanton to the Kimberley on horseback. There were only about 700 of them and their job was to observe and report and, if the Japanese landed, to harass but not engage. They became known as 'Curtin's Cowboys'. At least two other champion roughriders, Cecil Pearce and Arthur Winter, also joined the NAOU.

Most of the roughriders who joined up were assigned to remount units which broke in and trained horses for the army. In her book *Kidman — The Forgotten King* Jill Bowen estimated: 'One-fifth of each Remount Unit (forty men) were roughriders, horsebreakers and stockmen from the back blocks and also buck-jumping riders from the shows and circuses.'[10] Jack Dempsey, who had travelled with the Skuthorpes, Eronis and Martini, was one of them.

Jack Stanton was another. When he arrived at the Second Australian Remount Depot in Holsworthy, Sydney, he found plenty of roughriding mates there — rodeo champions, such as Colin Bell, and many of the great horsemen from around northern New South Wales. The unit had just 28 people, including cooking staff, office staff, a vet, two farriers and the breaking-in team. Jack broke in horses for the army for over three years and during that time he handled over 6000 horses, used for all different purposes both in Australia and overseas. The best of the horses were sent up to Doug Ramsay and the 'cowboys' patrolling the Top End.

Many roughriders were turned down by the army because of injuries sustained buckjumping. Dan Edwards discovered he had a skull fracture when he tried to join up, and Lance Skuthorpe Jnr had wrecked his feet leaping off bucking horses all his life. Lance shut down the show and drove a taxi in Sydney from 1942–44. Most of the showgrounds and racecourses were filled up with soldiers, particularly in Queensland, so venues were hard to come by. The Skuthorpes got involved with the Police Boys Clubs and ran rodeos to raise money for Boystown. Thorpe McConville closed his show down the day the Japanese bombed Darwin. He went back to his property, 'Clifton', outside Narrandera. He turned his horses out, lent his big top to the local armed forces catering unit, and the army took his trucks. His son, Doug McConville, enlisted and a year later was killed when his plane was shot down over France. He was 27.

After the war

Among the buckjump shows that continued on were the Skuthorpes, the Gills, Thorpe McConville, Ken Huntley, Noel George, Curley Bell, the Pigeons, Tex Morton, Buddy Williams, Mick and Dolly Lennon and the Sole Bros Rodeo and Circus. They were now all pretty much 'Wild West shows' and they were joined by a whole lot more. The public enjoyed a feast of touring roughriders, Country and Western singers, trick riders and ropers, whipcrackers, sharpshooters.

The 1950s were an affluent decade in Australia, particularly in the bush, where commodity prices were the highest they had ever been. Cowboys were big business in the late 40s and 50s, and these were golden years for travelling shows.

Lance Skuthorpe Jnr was back on the road by 1945, doing mainly small sideshows at the agricultural shows because straight after the war no-one had any money, and trucks and fuel were hard to come by. Dick Skinner, who in 1942, at 13, had run away from home and joined the Skuthorpes, remembers how he and Lance Jnr walked 50 buckjumpers from Sydney to Melbourne, showing in every town along the way. A couple of trucks would go ahead with all the gear and Old Lance, who was along for the ride. By the time Lance Jr and Dick got to town with the horses late each afternoon Old Lance would be snoozing happily in the only erected tent — his. Old Lance kept travelling almost to the day he died in

February 1958. Lance Jnr quit roughriding after the war and Dick, who stayed with the Skuthorpes for eight years, became their star rider.

Roughriders and performers Tex Mooney and Dan Crotty were both well known in the burgeoning rodeo scene. In 1946 they formed The Snowy River Stampede. It was a strange name for a show formed in Broken Hill, where they also took on Johnny Brady, a 15-year-old local who had been winning money off buckjump showmen like Ken Huntley and Thorpe McConville for the preceding couple of years. Timmy Harris from South Australia was also riding in the team. They lasted six months, went broke and chucked it in at Wagga rodeo. Lance Skuthorpe Jnr gave them all a job with his latest venture.

Lance's 1947–48 Rodeo and Circus tour of New Zealand, was his pièce de résistance. From December 1946, they toured for two full years and covered every bit of the country. Charging four bob a head at the door, Lance made a quarter of a million pounds in the first year. Mooney, Crotty, Brady and the Lennons, Dolly and Mick, were part of the team. Lance had a great string of bucking horses, including Cream of the Mountains, the old stalwart, Aristocrat and Violet's Baxter's Bay.

Baxter's Bay was a great bucking horse but she was mean. She had a nasty habit of attacking riders, ears flattened and jaws snapping. 'She'd eat you alive', reckons Johnny Brady. She was so vicious that they only used her for the exhibition to finish the show. Dick Skinner had that honour and he had his ear bitten off by the mare one night. Lance tied a bandanna round it while they finished the show and then took Dick to the hospital to have it stitched up.

It was a big independent show. 'See Australia's famous outlaw horses and those Daredevil Roughriders who *risk everything* for your entertainment', the newspaper advertisements screamed. 'High-class circus acts' included acrobats, wire-walkers, tumblers, ropespinners and aerial acts. There were '43 men, 32 horses, 4 mules, several marquees, 14 lorries, 9 caravans, 5 cars and considerable amounts of grain and chaff'. There was also at least one woman, Dolly Lennon.

Back in Sydney in 1949 Lance got together with Tex Morton and they showed up the coast, finishing up at the Brisbane Exhibition in 1950. That proved to be the final Skuthorpe show. Lance and Tex went to Canada and America. Dick Skinner was left with the horses, which he took to rodeos for a while. Aristocrat was retired and died at Dick's Coonamble property on Christmas Day, 1954.

Lance Jnr, they say, never wanted to be a showman, he was born to it. Always up and down, by 1950 he was sick of the constant hustle and wanted a change. Lance's first two marriages had ended in divorce. Then he married an American, Margaret Carruthers, and set up home in Los Angeles. He changed his surname to Thorpe, became a real estate salesman and lived the rest of his life in America. In 1973 he died of lung cancer. He was 57.

Violet Skuthorpe Jnr toured with her brother after the war but by this time she had married Max Miller, brother of champion boxer Mickey Miller. After the birth of their first child, Violet and Max started their own show. Violet Skuthorpe's Wild West Show toured extensively in Australia but it didn't do as well as it should have. After the marriage fell apart, Violet formed another show with veteran buckjump showman Noel George in 1953. Violet was one of only half-a-dozen women who were ever 'the boss' of a buckjump show. She married roughrider, trickrider and ace ropespinner John Brady and their professional and personal collaboration lasted 30 years until Violet died in 1990. Johnny Brady is still in show business.

Thorpe McConville got Wild Australia rolling again in 1946, opening in his home town, Narrandera. Dave Woods, Alan Cook, Jack Delahunt and Neville Bamblett returned to the show and Billy Cotter, John Burrows, Tommy Grace, Geoff and Wally Jamieson, Tommy Edwards and Thorpe's son, Noel McConville all started out for their first season roughriding. Art Creasy was whipcracking and ropespinning. The circus acts were back and Thorpe's sons Ray and Noel were clowning, doing gymnastics, rosin-back riding and whipcracking.

Thorpe's brother, Charlie, took on the job as advance agent. He and his wife, Stella, travelled two weeks ahead of the show arranging permits with the councils, booking sites and organising a stream of advertising. The four St Leons joined the show and in 1948 McConville went back to Queensland and toured for 18 months continuously. 'Fun in the Stockyard' continued to cause much merriment and the local riders continued to try to ride Thorpe's outlaws for £5 or £10 a win. His line-up of exhibition roughriders now included Bob Glover, Russell Rank, Bez Murray, Freddy Cull and lady roughrider, Audrey Croasdale.

In 1950 Thorpe decided he needed a holiday. He lent his buckjumpers to the Tumut Rodeo committee and he and his wife Violet took a trip to England. He was considering returning to showmanship when he developed was diagnosed with terminal cancer and died in June 1953. Australian roughriding and rodeo had lost one of its leading lights.

In 1957 Noel McConville joined forces with the St Leon family for one last season. Wild Australia and St Leons Circus and Rodeo went out on the road in New South Wales and Queensland. In the roughriding team was Kevin Nelson from Goondiwindi who won the Warwick buckjump in 1957 and the soon-to-be champion roughrider from Melbourne, Allan Hicks. Allan was learning his trade and he learnt it well. During the 1960s and early 70s he won six Australian roughriding titles, two for bullriding and four in the bareback.

Other shows on the road in the fabulous 40s and 50s included Queensland Harry, Skuthorpes' gun rider from the 1920s, who had his own show in New Zealand, and Jack Baker and Dolly Godfrey took up where the boys left off and formed Ma and Snowy Baker's Snowy River Stampede. They lasted through to the 1960s. Ken Huntley ran his show in Sydney during the war, then he and his wife, Beryl Riley (now Beryl Chick) toured around Australia and New Zealand until Huntley died from a heart attack there in 1951. Frank McFarlane was a roughrider in the 30s; he became a very good roman rider and had a buckjump show in the 40s and 50s, occasionally in partnership with Ron Anderson. Curley Bell was still going in Queensland in 1959. The singers went from strength to strength — Buddy Williams had a Queensland Wild West Rodeo and Variety Show and Tex Morton worked with everyone at some stage; he came and went to the USA, struggled with booze, had a somewhat disastrous comeback tour in 1972, then settled into acting until his death in 1983.

End of an era

By the 1960s only a few shows remained — the Snowy River Stampede, in Queensland the Kants family's Dad and Dave show and 'rodeo', and Larry Dulhunty, who was touring the west and the Territory; he finished with the horses in 1972. There was a Morgan Brothers Rodeo and the Brophy Brothers' Wild West Circus, and of course there were the Gills.

The Gills were working with Tex Morton during the years leading up to World War II. During the war they had a permanent set-up in Tamworth, entertaining the soldiers. After the war the Gill Brothers outfit was getting too big so Jack and Stan Jnr split it and each had their own show. Jack took the name Gill Brothers Rodeo and Circus and Stan had Stan Gill's Australian Round-Up. Jack showed up and down the east coast while Stan covered Western Australia, South Australia and Victoria. Occasionally they hooked up and combined. Doyle Gill worked with both outfits and was a notorious prankster. He and roughrider Allan Bennett were *the* practical jokers of the rodeo tribe.

According to Happy Gill, 'old showmen never die, they just fade away.' When his grandparents, old Stan and Violet, faded from the Wild West business in 1950, they settled in Bankstown, just around the corner from their good friends, Lance and Violet Skuthorpe Snr. They continued to work the small agricultural shows in and around Sydney until Stan Snr passed away in 1957.

Buckjump showmen always had the problem of drunken ratbags wanting to get in the ring and ride. In Queensland, where they drink a lot of rum, the problem was intensified. No professional showmen would put a drunk man on a buckjumper — it's too dangerous and a waste of everybody's time. They would generally use withering remarks to put a stop to the heckling of drunks or occasionally they'd escort them outside and thump them.

Contrary to folklore, Joseph Wain was not drunk on the night of 21 September 1957. But he was trying to hustle his way in through the back of the Gills' tent for free on the pretence of having a ride.

Jack and Stan Gill were showing together at Gayndah in Queensland. Jack was on the mike and Stan, who confronted Wain, wasn't having any of Wain's antics. There was a bit of a scuffle, Wain left but returned after the show with a gun. He walked straight up to Stan yelling, 'I'll shoot you, you bastard,' and did. Wain was tried and convicted of murder, but it was little consolation to the Gill family, most of whom were present when the incident happened, who were absolutely devastated by the loss of their father, brother, husband, uncle and great mate.

It was a grim and tragic end to Stan Gill's Australian Round-Up. Kitty Gill went back to the Wests and worked with Sole Brothers Circus until she injured herself badly when her trapeze rigging broke and she had to retire. Stan and Kitty had had three children, Stan Jnr, Patricia and Vicky. The two girls married out of the business but Stan Gill Jnr went on to become one of 'The Flying Waynes', which for years was the trapeze act in the centre ring at Ringling Bros Barnum and Bailey Circus — about as good as it gets in the circus world.

Jack and Gladys Gill had three children: John 'Happy', who was born in 1937, then Brian and Peter. They were all performing in their parents' show as soon as they could walk and riding in it by the time they were five and six years old. Happy, thus named by Tex Morton, specialised in somersaults and acrobatics; he had also inherited his grandfather's musical abilities and was a very good drummer. Brian specialised in whips and ropes, and Peter, who also did acrobatics was, as a child, a contortionist.

Gill Brothers Circus and Rodeo toured right through the 1950s and 60s with Happy, Brian and Peter roughriding every night. Each exhibition lasted 12–15 seconds; they rode with a chest rein or head rein and either without stirrups or no saddle at all. Generally they would buck six to eight horses and four to six bullocks, with different acts in between. They had trick ponies and a monkey called Tarz, who used to bite everyone. They had two particularly famous buckjumpers during this period, King of the Ring and Gravesend.

Gladys Gill died in 1961. A few years later Jack Gill and his sons took the buckjump show business into the next stage of its evolution when they segued from their tent show to producing full-scale rodeos. It was a natural progression as a tent show without a tent was halfway there. They removed the ropes, dropped the circus side of things, built portable, full-sized arenas and ran rodeos with professional events and standards. Happy and Peter later got into professional stock contracting.

Jack Gill 'faded' from full-time life on the road but stayed in the agricultural show business until his death in 1981. His middle son, Brian continued on in the buckjump show business.

Brian and his wife, Sylvia, and children, Brian Jnr, Malcolm, Justin, Jackie and Eddie, toured the show for six months of the year and stock contracted rodeos the other six months. Brian had a great sense of humour. He was the spruiker and the ringmaster and, as was the custom, the children did everything else. The boys also rodeoed on the professional circuit. The buckjump show stayed 'bush' in the more remote communities of north and western Queensland and the Northern Territory where life was still 'Wild and Western'.

Brian Gill was larger than life and very much loved by all who knew him. He died of cancer in November 1993. They called him the last of the tent-show men. Until now. His boys went off the road for a while; it was too hard on the heart to show without Dad, and they concentrated on stock contracting. But in the last year or two Brian's sons have resurrected their buckjump show. They've called it 'The Gill Brothers' Old Australian Buckjump Show'. It is living heritage, the only buckjump show left, and it's based entirely on the traditions that the Gills have carried for five generations.

The tent shows were a training ground, not to mention a breeding ground, for some of our greatest cowboys and bucking horses. Practically all of the early Australian roughriding champions spent some time riding in the tents. From World War II, Gill Brothers' Circus and Rodeo alone was host, mentor and boss to all three Woods brothers, Kevin McTaggart, Bernie Smyth Snr, Barry Gravener, Ken Coleman, Bob Hocking, Ken Healy, Reg Wiles, Kevin Lather and his son Errol Lather, Stuart McPhee, Kevin Nelson and Ray Hermann. There were innumerable others, both ARRA and Bushies — it was the normal thing to do. As the tent shows closed down, most of their bucking stock ended up with the established rodeo committees and some became the nucleus of the early stock contractors' strings. Both horsemanship and bucking spirit is in the blood and has carried down through the generations to today.

Meanwhile bushman's carnivals and rodeos were blossoming, and becoming more professional in the 1940s and 50s. As they proliferated, most of the travelling buckjump and Wild West shows, in fact much of the travelling live entertainment, was fading out. The introduction of television in 1956 was the biggest single reason for their demise. Television successfully challenged most forms of entertainment that relied on ticket sales. But there were many other contributing factors. The professional rodeo circuit was in full swing; their star 'circuit cowboys' were household names; and most Australians could see their heroes riding in a full-scale rodeo in their home town or a town nearby at least once a year. The automobile was being mass-produced and as it became more affordable it replaced the horse once and for all. Horses and livestock had long since disappeared from the cities and with them went an appreciation of horsemanship. With the demise of horse and stock sense, animal liberationists started to frown and scratch their heads about bucking horses in general. The 1960s also saw the start of the economic downturn in the bush. Mechanisation, motorbikes and choppers turned horsemen and horses into dying breeds. Bureaucracy flourished. It became complicated for the travelling shows to get council permission, and insurance — which no-one had ever bothered about before — became another worry and expense. All in all it was the end of the popularity of bushmen, horsemen and outback culture in general.

4

BUSHMEN'S CARNIVALS

There's an outlaw on Glenidol that is known through all the West,

And three men's lives are on his head, bold riders of the best;

And station lads have heard the sneer that travelled far and wide,

and flung the answering challenge, 'Come and teach us how to ride!'

Rodeo Carnival

TOWNSVILLE SHOW GROUNDS.

Saturday, 2nd July
Monday, 4th July

(Under the auspices of the Townsville and Warwick Show Associations.)

N.Q. BUCKJUMPING CHAMPIONSHIP   £40

BULLOCK RIDING CHAMPIONSHIP   £15

Complete Programme on Application.
ENTRIES CLOSE 13th JUNE.
W. B. DARLEY, Secretary, Townsville P.A. & I. Assen.

Townsville Show 5, 6, 7th July

Meanwhile back at the station...

THE MAJORITY OF CATTLEMEN and horsemen were too busy to go traipsing around the countryside chasing thrills and adventure. Despite considerable collaboration and competitions between them, graziers and their employees and the buckjump showmen lived in completely separate worlds. The latter were itinerant, promoting and riding buckjumpers for a living. The former were committed to home and hearth (or saving for it) and riding buckjumpers for work and sport.

Life on the land was not just hard slog. Entertainment was what they made it and the rural communities found plenty of ways of amusing themselves. The travelling shows and entertainers passed through from time to time. Meanwhile there were picnics, tennis parties and nights around the piano, cards and shooting and fishing. Pubs were gathering places for men when in town. Bush dances brought families together from miles around to party all night to the music of the concertina and violin. Horse and cattle sales also brought men together and the former often involved plenty of roughriding as horse dealers and their roughriders tried out and tested the horses.

Sport was a major pastime. Early outback newspapers were full of cricket, football, horseracing, foot races and boxing write-ups and scores. Although avidly followed by all, it was only the townspeople who could play team sports on a regular basis. Those on the stations stuck to individual sports, usually involving horses. To counter their isolation, graziers formed various committees and went to great lengths to throw annual bashes that gathered up far-flung friends and neighbours.

Horsemanship was the one common denominator in society so it was horse sports that brought the whole community together. The annual picnic races were huge affairs, lasted days, and involved plenty of carousing and revelry. Men and women and their families — of all colours and classes — caught up on each other's news, and sporting competition was fierce but friendly. The stations raced their grass-fed stockhorses, and the more affluent squatters pitched their thoroughbred blue bloods against each other.

From the mid-nineteenth century each colony formed an agricultural society and by the turn of the century many country towns had an annual agricultural show. Again these lasted three or four days — worth the long trip to get there. Graziers and their families converged from the surrounding districts and were awarded prizes for jams and cakes; needlework; leatherwork, such as saddles, harnesses and whips; new inventions; the most spectacular fruit and vegetables; and of course the best-quality wool. Dogs, hogs, chooks, sheep, cattle and all manner of horses were judged on both breed and utility. And then there were the horse sports.

Agricultural shows were an Anglo-Celtic tradition, and the horse events were too. Judges awarded ribbons and trophies to best lady and gent riders and best girl and boy in the various age groups. There were best pony and hack; prizes also went to the best horse and sulky and four-in-hand team. High-jumping was one of the most popular events and there was hunting (over jumps not after foxes) and hurdles, both single and teams of four. A game of polo might be held, and there were plenty of novelty events like billygoat races for the children.

In addition Australian bushmen invented contests based on their everyday work practices. There were competitions for sheep counting, shearing and woodchopping, and sheepdog trials. The cattlemen and stockmen had cattle drafting, which evolved into campdrafting, stockhorse trials and, in time, bullock throwing and tying contests. And any fool could go in the roughriding contests — on steers, bullocks and sometimes horses — and the resultant thrills and spills were the highlight of the day.

Both the horseraces and the agricultural show were the biggest social events on any bush calendar. Young people stayed up gallivanting every night and many hearts were won and broken. The climax was a ball in a hall if there was one or a dance in the woolshed if there was not. And there were always plenty of sore heads jig-jogging back home next morning.

Such was the celebration of physical prowess in pioneer Australia that most country towns had sports days or sports carnivals as well. There were foot races and high jump and long-jumping contests but it was predominantly horse sports. Like the modern-day gymkhana, there were all the hacking and jumping competitions, bending and flag races and rescue and relay races and plenty of games and novelty events. Riders galloped bareback to one end of the grounds, saddled up and galloped back, or grabbed an apple out of a bucket with their teeth and galloped back, or grabbed a light for a ciggie and galloped back ... anything that involved galloping. They also ran the bushmen's contests, including cattle drafting, roughriding and working stockhorse contests. The local men and women could display their skills and their clever horses to each other; the winners shouted the beer.

Occasionally, a town would throw a huge week-long carnival. There were horseraces and the usual horse contests and boxing, wrestling, dog- and cockfighting. People would come from miles around to bet, drink and fight; respectable families stayed out of the way. But generally sports days and carnivals were one-day family affairs and the emphasis was on fun and fundraising. Many 'Patriotic Sports Days' were held around the country during both world wars to raise money for the war effort — the Red Cross, veterans' hospitals and returning soldiers funds.

Around 1910 most graziers were seeing a return to more affluent times. This coincided with the expansion of the bushman's sports into what became known as bushmen's carnivals. Graziers had more time and money to get involved. Attending a show or a carnival often meant a week away from home, which is too long when in the grip of a drought. Committees and their meetings were one thing but to run bushmen's events took a lot of manpower, not only on the actual day but beforehand building facilities and amenities, fences for yards, and arenas and chutes for the bucking bullocks. Mobs of cattle for the drafting and roughriding were lent to the committees; they had to be in good condition and they had to be driven in on foot for the occasion and back home afterwards. Later it was the same for bucking horses.

Advances in transportation also boosted carnival numbers. Since their expansion in the 1880s and 90s the railroads had been the main mode of transport if anyone had to travel very far. Horses had their own special carriages at the back of the train. After World War I and throughout the 20s and 30s, automobiles began to replace horses on the roads. Agricultural shows and sports days became more accessible, which led to more contestants and more spectators. They grew from predominately local to more regional affairs and the cattlemen began to compete in earnest.

Let the games begin!

With the pressure off, the graziers could concentrate on horsebreeding and training. Cattle drafting was taken the most seriously out of the bushmen's sports and it was a contest between horses. Cattle draft associations were formed in Queensland as far back as 1916. R.F. (Roly) Munro from the Moree district in New South Wales won a hundred pounds with a horse called Joker in the cattle draft at Gayndah in 1918. Munro was one of the sport's instigators and later one of its most respected judges.[1] Cattle drafting was also a time-consuming event. As more people became interested in it, particularly in northern New South Wales and southern Queensland, sports days and carnivals gradually grew from one day to two — Saturdays and Mondays; Sunday was for church.

The Hunter River district has always been a hotbed of horses and horsemen. One-day carnivals were held regularly through the 20s. Murrurundi in New South Wales' Upper Hunter ran a sports day in 1921. George Hong won the buckjumping on a grey spinner called Snow owned by Mick O'Brian. Not long afterwards in an open paddock at Scone, the Upper Hunter Cattle Draft and Buckjumping Championships were held in addition to sprint races and the usual sporting events. Barney Haydon won the buckjumping championship on a horse called Ginger that belonged to Harry (Dusty) Miller, 'whose fame as a roughrider was world wide ... during the ride, Ginger bucked clean over the front end of a parked sulky'.[2]

As far as can be ascertained, there were few bushmen's carnivals as we now know them before the 1920s. By the 1930s a number were well established in northern New South Wales and Queensland at least. Certainly the term 'bushman's carnival' did not come into common usage until the late 1920s, early 1930s. A bushman's carnival was simply an extended sports day or carnival with more time for the four main bushmen's contests. Cattle drafting in particular, as it relied on a horse's stock sense and skills and contests were won with the best bred and trained horses. Bullock throwing (by the tail from horseback) and tying was a stockman's method for catching wild or intractable cattle. Riding buckjumpers was also part of the stockmen's and horsebreaker's trade. Bullock or steer riding was a lark, an excuse to get dirty and a laugh for the crowd.

Murrurundi ran its first Bushman's Carnival in 1932. All the normal horsy events were conducted, Jack Stanton of Tamworth won the open buckjump championship. Ruben Smith of Singleton won the open bullock riding championship. There were plenty of competitors in the roughriding, including Jack Palmer, Arthur Winter, Ken McDonald, Alex Henderson, George Hong, Jack Charlton and Harry Green.

The carnival was a great success, socially and financially, and the following Sunday a meeting was held to draw up a set of rules. Attended mainly by the men from the White and Haydon families, interested parties from Warwick's Bushmen's Carnival Committee were also there, including renowned all-rounder, Cecil Pearce and E.J. 'Ned' Portley, who became the secretary of Warwick rodeo from 1935–45. A booklet containing the *Murrurundi Bushmen's Carnival and Show Association Rules* was published. The following year the Australian Bushmen's Carnival Association, which was affiliated with the New South Wales Royal Agricultural Society (RAS), adopted the rules.[3] Warwick and the men of central and south-east Queensland and Sydney RAS and the men of the Hunter and north-eastern New South Wales were the bushman's carnival establishment for the rest of the 1930s. Both Warwick and Sydney became yardsticks in the development of rodeo in Australia. They were instigators and innovators, they had the best prize money and the most prestige and their shows attracted the leading horsemen of the era. As Australia's oldest continually running rodeos Warwick and Sydney hold pride of place in the sport's history.

Although we like to view Australia as an egalitarian society, in the bush where smaller numbers of people make the truth easier to see there were (and still are) huge class distinctions between the 'haves' and 'have nots'. On a cattle station the boss and his men often worked side by side, but did not socialise, live or even eat together. Successful squatters and graziers might have had the resources to breed and rear flash horses for racing, polo, high-jumping, hacking and to a certain extent campdrafting, but their workers — the station hands, stockmen and horsebreakers did not. These men were mostly itinerant, rode the station's horses, and their skills lay in mustering, drafting and doctoring cattle and mastering and educating rough horses, not well-behaved ones. Most cattlemen were excellent horsemen and stockmen and competed in all events, but the workers were drawn to the roughstock events because you didn't need anything other than guts and determination to win. Everyone could have a go. Aboriginal stockmen were always welcomed and had great success in the bushmen's carnival and rodeo arenas, particularly in Queensland, in the 1920s, 30s and 40s. It was about how good you were, not who you were. The itinerant and disenfranchised — of all races and backgrounds — the workers and the bosses competed together. Roughriding is a great social leveller.

During the 1920s and into the early 30s, there were some outstanding and well-known roughriders competing in the bushmen's carnivals in northern New South Wales. Harry McPhee of Belltrees Station was one of the greatest, as was his brother, Ron. Other top-class riders were Jack Stanton and his brother Les, Dan Edwards, Hilton McTaggart, Tommy Kelly, Arthur Winter, later his wife, Gwen, and Billy Timmins, father of 1950s buckjumping legend, Stumpy Timmins. There was Arch 'Bung' and Neil McInnes, Ruben Smith, George Hong, Laurie Harris, Ben Singleton, Barney Haydon, Harry Evans, Lance Stockdale, Bruce Lee, Arthur Bowd, Tony and Joe Purcell, Aub, Les and Terry Hunt, Gerbie Trindall, Jack Nolan and Jack Palmer the great all-rounder from Scone. Sep Clarke from Kempsey was another well-known roughrider during the 1930s. He travelled with Thorpe McConville, competed in competitions all over New South Wales and won an Australian Championship bullock ride at Sydney Showground in 1933.[4]

Most of these men spent time riding with the travelling buckjump shows during the 1920s and 1930s. In 1937 Jack Hay had his buckjump show set up at the Murrurundi Bushmen's Carnival which suggests that the travelling showmen took advantage of all gatherings of bushmen and horsemen, not just the agricultural shows.

There were some pretty handy bullock throwers and tyers in the Hunter Valley area pre–1935: Arch 'Bung' McInnes and his brother Neil, Ken Campbell, Bill Scriven, Jim Callinan, the Haydons — Fred, Barney, Hilton and Jim, Alec Wiseman, Alex Henderson, Jack McPhee, Jim Purcell, Arthur Davis, Carl Mitchell, Ken Mackay and Colin Bell, who often came down from Queensland. Winning times ranged from 45 seconds to a minute.[5]

Whereas American cowboys had embraced showmanship from the word go, most Australian stockmen did the opposite. The American working cattlemen and cowboys who contested in their local tournaments and rodeos appropriated entertainment styles from Wild West shows, drawing upon the showmen's flair for promoting their attractions. Their rodeos were quickly recognised as a means of promoting tourism and business and by 1915 major rodeo events had become annual occurrences in Cheyenne, Pendleton, Salinas and Calgary. Rodeo as a huge Western spectacle never looked back.[6]

In Australia, despite the presence of plenty of Australian and American Wild West showmen and contests between the American cowboys and Australians over the years, our bushmen did not incorporate showmanship into their weekend sport. Our working graziers and stockmen had a more utilitarian and low-profile approach. The laconic boys of the bush were rather modest and shy, until the rum kicked in; self-promotion wasn't even an option. They were isolated, insular, wary of change, and were both suspicious of the 'cowboy' flamboyance and too busy to take much notice.

Until the end of the 1920s Australian bushmen pretty much ignored the showmen except as a gimmick, or an occasional challenge. They got on with their own weekend horse sports and created their own milieu. They were not concerned with selling themselves, only entertaining and competing against each other. If they were charging at the gate it was to raise money for charity.

However from the mid–1920s, Thorpe McConville was hard to ignore. He was running full-blown American-style rodeos, both exhibitions and competitions in showgrounds and sports grounds and indoor venues around the country — and packing them in. Over the years Australian and American roughriders and cowboys had been invited to give exhibitions of buckjumping, whipcracking and ropespinning at shows, but now the showmen began to get more involved with the bushmen 'establishment'. The agricultural societies, not the bushmen's carnival committees, led the way because they needed the money to promote and run their annual shows.

Making a buck

The early 1930s saw the awakening of the idea that bushmen's carnivals and agricultural shows could be popular entertainment. With the money from the gate they could graduate from the paddocks and open flats and build better facilities. They could award more prize money to attract the best competitors from around the country and further lift their game. Campdrafting, unless you're an expert, is too slow to be a spectator sport. The other three bushmen's events were exciting and dangerous and often hilarious and in the interests of selling tickets it was the roughriders who were promoted as the gallant and daring stars. The ever-present buckjump showmen helped of course. The evolution to professional rodeo took another 40 years but the seeds were sown at this time.

The 1930s saw a worldwide cowboy craze grow out of the Depression years, fed by the mass marketing of American western popular culture. Australian bushmen were not necessarily wowed by cowboys, their methods or their antics, but our general population — the paying public — were. The promoters, committees, agricultural societies and their accountants woke up to what our travelling showmen had known for years. There was money in it. Cowboys and cowgirls appealed to a broader population. If the townies and city slickers would pay to marvel at American-styled spectacle, then that's what they should have. The Australian bushmen's carnival community slowly but surely began to absorb the American cowboy's ways and means of gaining recognition and making money. Marrabel in South Australia and Lang Lang in Victoria are two famous Australian rodeo towns that exemplify this.

In South Australia Kidman was king of the cattlemen and many of his horses and cattle found their way into rodeo arenas. In 1934 the Marrabel Tennis Club needed to raise money for new courts. They organised a gymkhana incorporating a roughstock riding competition, inspired by a similar event at neighbouring Saddleworth, from whom they borrowed buckjumpers bought from one of Kidman's horse sales. The event was held on the football oval and it was a great success.

The following year an official committee organised a proper rodeo; a successful annual event was born. By 1939 Marrabel had their own string of buckjumpers, also tough Kidman station horses, and roughriders were travelling from all states to compete. Years later the feats of their legendary bucking mare, Curio (who bucked professionally from 1945–64) made the name of Marrabel synonymous with rodeo in Australia.

Lang Lang started its annual Pastoral, Agricultural and Horticultural Society's show in 1901. Public interest was waning so in 1939 the committee secretary asked the Kirkham brothers of Hallam to assemble a 'boxing troupe' for the show. As dedicated roughriders who travelled the bushmen's carnivals, the brothers argued successfully for a steer ride instead. It went brilliantly and they made £130 on the gate. Jim Ridgeway took over as secretary in 1941 and found that the bank overdraft was still £200. He instigated a 'Steer Riding Championship of Victoria'. Twenty riders from the local Remount Depot competed, and the poster advertised all the 'fun and excitement of a Wild West Rodeo' on top of the usual hacking and hunting events, the flag, barrel, bending and vegetable races, and musical chairs. Nominations jumped by 300 from the previous year. Cars were parked five or six deep facing the arena and many had to park outside the showground. It was a roaring success; the committee bank balance returned to the black.

And so it went all over the country. Rodeos popularised bushmen's carnivals and agricultural shows.

Wild and Western for the people

It is arbitrary and pedantic to speculate on who ran the first 'rodeo' in Australia. It's a question of semantics and would involve a search through the historical records and local papers of every town and city in Australia to authenticate. There is an unsubstantiated claim that it was held in Gayndah in Queensland in 1897. What events were staged, who ran the show and what it was called are unknown. Rodeos were more or less the American version of bushmen's carnivals. They had been capitalised upon by the Wild West showmen who brought the term to Australia sometime after 1890. McConville definitely used it from 1924, after the international rodeo at Wembley and not before.

Merriwa, New South Wales, held its first 'rodeo' in March 1928. It was staged in conjunction with the annual agricultural show and was reported as a 'most thrilling and spectacular event'. Prize money of £25 each was put up for the bullock ride, the buckjumping and the throwing and tying. There was also a draughthorse race and the usual flag races and whatnot. Colonel G.C. Somerville, the secretary of the Sydney RAS, was there to see whether 'this sort of thing' might be good for the Sydney show. People travelled from Sydney, Singleton, Muswellbrook, Scone, Tamworth, Denman, Coolah, Mudgee, Bathurst and everywhere in between to watch competitors from all over New South Wales, Victoria and Queensland.[7]

It was so successful that the Merriwa Show and Rodeo Committee ran an Australasian Championship in buckjumping and bullock riding the following year, attracting riders from all parts of the Commonwealth and New Zealand. Record numbers turned out — about 800 cars parked in the grounds on the second day. The event was even broadcast live on ABC radio. Typhoon, ridden by Scone's Harry McPhee, caused a 'sensation' when he jumped through the ring ropes and McPhee came off with his chin caught under the top strand.

The horse then careered around the grounds causing a panic among the spectators. Tom Handley, 'one of the best riders in Australia', failed to qualify for the final. Dan Edwards was declared 'Buckjumping Champion of Australasia' for his 'fearless exhibition on a snorting brown horse called Sudden Death'.[8] Tommy Kelly (Rockhampton) and Hilton McTaggart (Singleton) tied for second. Of the £400 that had been donated for prize money Edwards pocketed £100 — a fortune in 1929 when the country was heading into depression and the average wage was between £2 and £5 a week. Dan bought his mother a house in Sydney with the winnings. Other contestants in the championship buckjumping that day were Ross Berry (Merriwa), 'Snowy' Birrell (Condobolin), Tom Barrett (Moree), E. Harrison (New Zealand), and Harry Phillips who Dan Edwards remembers as 'a big black fella with big white moustache'.[9] Merriwa was a good example of the developing relationship between the showmen and the graziers. It was an open competition run by a buckjump showman hired by an agricultural show committee. Handley hired out his ropes, his horses, and himself. His show was on the road at that time. He competed, as did his then gun roughrider, Dan Edwards. It was just another gig for the showmen, but it certainly put Merriwa's agricultural show on the map.

Following Merriwa's success, a committee was formed in Warwick, Queensland, to organise a Bushmen's Carnival and Rodeo to raise funds for the annual agricultural show. It took place in November 1929 and included the four standard bushmen's contests and numerous novelty events. The cattle drafting prize was 50 sovereigns and a trophy, the buckjumping was 15 sovereigns and a trophy, the bullock ride £15 and a cup, and the throwing and tying contest was £10 and a cup. The buckjumping and bullock riding contests — also the 'Australian Championships' — were won by Archie Trott and Frank Ebzert respectively.[10] Whether the buckjump showmen or their bucking stock were involved or whether everyone brought their own buckjumpers is unknown. But the Warwick committee quickly built up a string of great bucking horses that they transported to other bushmen's carnivals and rodeos in the state during the years to come. Among Warwick's early buckjumpers Knickerbockerbuckeroo and Arrawidgee (The Grey Ghost) became the most famous.

In 1930 Warwick again announced itself the 'Australian Championships' in buckjumping, campdrafting, bullock throwing and tying and cattle draft. This year they added other acts and American-style contests to entertain the general public, notably clowns, trick riders and ropers.

Sydney, Melbourne and probably Brisbane RAS had hosted roughriding competitions on and off for years. Lance Skuthorpe Snr was captivated by his wife-to-be, Violet, when he saw her riding bullocks at Sydney in 1911.[11] Colonel Somerville must have liked what he saw at Merriwa and Warwick because the Sydney Royal added a 'Grand Rodeo' to its attractions in 1931. It included buckjumping, steer riding, cattle throwing and tying and a mule race. Hilton McTaggart won the buckjumping, ahead of Billy Reynolds, George Handley and C. McAuliffe. The society provided the horses, the (poley) saddles and the (blunt) spurs. Stirrups were optional, horses wore a headstall (no bit) with reins. It was one-handed, the other hand carried free. The steer ride was won by Col Shutes, with Ben Singleton, Hilton McTaggart and J. Riley placing second to fourth. Also one-handed, competitors had to take their surcingle with them when dismounting. From then on the Sydney Royal always had campdraft, a throw and tie and at least one roughriding event in their program.

Outside of the cities the average Australian stockman was never considered glamorous. Larry Dulhunty was a Queensland ringer in the 1930s, and he swears the girls avoided him like the plague. In town for a dance on a Saturday night, they would take one look at his boots and be gone. Ringers or stockmen were considered to be 'hicks' and not good marriage potential. There was nothing special about them as far as the bush girls were concerned; they could ride and muster as well as the boys could any day.

Neither were our stockmen ostentatious. In the arena the roughriders wore more or less what they wore to work. Plain cream jodhpurs or moleskins, unadorned boots, plain white or blue shirts with a tie or, if flash, a scarf, and their hats were smashed up and sweat-stained. But there were those who were dabbling. At Warwick, in 1930, the crowd became 'suddenly alert' when they saw a 'Tom Mix figure resplendent in sombrero, buckskins, leather gloves etc enter the ring'. He 'placed a big Mexican saddle on a diminutive nag', but a few seconds later 'rider, saddle and all were sprawled on the ground as a stirrup had broken' [perhaps they meant girth]. Undaunted, the quickly dubbed Western Terror (H. Beeston of Warwick) borrowed another saddle and his second attempt saw the mount 'subdued'.[12]

Cowboys, the heroes of the silver screen, were quite something else. However, as rodeos continued to evolve so did the stockmen's image and desirability — the cowboy's glamour began to transfer to those who competed at the shows.

'Rodeo fever', as it was called, took off simultaneously all over the country. Bushmen's carnivals were popularised as bushmen's carnivals and rodeos. The general public poured in looking for thrills, spills and entertainment. And they got it. At Oakey in 1932 a horse crashed through the arena fence and 'kicked viciously at a parked motor car full of spectators'. In the same year 8000 people turned up to Toowoomba's Royal Agricultural Society's Rodeo and Bushmen's Carnival. With an eye for a buck, some intrepid individuals put on their own rodeos. Over the years Australia has had plenty of dubious rodeo promoters but there are, of course, the exceptions.

New entrepreneurs

Saint John Robertson, or 'Old Robbie' as he was also fondly known, owned a zoo at Mount St John outside of Townsville. There he bred alligators among other things and had a performing alligator called Mickey. He was a great showman, 'a bit of an old con', but a good one. In 1932, 33 and 34, Mr Robertson ran rodeos on an open flat paddock next to his zoo. According to newspaper accounts, although these 'big carnivals' had been popular in southern Queensland 'for some years', there had only been a few 'spasmodic' cattle drafting competitions in the north so far, in big cattle towns such as Charters Towers and Mareeba.[13]

In 1932, 'Bill Bowyang' wrote in his Townsville newspaper column that there was a: 'Rodeo craze now sweeping the North ... Mr St John Robertson, a great buckjump rider in his day, was the first to start the ball rolling, and backed up by an enthusiastic band of workers his effort was a wonderful success'.[14]

Only a few weeks later the Townsville Show Association, in conjunction with the Warwick Show Association, put on a rodeo carnival at the Townsville Showgrounds. It was advertised as the North Queensland Buckjumping and Bullock Riding Championships and fifteen thousand people passed through the gates in two days. The team from Warwick, committee men and buckjumpers, were fresh from organising a successful show in Brisbane which 42 000 people had attended.[15]

Despite the success of the Townsville show, the use of the Warwick buckjumpers, saddles, judges and announcers was contentious. As we glean from 'Bill Bowyang' buckjumping contestants used their own saddles in the preceding rounds but Warwick committee's for the finals. The buckjumping finalists were 'northerners'; W. (Billy) Bargo, Roy Oram, Roy Jansen, L. George and Jack Williams. As they waited by the snubbing post for the 'Warwick Men' to saddle the horse, 'each of the five in turn looked hard at the saddle ... so small and polished that it glittered round the ring — and there was not the slightest sign of a knee pad'. Not one of them lasted a second. 'Which made our good horsemen look fools to the crowd.' After each rider was thrown the 'Warwick Man' would announce, 'no-one has ever ridden this horse!'

'Bill Boyang' concluded that next time they should use 'northern horses' not the southern 'trick corn-fed horses', and each man should compete in his own saddle. 'I have watched many rodeos and gazed at buckjumping events in calico arenas, and in the latter place one naturally expects a good rider to get something "put over him". When he comes to a rodeo out in the open that is another thing, but ... the Warwick turnout went one better than the travelling buckjump shows.' Best buckjumper, however, was won by a local 'outlaw', Ginger Meggs, belonging to J. Brabon.

The Warwick team, men and horses went off to Rockhampton to stage another 'rodeo and bushmen's carnival' — the Central Queensland Championships — in collaboration with the Rockhampton Agricultural Society.

Rockhampton made this an annual event from 1938, in which year they hosted the Queensland State Titles. The Rockhampton rodeo was billed as the Australian Titles in 1941 and (with official sanctioning) 1949, when the event was renamed 'The Rocky Round Up'. The self-styled 'Beef Capital of Australia', Rockhampton has always had successful rodeos. Their two biggest were in 1951 (featuring a National Buckjumping Title with a prize of £1000, at the time the largest prize ever offered for a rodeo event in Australia) and in 1981 with the World Roughriding Championships. Both rodeos were organised by the indefatigable Rex Pilbeam.

In north Queensland, like everywhere, these new carnivals and rodeos added to or replaced our traditional Anglo-Celtic horse events with those that were either associated with the cattle industry or the American Wild West shows and rodeos.

'Decorating the steer' was a new invention which almost always saw the steers victorious. A team of two on horseback, chased and threw a steer then 'decorated' it with a blue ribbon around its neck and an orange spiked on each horn! 'An amusing but futile exercise,' a paper said, and 'whilst chewing their reflective cud that evening', the bullocks could 'gloat over at least some victories over those unfathomable beings — men.'

The rodeo express race involved each rider galloping three laps of the grounds, changing horse and saddle at each lap. Five men per heat made a 'thrilling spectacle' as they thundered around the track. Steer and calf rides for the novices and juniors became more popular. Aboriginals often had their own 'Black Boys Bullock Ride' or buckjumping contest and they also rode in open competition with the whites. There were plenty of exhibition buckjump rides and challenges on local outlaws. A Mrs Crawford gave exhibitions of steer riding 'completely decked out in cowgirl gear'. Mr James White gave performances with his trick ponies, who lay down as he clambered over them cracking whips and so forth and then got up and bucked off all the local children.

Bullock riding remained the crowd favourite. Chutes instead of the snubbing post used for horses, made it faster action and the bullocks, once ridden, were left in the ring together until the round was over. They took revenge on the ambulance men and photographers who generally based themselves at the centre of the arena, next to the judges high seat, which only fitted one. The public loved a good chase; even better if the bullocks charged them as well. Amid the shrieks, yells and laughter, 'the way small boys flew over the rails was suggestive of a sudden flight of budgerigars'.[16]

Bullock riding was now a one-handed contest with extra points given for releasing and taking your surcingle or rope with you. Otherwise there was no choice but for the attendants to throw each beast (by the tail) to get them off, no easy task when the bullocks are in a mob and running amok. As the attendants were butted and trampled into the dust there were always cheers and 'howls of delight' from the crowd. Horses were also known to cause chaos. At Rockhampton one year, Dandaroo delighted the crowd by pelting his rider then sprinting round the track, sending the peanut vendor dashing for safety 'with his tray held rigidly out in front of him'.

In 1933 some 13 000 people turned up at Mount St John for Old Robbie's Charity Rodeo Carnival. The climax of the show was supposed to be a spectacular bullfight. This was merely a mock battle with no weapons, just a red cape. The 'toreadors' were apparently found among some local 'Spanish-looking' canecutters, and could hardly speak English, so they didn't know what they were getting into. The bulls were huge stags with impressive horns. The first 'bull' and 'toreador' had a great dance until the bull horned the poor man in the stomach. The second 'toreador' saw this and 'dogged it'; he refused to enter the ring and begged for mercy. Robertson managed to get one of the stockmen to have a go, but the second bull was not to be taunted and stood balefully eyeing the crowd. The third bull was also half-hearted despite the efforts of the various maniacs who danced around it with the red cape. They eventually all gave up and went home.[17]

In north Queensland roughriding contests were attracting around 30 riders each, mostly locals but a few roughriders were obviously travelling about. Among the winners were Billy Bargo, Bill and Roy Oram, Charlie Edmunds, Vic Jensen, Roy Jansen, Sam and Dick Hill, A.W. Harris, who was usually attired in 'approved cowboy style', Sam Watson, A. Black, Teddy Naylor and Charlie King. Joe Atkinson, Harry Tullipan, Jack Hay and Tom Handley were also winners and all had their buckjump shows on the side

Championships attracted a lot more competitors. In 1934 Mount St John hosted another North Queensland Championships over two days. The venue was again the open flat next to the zoo, six or seven acres walled in with cars and a 'splendid' crowd. The stock for the rodeo included 87 bullocks, principally Brahmans, 78 cows for the novices, 25 calves for the boys and 150 horses. There were 320 competitors entered in various events but it was Joe Atkinson 'Australia's Champion Roughrider', Cecil Pearce (another champion roughrider), Frank Maynard (an American cowboy) and Eva Smith (lady roughrider) who were being touted about as celebrities.

In a field of 52 Joe Atkinson won the open buckjumping championships with a 19-second ride. Governor Bower, the local and favourite, gave a good hard 20-second ride for second, and Jack Gorry and Jimmy Moore were third and fourth. Cecil Pearce won the bullock riding championships — riding one-handed and cracking a whip in the other.

But it was the bullock throwing and tying — won by C. Wordsworth — that the newspaper reporter 'Cestus' loved that day:

> *A great business, men and bullocks flying in every direction, and the crowd howling with glee. Everybody was at fever point, the air was electric and men, horses and bullocks rose to the occasion. It was an open slather, devil may care sort of ending to a first rate day's sport.*[18]

'Cestus' was terribly proud of them all. Behind the scenes, 'men worked like Trojans'. In the ring, it was 'grim nerve and determination right through the day

... not one unsporting action, not one unsporting word'. Quite the philosopher, he praised the great numbers of Aboriginal roughriders who had turned out and were riding 'gallantly and bravely' and observing all the traditions which govern the game. This code he summed up as:

> *To show well always, to smile gently when in luck, and to own up, pay up, and shut up, when out of luck — the necessary qualifications of a sporting man ... We may well be a White Australia, but in the heart of all real bushmen is an affection, and a big friendliness for this disappearing race.*[19]

Displeasure

The burgeoning American influences were more than just new arena events and styles. It was lingo too. Speaking at the official opening of the rodeo in Maryborough in 1934, the Governor of Queensland, Sir Leslie Orme Wilson, said he disliked both the term 'rodeo' and 'rodayo':

> *He would prefer that these contests be called 'Bushmen's carnivals'. They had nothing in common with the rodeo of South America as they were typically Australian in character. What he liked about them was that they gave the people an opportunity of witnessing the splendid horsemanship of Queenslanders, and also the opportunity of bringing the people together.*[20]

The newspapers were calling buckjumpers, outlaws and broncos and roughriders, cowboys. 'Cestus' himself could not help but notice:

> *... instead of cries of 'Stick to him,' you now hear: 'Ride him, cowboy.' The slang of the States has permeated the idiom of our bush boys, but, thank goodness, we still call a cattleman a stockman, and not a cowboy, a horsebreaker a horsebreaker and not a bronco buster, a cattle dog a cattle dog and not a cow dog and a brumby a brumby and not a mustang or bronco.*[21]

He didn't like the new clobber either: 'A new style in bush costumes has descended upon us, evidently moulded on Mr Tom Mix and other "two gun cowboys" of the cinemas.'

Lots of competitors were sporting 'great sombreros, in grey, brown and black' and 'butcher's blue' shirts. 'Cestus' longed for the sight of a cabbage tree hat, which 'years ago were the insignia of the cattlemen'.[22]

1934 was the first time a cattle drafting competition was held at Mount St John. Most of the cattle drafters had come straight from the Sydney Show. The winner was W. 'Bill' Gough, father of the great all-rounder Vic Gough, with a mare called

Actress. The cattle drafters were wearing traditional Australian gear and looked 'just like normal working men'. To this day the cattle drafters (now known as campdrafters) have remained staunchly traditional in their approach to their sport. Not so the roughriders.

American imports

Although it never took place, the events on the program for Stuart McColl's Centennial Stampede were good examples of our earliest rodeos. High jumping, cattle drafting, buckjumping (saddle and bareback), calf roping, covered-wagon race (Cowboys and Indians in a chuck-wagon race) wild cow milking, ladies roughriding, Aboriginal roughriding (Aborigines also rode in the open event), steer decorating, (Australian style) steer riding and a wild horse chariot race. Bulldogging and Russian Cossacks trick-riding were planned as exhibitions. It was supposed to be a lively mixture of Australian Bushmen's Carnival and American rodeo events.

Before the downpour in Melbourne, American cowboy Johnnie Schneider found time to teach Queensland graziers and great all-rounders and siblings, Owen and Penny Perrett the art of bulldogging. Invented as a stunt in the 1880s by African-American cowboy showman Bill Pickett, bulldogging was the Americans' version of catching and decorating a beast, instead of flipping it off its feet by its tail as we did. On their way home from Melbourne the Perretts stopped in at Murrurundi's Bushmen's Carnival to compete and gave a bulldogging exhibition which was described by the local paper as follows:

> *Bulldogging and Decorating ... the idea being for the two to pursue a bullock, the lady rider {hazer} keeping the bullock well over to her partner, who racing alongside slips from his horse at full gallop, seizes the bullock by the horns, throws him and decorates his horns with ribbons or rosettes, while his partner catches and brings back his horse. It is a most spectacular and thrilling event, and — to the spectators at all events — very dangerous. It was certainly a most attractive feature, and the daring and dashing horseman and his graceful and intrepid sister were applauded again and again.*[23]

Both Skuthorpe Snr and McConville claim to have displayed bulldogging prior to this in their travelling shows but the Perretts' display is widely regarded as being the first time bulldogging was seen at a bushmen's carnival, rodeo or agricultural show. After Murrurundi, the Perretts accepted invitations to give exhibitions of bulldogging wherever they were competing, including the Sydney and Brisbane Royals.

In 1935 Johnnie Schneider and the other cowboys who stayed here after the demise of the Stampede, along with the Perretts, gave exhibitions of bulldogging at the Sydney Easter Show. In 1936 it was one of the show's 'international' competitions, and the American team won. In November that same year it was contested at Warwick's annual Bushmen's Carnival and Rodeo (American Frank Maynard won). Bulldogging went on to replace our traditional bullock throwing (by the tail) and tying as an event. In the 1980s bulldogging became known as 'Steer wresling.'

In the beginning women occasionally hazed for their husbands, brothers, fathers and friends. Cecil Pearce competed in the bulldogging at Sydney in 1937, with a 'slip of a girl from Boggabilla', Bessie Scott, as his hazer. Women hazing was banned in the 1960s perhaps because no-one could beat Jim McGuire when his wife Margaret was hazing for him. According to Penny Perrett (now Penny McAulay), hazing is not such a hard job, 'but you had to have your wits about you and be in the right place at the right time, or you could blooming well kill your poor old brother'.

Calf roping was another new event on the program for the Melbourne Centenary Stampede. It was first contested at Warwick in 1937 but other than fits and bursts during the 40s and 50s, led and dominated by the legendary Dan Crotty, roping did not really take off as a sport in Australian rodeos until the 1960s.

For an event that never actually happened, the Melbourne Centenary Stampede certainly got people thinking. After the 1934 Murrurundi Bushmen's Carnival, where the numbers of competitors swelled with thwarted 'Stampeders' — and in which Owen Perrett won the buckjump, came third in the campdraft and was named as Murrurundi's first all-round champion — the front page of the local paper had this to say:

The objects of the carnival are twofold — primarily to perpetuate for all time the sport which is typical of the back country, that intrepid spirit which lifts our fine bronzed daredevil young fellows to the saddle of the most fearsome outlaw; to demonstrate how, single-handed, they pursue and deal with the wildest cattle in the scrub or pear country; to show their skill in cutting out on the camp those cattle which they desire for any particular purpose; and, finally after all this is over, how they can join with their lady friends in the graceful mazes of the dance in the ballroom under the glitter of the most brilliant lighting ... as they join in the fun which is clean, manly and without the corrupting influences which have intruded into so many other

> *branches. The danger of it getting under the domination of professionalism is far remote, as hundreds of our young bushmen will always be found who will be able to hold their own in any company and besides there is always that element of luck which makes it no certainty and adds to the thrill of excitement and expectancy, and proves how men can be the best of sports in adversity as well as in the glare of glory.*[24]

Stirring words indeed. But here, too, is an early flicker of the stubbornness that characterised the battle of traditionalism versus professionalism that would confront ABC committees ten years later, when roughriders started pushing for improvements to their sport. Something about professionalism was corrupting. Perhaps the article was referring to showmen who *paid* their 'bronzed daredevils' when they went on down the road. Ultimately the roughriders themselves would rebel against the system — the bushmen's carnival committees — and form an association that went in direct competition to them.

The second object of bushmen's carnivals, according to the Murrurundi paper, was their 'distinct tendency to improve the breed of horses'. It lamented the passing of the good old stock-horse that would carry a heavy man all day, day after day, in the roughest of country and claimed that as a society we were becoming a 'joy riding luxury-loving crowd that looked to the stream-lined motor car as our means of transport'.

That was undeniable. The 1920s and early 30s were, for those who could afford it, when motor vehicles started replacing the horse on the road and was even used for mustering on some sheep stations. However, motor vehicles made little difference to the working methods of the cattlemen until the early 1960s, with the advent of motorbikes and aeroplanes for mustering stock. Mechanisation has since considerably reduced the numbers of stockmen and horses but the transition was not complete until the 1980s.

Cattle drafting, or campdrafting, lives on — as a sport. It remains the integral event at all bushmen's carnivals today. Consequently stockhorse breeding and training has continued over the years, despite the machinations of progress.

This is the main reason the Australian stockhorse, albeit a somewhat mongrel breed to start with, has evolved into the handsome and clever creature of today and was officially recognised with the formation of the Australian Stock Horse Association in 1971.

Horses had practically disappeared from cities by the end of the 1920s leaving only the races and the annual agricultural show to celebrate horses and horsemanship. In 1934 cattle drafting and steer riding events along with exhibitions of cattle throwing and tying 'topped the bill of popularity' at the Sydney Royal and journalists were already nostalgic:

These and similar events stand for a national sentiment that is written deep in to the very name of Australia. The crack of the stockwhip, the thundering hooves of horses and herd. These have come down to us from the epoch making days of our hardy forefathers. Cattlemen and horsemen — our forbearers — they were the pioneer captains of the Commonwealth. Generations of young Australians knew the saddle almost as soon as they could walk.[25]

By 1937 they were saying:

... there is no longer any doubt about the enthusiasm of the public for this relatively new side of the show. In fact there may even exist some alarm among officials that, as had been the case in country centres, this spectacular roughriding carnival may become The Show, to the detriment of trots, pigs and pumpkins.[26]

From 1935–41 the Sydney Easter Show went Wild and Western. American and Canadian Cowboys and showmen, Indians, Canadian Mounties and Russian Cossacks were invited to perform stunts, give exhibitions and compete in teams against Australians. Rodeo, as a sport and culture in Australia, never looked back.

Out-flashed — but not out-ridden

The American cowboys had showmanship down pat. They had developed their sport seriously, had a very high standard of competition but they had always presented it as entertainment. The Spanish/Mexican influence had produced extravagant costumes and riding gear. American exhibitions and competitions had developed from working cowboy and vaquero skills, been adapted for glamour, speed and spectacle and had been gradually perfected over 50 years.

Mainstream Australian audiences loved them. Lots of pomp and pageantry, fancy costumes, flags, stirring music and larger-than-life action and drama. This excerpt is from a newspaper clipping regarding the Sydney Easter show in 1935:

WILD WEST RIDERS

The youthful section of the ringside crowd last night left no doubt of their favourites. The youngsters were rather vague as to just what a Cossack was, but the cowboy is every lad's hero, and there were roars of applause, shrill whistles, and all the noises concomitant to youthful Australian appreciation, when the riders from Canada and the United States thundered past the stands, waving 'ten gallon' Stetsons, with bat-

> *wing chaps, coloured neckcloths, riatas, high horned saddles, and all the colourful paraphernalia of their craft* . . .[27]

The Australians won the three 'International' events that year, the campdraft, steer ride and the bareback buckjumping. The presence of American cowboys at the penultimate show of the year had a dramatic influence, which further changed our bushmen's carnivals and agricultural shows. Not only did they alert the public to the Wild West but they were often here for a month or two, mixing and mucking about with Australian horsemen. They stayed at graziers' homes, borrowed and trained their horses, practised with our roughriders and competed in small shows around New South Wales leading up to the Sydney Royal.

The Americans had a lot of trouble adapting to our small flat 'postage stamp' saddles and the style of riding required by them. Their bronc saddles were like 'armchairs' in comparison. The first year the international buckjumping contest was conducted bareback — we won anyway. Thereafter during the lead-up to the RAS each year the Americans stayed up at Merriwa and practised on the RAS buckjumpers in our saddles. They trained Australian horses to do their tricks and stunts, they shared their ideas and experience. They taught the Australians and their horses to bulldog, rope and do trick-riding, how to build proper chutes for the buckjumpers and how to pick up buckjump riders from horseback after each 10-second ride. The Australians realised those flapping chaps gave a bit of added grip and more importantly gave the illusion of more fancy footwork and spurring action. As with the pick-up men they also looked good and livened up the show.

Arena acts were copied by Australians. Performing horses and dogs and ropespinners and whipcrackers and trick-riders, formerly mainly employed by the circus and buckjump showmen or vaudeville shows, now sprang up in the rodeo arenas. The Australians got on well with the Americans and especially admired their jeans. They only cost a dollar a pair in America in those days and the cowboys would bring over suitcases of them. Doug Ramsay was one who used to buy them, 'before anybody out here ever wore Levis'.

Jack Scott was there in 1935 and tells us of the consequences in his autobiography, *Fair Crack of the Whip*:

> *Rodeo Mania spread like wild fire, altering customs, speech, dress, terminology and attitudes . . . Blokes and coves became 'guys', girls were called 'Honey'. Moleskin trousers, breeches and jodhpurs, the traditional blue shirt and tie, concertina leggings, plaited belt and goose-necked spurs were discarded . . .*

> *This revolutionary transition was not confined to the rodeo circuit. Stockmen in the Kimberleys, Northern Territory, Cape York, Western Queensland, Darling Downs, Hunter River Valley, in fact nearly everywhere in Australia, Americanised themselves with a completeness that makes it difficult now to find one of the original breed.*[28]

Every year until 1940 Americans, Canadians and Australians competed against each other in teams of three, in roughriding (bareback, saddle and steers) campdrafting, releasing the surcingle, bulldogging and wild cow milking contests. The Australian roughriders who were selected to represent Australia over these years were from New South Wales and Queensland. Harry McPhee (three times), Owen (twice) and Penny Perrett, Roy Oram, Cecil Pearce (three times), Fred Lawton, Colin Bell, Alec Haydon and his cousin Jim Williams, Jack Palmer (twice), Ron McPhee, Arthur Winter (twice) and Grove McDonald.[29]

Oram was a Pacific Islander and Lawton, Haydon and Williams were Aboriginal. All were highly skilled and well-known roughriders; all were Queenslanders. Racism may not have been glaringly obvious among competitors in bushmen's carnivals and rodeos in the backblocks and pastoral zones. There were plenty of big cattle stations employing Aboriginal stockmen and roughriders, but it was a different story away from the north, west and centre. On the smaller blocks in the south and east there were very few Aboriginal stockmen and horsebreakers. Aboriginal roughriders had always been stars of the travelling buckjump shows but down south racism was untempered by familiarity and respect for horse and stock skills. The Sydney Easter Show exemplifies this. It was the ultimate horse show in Australia's biggest city, yet it was full of people who knew little about the bush, its traditions and life skills. In 1937 a Sydney newspaper published this load of bigoted babble: 'The outstanding rider of the Australian team is Cecil Pearce, of Warwick, the other two — dusky descendants of our oldest families — hardly measure up to the high standard demanded in an international contest.'[30] 'The other two' were Alec Haydon and Jim Williams. Haydon was undoubtedly one of Australia's greatest roughriders — ever. The previous year he had won one of the most coveted titles in the country, the Warwick buckjump (which made him Australian champion at the time the journalist was writing) and he became the only person other than Cecil Pearce to win it three times. Jim Williams was also a tremendous roughrider, why else would he have been chosen alongside the other two? Given the enormous respect they garnered for their horsemanship it is surprising how few Aboriginal roughriders pursued rodeo as a profession over the next few decades. Racism obviously had a lot to do with it, but it came more from outsiders than from their peers in the game.

Throughout the 1930s until war began to again get close to home, more and more bushmen's carnivals and agricultural shows aded 'rodeo' events and styles to their programs. These were mostly in cattle country, or towns where cattle were shipped to markets or meatworks, and in the capital cities. Queenslanders loved big rodeo-type carnivals, which were held at Townsville, Oakey, Esk, Ingham, Charters Towers, Toowoomba, Bowen, Richmond, Hughenden, Pentland and Goondiwindi for starters, and the big three, Warwick, Rockhampton and Brisbane.

Apart from those already mentioned other great roughriders from Queensland in the 1930s and early 40s were Warwick's 'Bushman Bill' Harris and Greg Canavan, Charlie Edmunds, Bob Campbell from Bonshaw on the border, Bill Hilton, Colin McLeod, Grove McDonald and Archie Trott. Trott, who won the first ever buckjump championship held at Warwick in 1929, won the Warwick Gold Cup campdraft in 1935. He, Jack Palmer and Stumpy Timmins are the only three men to have won both these prestigious competitions. At the end of the 1930s, roughriders such as Les McNamara, Basil Gollan, Gib Bloxsome, Ron Woodbridge and New Zealander, Steve Laird were heading north from New South Wales for the big ones.

Most of the best roughriders were professional horsebreakers and/or stockmen and drovers. Some were graziers. You couldn't earn a living as a rodeo roughrider in Australia at this time unless you took your roughriding skills and made a business out of it with a buckjump show. But the few proper rodeos that were around were lucrative. £100 to win the buckjump at Merriwa in 1929! £25 for Warwick and Sydney during the 30s, but it was generally 15–20 pounds and you'd have to pay 10 bob (a dollar) to nominate. You could always try your luck in the tents. In a standard contest if you rode well 'in the shade' you'd get a pound, which doesn't sound like much but, as Larry Dulhunty says, he was earning a pound a week as a ringer up in Queensland's basalt country in the late 30s: 'There were no unions. If your boss didn't like you he'd give you the bloody sack; the only thing you could give him was a left hook.'

Queensland's Royal National Agricultural and Industrial Association had an annual show, later called the Brisbane Exhibition. Sydney's rodeos were so successful, that the Brisbane Royal put on similar programs, but never matched the size, scope and competitiveness of Sydney. With Adelaide being the main cattle market and port for the central pastoral zones, it is surprising that South Australia's Royal Agricultural and Horticultural Society did not feature roughriding or rodeo competitions or exhibitions as part of their annual show. Jubilee Oval, which used to belong to the Society hosted many rodeos put on by independent promoters and buckjump showmen including McConville and Skuthorpe. In 1932 Sir Sidney Kidman's employees threw him a huge 75th birthday party rodeo where, according to Kidman's biographer Jill Bowen, 'more than 50,000 crammed in and around Jubilee Oval — a fair slice of them had behaved like stampeding cattle and knocked over the fences to get into the ground. A further 10,000 were reported to be lowing fractiously in the streets outside because they could not gain admittance.'[31]

In Victoria the RAS in Melbourne ran roughriding contests from 1886–90 before 'adverse publicity in the press' changed their minds. They tried again from 1949–53 but despite its enormous popularity with the people of Melbourne, a particularly active animal welfare group scared the society off. Melbourne RAS have only run the occasional rodeo contests and exhibitions since then.

There was plenty of Wild and Western activity in Western Australia. In 1936 readers of the *Western Mail* were treated to a long-running discussion in the 'Highways and Byways' section as to who their top roughriders were. Harry Farber, Frank Lucas, Jack Evans, Billy Skinner, Ted Graham, Harry Connors, Andy Everett, Donald Cronin, Tommy Davidson and Tommy Cocking were the names bandied about. It was generally agreed that ex-Queenslander and current buckjump showman Farber was the best bareback rider. In the saddle Bert Fletcher, also formerly from the eastern states, was regarded as the best — while touring with Broncho George's show he'd won a West Australian Championship. He repeatedly rode horses that could 'buck their brands off', and this account of Bert's performance in the stockyards leaves little doubt:

> *Buck! by Christmas. On her side, straight ahead, backwards, round and round, and as high as your bloomin' head every time. You couldn't see her or Bert for dust. Just like a big whirlwind, tearing up the yard. Excitin'! Ghost, we climbed the*

fence out of the road. The saddlecloth went first, then Bert's boots and belt left, and his shirt and trousers came flying out of the dust. We thought it was Bert for a moment. Then we started cheering, being mostly British, and the blooming mare started squealing and grunting — sort a hooting. By gad! 'Stick to her, stick to her,' the boss was yelling and getting louder every time until Bert's saddle hit him hard in the waistcoat and knocked him back off the top rail and silenced him. Cripes! We got down off the yard in quick time before getting one with Bert. But he never came off. Not he! The mare gave in, and when the dust cleared away there he was sitting across her neck with short holds on the reins and his toes in the bridle rings for stirrups, and smiling![32]

In the ring

Buckjumpers came from everywhere. Graziers mustered up the horse paddock, drafted off the likely looking suspects and sent them in. Drovers were known to do the same. In some parts of the country, brumbies were run in for the day. Showmen hired or lent their horses or brought them in to ride themselves or back against the others. Prizes were given for the best bucking horse, and most stations and properties had reliable rogues that were kept for such occasions; most towns would have had the same. It was pretty common for buckjump horses to be named after the station or town from whence they came. Many individuals, usually ex-roughriders, collected bucking horses as a hobby, which they lent or leased to shows. There would always be one local irascible, unrideable buckjumper that was legend enough to be the feature horse of the day. Buckjumpers were driven from place to place on foot, or sent by train.

A buckjumping score is judged 50:50 on horse and rider. With all of the above there was no guarantee that a horse would buck at all, let alone well enough for a good score. Any serious roughrider had his own buckjumper, kept exclusively for competition. Owen Perrett had two fast bucking horses — Vinegar a spinner, and Velvet, who was a shoulder bucker. They were corn-fed and kept fat and happy for carnivals and rodeos. Dan Edwards had a creamy pony called Calico that he'd bought in Newcastle for £10, together they scored 98 on two occasions which would have been hard to beat.

If a roughrider didn't have their own buckjumper, many simply flanked their riding horse — if they knew it would buck. Not all buckjumpers were unbroken or intractable, some were perfectly rideable but knew how to buck when the flank rope went on. A competitor could always beg, borrow or rent a horse from the locals or preferably the nearest showman who would have something more reliable. Dan Edwards would sometimes pick up a truck load of horses from a 'mate' at the knackery in Newcastle and take them to a rodeo. Roughriders could use one for £2 which covered their freight. If they bucked well, they got a reprieve. Horses were plentiful and dispensable. There were buckjumpers stashed all over the place; by stockmen, horsebreakers, drovers, graziers, roughriders, showmen and schoolboys.

Rodeo events within normal bushmen's carnivals and agricultural shows flourished in all states. Rodeos themselves, or Paddock Shows as they were also known, were still thin on the ground. The sport grew haphazardly. It was still intricately connected with the showmen, who had the horses, the acts and the know-how, but it was casual and inconsistent.

The term 'championship' was still used very loosely — it sold tickets after all. There were at least two annual Australian Championships. Hilton McTaggart won the Australian buckjumping title in Sydney in 1931; later that year Owen Perrett won it again at Warwick. Prior to and during World War II a lot of shows and carnivals promoted their contests as championships — international, national, state and regional. And of course the buckjump showmen did the same. Despite the fact that the bushmen's establishment regarded the buckjump shows as a bit of a gimmick, the roughriders viewed them otherwise. The showmen had the horses that they wanted to beat and paid well for a challenge won.

The burgeoning sport lacked uniform rules — despite the existence of Murrurundi's rule book, and the Australian Bushmen's Carnival Association (ABCA) 'rules were Rafferty's'. Each committee made its own decisions about what events were run and how. It was an experimental time as our bushmen's and horsemen's events were melded in with the American rodeo events. Even so, slowly and surely the concept of rodeos was formulating. To what extent the ABCA influenced or monitored their individual committees is unknown. Sydney and Warwick had the same rules but it is doubtful that any committee *had* to follow any particular rules. The further away from the establishment you headed, the more slipshod the rules became.

There was the constant problem of different saddle types and shapes. Riders mostly rode in their own poley or stock-saddles held down by a crupper — the back cinch was an American device adopted along with their style of saddles and riding in the 1960s. The bigger shows provided a set of saddles, particularly for the finals. Roughriders rode with or without stirrups, with more points often given for riding without. In the buckjump competitions in the open arena, they rarely used a chest rein. They used a halter with a rope rein. You could hang on to any old rope for the bullock and bareback riding event: but most made their own leather surcingles with a handpiece and wrapped hankies — no gloves — around their hands.

Originally riders could hold with two hands; by the 1920s buckjumping was always a one-handed contest. The free hand wasn't allowed to 'touch leather' or anything else for that matter. Bullock riding was one-handed in the big competitions, elsewhere there was still two-handed bullock riding until the 1950s. All roughstock were flanked and spurs were optional but had to be blunt. The judges would signal disqualification with the crack of a stock whip. Riders could be 'cracked off' for failing to spur enough or if the ride was deemed 'uncontrolled'. If a horse didn't buck sufficiently they could award a re-ride. Times were nothing. To start with, you either rode the horse until it stopped bucking or bucked you off. Most horses eased up after 10 or 20 seconds, but a ride could go on for minutes. Gradually times were introduced and thanks to the Yanks ten seconds became the standard by the end of the 30s.

In the early days crushes, hefty but often portable, were used to mount the bullocks or steers but not the horses. They were either held by attendants or tied to a snubbing post, and blindfolded with a hessian sack or cloth while the competitors saddled them in the open arena. It was a ride to the end then fend for yourself. Pick-up men weren't universally used until after the war. The rider would leap from the buckjumper onto the back of a mounted 'pick-up man'.

It was time-consuming but most old-timers miss the saddle and mount-in-the-ring days. They see the art of saddling and mounting a fractious horse as a sign of real horsemanship. Most buckjumpers would turn it on the second your boot hit the stirrup iron or, if you jumped straight up and into the saddle (which was the go) the second your rear hit the leather.

Knowing where to place the saddle, how far back or forwards and how tight your crupper should be, and getting on were all part of the contest. If someone else saddled your horse (like the Warwick men at the finals in Townsville in 1932, for example), slight variations could give the rider no hope — too far forwards and you go over the front, too far back and you got the full impact of a high kick. A saddle had to be able to move so you could move with it. The 'balance riding' style of the times relied on being able to read a horse and go with it, not against it. Dan Edwards explains:

> *You ride with your knees and your calves. When the horse comes down you're loose, when he hits the ground you take up because that's when he's going to change attitude ... It was all done with the feet. When the horse drops his head, he's going to kick high so your feet go forward and you lean back. It's a matter of riding your iron, your pedal. The horse drops his shoulder, you put that foot forward, more weight on that iron.*

The trick was to minimise the impact of the horse's plunges and high kicks. If you were good enough you allowed yourself to be fluid, using your legs and feet to counter shoulder drops, spins and twists. You stayed ahead of it by always being ready as the horse took off in its next manoeuvre. It was unlike bareback and bullock riding where you simply pulled yourself down hard onto a beast's back and hung on like grim death, and spurred for more — if you were up to it. You didn't try and pull yourself down with the saddle as that would make the jarring worse and you only punished yourself. If you were good, you didn't fight the horse, you let it have its head. If you were lucky, balance riding was the way to top-score.

Saddling and mounting in front of the crowd was also good for suspense. Penny Perrett remembers the hushed tension as each roughrider saddled their mount, the horses twitched taunt and expectant, the riders tightening and adjusting their gear. 'You could hear a pin drop', in the lead-up to each ride.

In the late 30s we adopted the American method of using crushes and chutes to mount the horses. Warwick and Sydney again led the way with permanent fixtures. These early 'shotgun' chutes faced into the ring. They were two gates which came together then opened both sides simultaneously so the bullock or horse could go either way first leap. The roughriders now saddled and mounted their horse from the rails above a penned horse. The audience could see little other than hats clambering about the crushes and chutes until the gate opened. The roughrider either stayed 10 seconds or not, after which they jumped on the back of the mounted, pick-up men. As spectacular and efficient as that was, it didn't impress the experts — a horseman didn't even have to vault off in style any more.

'Well that was all very good and exciting,' as Penny Perrett puts it 'but no great skill.'

The war years

Many of the bushie horsemen felt that it was the end of their era. They couldn't relate to 'rodeo' with its flashiness and fanfare, American traditions and events, let alone have to cop all the new rules and regulations that were coming in. Traditional 'bushmen' and 'horsemen' were derisive of the instigators of change, the hot new roughriders with their 'professional' ideas and methods. They called them 'Queen Street cowboys'. They might be able to ride buckjumpers if they climbed aboard from the top rail, but they weren't 'horsemen' or 'stockmen' — look out if you dropped them in the middle of a paddock and said, 'go muster'. Soon they would have to be a member of an association and pay fees plus entry money just to compete in their own local show. As 'rodeo' consolidated and developed in the early 1940s, a lot of the bush boys dropped out of the game. And of course the war changed a lot of things, too.

Contrary to this generalisation, many of the younger roughriders — who were getting going in the early 1940s — were extremely gifted 'horsemen'. Gib Bloxsome, Ray Crawford, Stumpy Timmins, Tom Willoughby and Dan Crotty spring to mind. This generation, too, eventually lamented changes to their sport, and with every new generation, the ones who rode before think they had it tougher on rougher horses and were better at it.

In 1942 World War II found Australia. For the next three years most of the travelling showmen shut down; as did the bushmen's carnivals and rodeos.

After the fall of the Philippines, US General Douglas MacArthur directed the war in the Pacific from north Queensland. Over a million American servicemen passed through Sydney on their way north, among them Lieutenant Colonel R.S. 'Dick' Ryan, a former cowboy showman and stunt performer in Hollywood films. While stationed in Queensland he promoted rodeos at Charters Towers, Townsville, around Brisbane and the south-east corner. Dan Mahon, a grazier from Gowrie and Penny Perrett's champion wild cow milking partner, teamed up with him and organised the bucking stock. Everywhere the crowds turned up in the thousands. Ryan also led the American team in an international rodeo at Sydney showground in April 1944.

Despite wartime belt-tightening, manpower shortages and the fact that the army commandeered most showgrounds and sportsgrounds for training and housing soldiers, quite a few committees still held sports days and bushmen's carnivals and rodeos for charity. In north and central Queensland, where tens of thousands of troops were stationed, it was much needed entertainment. The town of MacKay's 'Patriotic Rodeo and Sports Day' in June 1941 featured Billy Bargo fresh from winning an 'Australian Buckjumping Championship' at Sydney Show (not RAS) just before he won Warwick in October. Other competitors included local legend George Mellor (aka The Arkansas Kid and Bronco George) and Frank Williams, another north Queensland 'Champion'. The sum of £650 was raised for King and Country.

Towns like Hughenden, Richmond, Charters Towers, Ingham, Pentland, Rockhampton, Toowoomba, Goondiwindi and Caboolture also managed to put on rodeos during the war. There were scores more communities using rodeos to raise money for returning soldiers and hospitals. Marrabel (a name synonymous with rodeo) only skipped their show in 1942, Warwick had no rodeo from 1942–45 nor was there a Sydney Royal Show from 1942–46 as the army occupied their showgrounds. Lang Lang did not have an agricultural show in 1942 and 43 but were back in action in 1944 with a 'Steer Riding Championship of Australia'.

There were an enormous number of somewhat dashing American servicemen about during the latter years of the war. They were fresh, brash, affluent and charming — the Australian women loved them. As our boys saw it, the Americans were 'over sexed, over paid and over here' and there was a fair amount of animosity.

When Cooma Bushmen's Carnival committee put on an 'international' Grand Easter Rodeo at the Sydney Showgrounds as a fundraiser for the Australian Comforts' Fund, it gave our boys a chance to flaunt their prowess.

Sydney was the hotbed of rodeo in 1944. It was home to the Ladies' Rodeo Club, and the Skuthorpes were based there. Lance Snr was organising buckjumpers for carnivals for Boy's Town. Ken Huntley was showing six nights a week at Mick Simmon's Corner (George Street). Beryl Riley (now Beryl Chick) said there was something on nearly every weekend. All the usual suspects were there, including Lance Jnr, Gib Bloxsome, Jack Watson, Doug Ramsay, Tom Willoughby, Milton Noble, Ron Boardman, Dan Edwards, Tom Smyth, Jim Smythe, Frank Maynard, Cecil Pearce, Jack Jamieson, Tex Mooney, Billy Bargo, Ron Richards, Reg Lindsay, Eric Willoughby, Johnny Pierce, Noel Bottom and Jack Reilly. Lieutenant Colonel Dick Ryan led a whole host of American cowboys from Texas, Arizona and California. The ladies buckjumpers included Marge Bratby from Warwick, 'Bub' Forbes and

Constance Hammond from the Ladies' Rodeo Club in Sydney and Gwen Duncan, who became Gwen Winter.

Prizes totalled £1000 and the competition was held over two days. Six thousand people were lined up waiting for the gates to open at 10.30 am on the Saturday; eventually 40 000 people turned up and 50 000 attended the finals on the Monday. Lance Skuthorpe Jnr won Buckjumping Championships of Australia with Cream of the Valley, a horse he later bought and took to New Zealand. Lance was 29 years old at the time. He broke his ankle in the semi-final and won the finals of both the bulldogging and the buckjumping with his right leg in a plaster cast. He donated his buckjumping prize money of £150 to Boy's Town. As Jack Pollard records:

> 'I became very full of myself over this feat,' young Lance reflected. 'I thought I was famous, but as I went around the country with Dad, I soon noticed that it was not my hand people wanted to shake. I thought to myself, "Why are they so eager to shake his hand? — He's an old man." And then it dawned on me that the reason they wanted to shake his hand had nothing to do with any title. They wanted to tell their friends about it because he was a legend.'[33]

Later that year the Federation of New South Wales Police-Citizens' Boys Clubs held fundraising 'rodeos' at Wagga, Tamworth, Newcastle and Sydney in aid of Boy's Town. Sydney was to host the (Australian Championship) finals, held over the New Year 1944–1945. Sydney Police Sergeant Jack Reilly, a champion bulldogger and rodeo organiser, was heavily involved. So was Lance Skuthorpe, whose son Lance Jnr competed along with the Gill brothers, Jack and Stan. The rodeos drew huge crowds — 10 000 at Tamworth, 8000 at Wagga and 10 000 then 15 000 in the two days of the championships at Sydney.

'The (ABCA) Establishment' was based in Sydney. R.F. Munro, R. Schmidt and B.B. Haydon were the judges, T.B. Macfarlane was the ringmaster, and the riders competed in teams — Eastern District, Western District and Northern District, Victoria, Northern Rivers, Hunter Valley and so on — which is how the Australian Bushmen's Carnival Association was sectioned, too. Unfortunately the newspapers only mention the ladies' buckjumping winners. There were eight or nine contestants. Beryl Riley from the Ladies' Rodeo Club rode Violet Skuthorpe's horse, Baxter's Bay. Kitty Gill won the day, Constance Hammond came second and Mrs Marge Bratby from Queensland was third.

The 'cowboys' competing in this series of 'rodeos' represented both the old and new generations — bushmen, horsemen, roughriders, 'Queen Street Cowboys' and showmen. At 42, professional horsebreaker and roughrider Dan Edwards, who had started with the Gill Brothers in 1918, was probably the oldest competitor. Dan won the buckjumping at Newcastle, Tamworth and Wagga but was bucked off in the Sydney finals. The youngsters included Tom Willoughby, Terry Hunt, Jack and Stan Gill, J. Purcell, P. Bell, Arthur Bowd, Greg Canavan, Basil Gollan, Sgt Jack Reilly, Lance Skuthorpe Jnr, Tex Mooney, Ron Boardman, Jack Agnew, Harry Myers, Noel Bottom, Johnny Pierce and Dan Crotty. These were the roughriders who went on to define, unify and solidify Australian rodeo. Most of them became household names — and for those in the know, they still are.

Quintessentially Australian, especially the poley saddle

Parade of American, Canadian, Indian and Australian riders at the Sydney Easter Show, 1939

Cecil Pearce, Upper Hunter Buckjumping Champion, 1937

Mount St John Rodeo, near Townsville, Queensland, 1934

Alec Haydon on 'Arrawidgee', The Grey Ghost, 1938

Sydney Royal Easter Show roughriders, 1932.
Left to right: Laurie Harris, Mick Woods, Alex Abdulla, Jack Maidens, unknown, Arthur Winter and Tom Kelly

Left to right: Unknown, Owen Perrett, Penny Perrett, unknown, Cecil Pearce and Steve Laird, Maryborough, 1934

Stumpy Timmins

Dan Crotty

Tom Willoughby, Johnny Pearce and Noel Bottom, late 1940s

Kitty Gill

Buddy Gravener on 'Cloudbuster'

Pat Elder (now Pat Peters) with Chilla Seeney (*right*)

Gwen Winter

Enid Bennett

Left to right: Pat Elder, Betty Urquhart, Enid Bennett, Norma McDonald, Buddy James, Audrey Croasdale (partly obscured) and Ray Mattei (aka Texas Lil), early 1950s

Wally Woods

Winners, 1956 Rocky Round-Up. *Left to right:* Chilla Seeney, Vic Gough, Ray Crawford, Wally Woods, Lindsay Black

Bulldogging – Vic Gough (hazing) and Chilla Seeney (dogging)

Allan Woods rides Curio, 1953, as photographed by the masterful Keith Stevens

Left to right: Allan Bennett, Kevin McTaggart, Basil Gollan and Max McTaggart

Lindsay Black

Barry Gravener

At Warwick Golden Jubilee Rodeo, 1956.
Left to right: Vic Gough, Dally Holden, Col McTaggart, Wally Woods and Bo Crawford

Ray Crawford

Bernie Smyth Jnr

Neville McCarthy

Bullfighting clowns Pat Speedy and Russell (Rusty) Frame in action at Kooralbyn, 1976

The 1965 ARRA board of directors holding their first meeting after being elected

5

THE DAWN OF PROFESSIONALISM

A demon to handle! A devil to ride!

Small wonder the surcingle burst;

You'd have thought that he'd buck himself out of his hide

On the morning we saddled him first.

Associations and ultimatums

THE 1950s WERE THE golden years for rodeo in Australia. Australian soldiers had returned from World War II and those from the bush went home to farms and stations their wives and children had been running in their absence. Prices for wool and beef had recovered from the Depression; they remained strong throughout the war years and then boomed. At the height of the Korean War in the 1950s Australian wool was fetching the famous 'pound for a pound'. The bush had plenty of money, work, horses and horsemen.

Many of the big stations were slowly broken up, first with soldier settlement blocks and later with additional balloted blocks. As leases ran out governments subdivided stations to encourage rural settlement and development. There were more people in the bush than ever before and the 20 years of prosperity was good for the rodeo business.

When the bushmen's carnivals and agricultural shows resumed after the war they were still community affairs. There was limited horse transport other than trains so most people rode in for the weekend. They ran traditional events, hacks, hunting and high-jumping. The flag and bending and relay races were just as hotly contested. People kept special horses for each event. Campdrafting was extremely popular — it was an Australian tradition, a stockman's job and as the stockhorses competed, it was a good opportunity to see what sort of horseflesh the other stations were breeding.

The people involved in the bushmen's carnivals and agricultural shows in the 1930s viewed rodeo cowboys as a fad. Most of the smaller towns had ignored the rodeo community influence — they'd got plenty of that sort of hype from the travelling Wild West showmen. After the war the shows and carnivals still ran the popular bullock and steer rides and most had buckjumping contests which were mostly BYO (horse and saddle), and 'give us your best shot'. Graziers would bring in their buckjumpers and match them against the local stockmen. For most bushmen's carnivals, roughriding was only ever intended as local contests with amateurish efforts.

The bigger shows and carnivals that had led the way with rodeo events before the war continued to run the standard four bushmen's events — campdrafting, buckjumping, steer riding and bulldogging, which had now replaced bullock throwing and tying.

Bushmen's carnivals were run by local committees under the auspices of the Australian Bushman's Carnival Association. The ABCA was closely associated with the Sydney RAS, who in turn were the headquarters for all the New South Wales agricultural shows. These two umbrella organisations — the ABCA and the RAS, 'the establishment' — were predominantly run by northern New South Wales graziers who competed in all the events but were particularly avid campdrafters.

Dissension

The alliance between roughriders, committees and rodeo promoters had often been uneasy — and not simply because judges were often lackadaisical or biased or prudent enough to award the prize to the man who supplied the beef for the barbeque. Independent promoters frequently failed to deliver on their promises. Entry fees were used to line committees' pockets. Often the prize money at shows and carnivals was less than the total of the roughriders' entry fees. In the early 40s the roughriders were also dissatisfied with the prize money they were getting, compared to the campdrafters. The standard prize money at a small agricultural show or bushmen's carnival to win the buckjump was between £2 and £10, at a big one it was £10 to £30 and for big roughriding championships, £50 or £100. The campdrafters, however, were winning £100 and £200 all the time. Dan Edwards remembers how put out the roughriders felt and why they took their expertise away from the establishment and made rodeo their own.

~THE DAWN OF PROFESSIONALISM~

> *... it was all about money, that's the real thing. Well, what's £10 when you've got to supply your horse?... See, the campdrafters, they could use their horses for work during the week and then compete on them during the weekend. The roughriders had to keep and feed and travel their buckjumpers just for the competitions on Saturday nights — expensive if you only got £10 ... What's a buckjumper going to earn me? Without him I can't win much. It's like going to the races. If I haven't got a good horse, what's the point of me going and backing him? It's the same with a buckjumper.*

Campdrafting enjoyed a privileged position as it was a favourite sport of the squatters and graziers, landowners (the bosses) and their families. They made up the committees and they ran the shows and carnivals as they saw fit. By contrast the roughriding specialists were rarely on committees. There were plenty of sons of graziers who rode buckjumpers but generally the ones who really embraced roughriding and later furthered it as a sport were the working men — usually itinerant — stockmen, drovers and horsebreakers.

The small band of roughriders and buckjump showmen who had been doing the miles as the nucleus of the fledgling rodeo scene prior to and during the war knew they had an advantage. As Dan Edwards puts it:

> *Campdrafting, as a spectacle to the ordinary person, from the spectator's point of view, it's boring. Rodeo's the thrills. The audience would go out and see the sideshows while the campdraft was on, but when the rodeo was on they'd stand up and watch the show.*

The roughriders were the drawcard and yet they were not being paid accordingly.

Similar sorts of issues and conflicts had come to a head in the USA in 1936 when about 60 rodeo cowboys went on strike and walked out on Colonel W.T. Johnson's rodeo at the Boston Garden because the total prize money he offered was less than the sum of their entry fees. In November 1936 the US cowboys formed the Cowboy's Turtle Association — 'Turtle' because they had been so slow to get organised.[1] As a union they got Johnson to agree to their demands.

Over Easter weekend in 1944 at the big 'international' rodeo at the Sydney showgrounds, the American cowboys — soldiers mostly — were able to explain more about the Turtle Association. Later that year the Police Boy's Club rodeos were held at Newcastle, Wagga, Tamworth and the finals in Sydney over New Year 1944–45. At Newcastle roughriders Dan Edwards and Basil Gollan approached 'Ken Mackay and his association' and lobbied for an increase in prize money. They refused. Dan Edwards states:

So we went to the RAS. They turned us down, too. Then some of the committees said they were having a meeting and so we asked them if we could attend, Basil Gollan and myself. We were never educated much and Reg Williams was pretty educated and pretty smart. And he said, 'I'll come along with you.'

Well-known bushman, businessman and rodeo aficionado R.M. Williams, helped to steer the process. He recalls:

... when the boys approached the Sydney Show about a rough rider's association they figured it was a union thing, which in a sense it was, and they didn't like it one little bit. They thought the crowd was only interested in seeing the boys come a cropper so who cared about rules and regulations.

Dan Edwards takes up the story again:

We weren't satisfied with that and told them we were not going to continue with it. We won't ride! We went and had a cup of tea and Reg said, '... Well, what do you reckon?' ... Better form an association of our own, see. R.M. said '... Well, I'll finance it.' Basil Gollan and myself, we had no money and course he had the money ... with a big business in Adelaide.

United we stand

At the next rodeo in Wagga, they formed the New South Wales Rough Rider's Association.

With the help of Lance Skuthorpe Jnr, artist Virgil Reilly and newspaperman Sir Keith Murdoch, R.M. organised a newssheet which was eventually called *Hoofs and Horns* — '"hoofs" because it set out to record the activities of horsemen and horsemanship in Australia, and "horns" because it was also devoted to the cattle industry.'[2] Under the editorship of R.M. Williams and later the legendary rodeo photographer Keith Stevens, the publication became an effective means of promoting roughriding as a sport. Apart from money and uniformity of riding rules and conditions, the November 1944 edition of *Hoofs and Horns* proclaimed that the aim of the Rough Rider's Association was, '... to improve the standard of judging, to provide an insurance fund for injured riders, and to see that the standard of gear supplied is up to scratch.' They invited roughriders from all of Australia to join them for a meeting in Sydney at the Police Boy's Rodeos Sydney finals.

About 40 people attended the meeting on 1 January 1945 and a national body, the Australian Rough Rider's Association (ARRA) was formed.

Membership cost £1.00. Gib Bloxsome was the first to sign on, then Jack Stanton, Dan Edwards, Ron Boardman and Johnny Pierce was number five. Ron Boardman became the first chairman. R.M. became the official secretary, a position he held until 1956, but he said, 'Mary did all the work'. Mary Dollard, who became Mrs Mick Young, was the voluntary secretary/public relations officer — she did the job for over 25 years and received the first-ever life membership gold card. Toby Jones, who was R.M.'s publicity man, also put his shoulder in behind the association and *Hoofs and Horns*.

The first generation of ARRA roughriders were the stars of the bushmen's carnivals, rodeos and tent shows. They included Dan Edwards, Basil Gollan, Lance and Violet Skuthorpe Jnrs, Jack Stanton, Gib Bloxsome, Noel Bottom, Tom Willoughby, Johnny Pierce, Dan Crotty, Tex Mooney, Milton Noble, Billy Bargo, Alec Haydon, Ron Boardman, Noel Hargreaves, Frank Maynard, Bob Dodge, Matt Salman, Greg Canavan and later his brothers Terry and Brian. Jack, Stan, Doyle, Kitty and Gladys Gill, Alan and later Ron Hentschke, the Frame brothers, Jack, Angus and Bob. Jack and Angus in particular were renowned roughriders; Angus Frame had his own buckjump show from 1944–45, was ARRA buckjumping champion in 1946; and Jack became 'the man behind the bulls' in the 60s. There were Dick Hawkins, Charlie Christensen, Bill Wilson, Allan Woods, Kevin McTaggart, Johnny Roberts, and Tom and Bernie Smyth (Snr), Jack Agnew, the Jamieson brothers, Jim Bullock, the Kirkham brothers, Frank, Harry and Jack, Ron Woodbridge, Ron Richards and Rupe Richardson, who later became a gun pick-up man. Norm and Graham Cakebread were part of it and so was Ron Anderson. In South Australia, where they first kicked off, they were joined by Alec Draper, Allan Gottfried, Johnny Cadell, Leo Reichstein, Allan Vater, Norm and Dick Webster, the fabulous Les Cowan, and of course 'Big Benny' himself, Allan Bennett. Dally Holden, Wally Woods, Stumpy Timmins, Wally Mailman and Lindsay and Gordon Black were competing with the ARRA by 1950.

The formation of the ARRA put Australian rodeo on a cohesive and professional footing. Within five years there were enough rodeos with enough prize money to support a small but determined group of rodeo riders who toured Australia more or less full-time.

In his autobiography R.M. Williams said of the early ARRA:

It may not have been an organisation of 'gentlemen', but its members were men who slept in uncomfortable beds, if any. Men who risked their lives day after day on the wildest of horses, leaping headlong onto wild long-horned cattle and facing up to the fiercest bulls that could be found. Men like these are not to be abused, and one is proud to call any of the breed one's friend.[3]

The first year of competition under ARRA rules and conditions was 1945, starting in South Australia with Prospect, Hahndorf, Kensington and Marrabel. At the championships in Prospect, Warwick's Greg Canavan won the buckjumping and the bullock ride, American Frank Maynard won the bulldogging and Tex Mooney won wild cow milking and the all-round.

In October 1946 Warwick (Queensland) ran the ARRA championships. That caused a domino effect in the cattle towns of Queensland and north-west New South Wales. Whether they ran a full rodeo or just a roughriding competition in conjunction with their show, many agricultural shows, sports days and carnivals around Australia had affiliated with the ARRA by the end of the decade. North-eastern New South Wales and southern Queensland, however, were the domain of the Australian Bushmen's Carnival Association and *that* was a whole different story.

Separate camps

The ARRA barred their riders from competing at any carnivals, shows or rodeos that were not affiliated with them, and would not assist by loaning buckjumpers. Committees affiliated if they wanted the 'star riders' to compete at their shows, which of course drew the crowds. The northern New South Wales bushmen's carnival committees didn't approve of the 'unionised' roughriders or wish to be dictated to about rules and regulations. They started their own association in March 1946.

By most accounts Ken Mackay was one of the greatest of people. He was president of the Dungog Bushmen's Carnival Committee and was also the ringmaster of the Sydney Royal Show for many years. He was the first and longest-serving president of the Northern New South Wales Bushman's Carnival Association, which he instigated, lasting 30 years. When Mackay set down his account of the impact of the ARRA he merely wrote: 'The ultimatum did not appeal to most of the long established committees in the Hunter region and northern areas of New South Wales who objected to being told how they should run their own carnivals. Feelings became strained...'

The Northern New South Wales BCA became affectionately known as the 'ABC' or the 'Bushies'. The ARRA were simply referred to as the 'Pros'. The

Bushies had similar aims to the Pros — to standardise rules, regulations and saddles, and to provide insurance for riders. But they were graziers and campdrafting enthusiasts. They had no intention of increasing the roughriders' purse. The ARRA declared their rodeos 'black' until such time as they improved their prize money. In the words of R.M Williams: 'so began the war between the ABCA and ARRA which lasted 40 years and which the ARRA won because they pretty much got all the good cowboys in the end.'

Committees didn't have to affiliate with either association. The Sydney Royal didn't. But most committees signed up with one or the other because it helped with the logistics of getting bucking stock, judges, saddles and insurance for riders.

The differences between the two associations boiled down to two things. Firstly, the ABC was an umbrella organisation for committees around the country. It was formed and run by 'committee men'. The ARRA was formed and run by the roughriders themselves. Its aim was to improve their lot. Secondly, it was a different choice of lifestyle. ARRA riders were 'professional' in that they were attempting to consolidate their sport and make their living out of it. They travelled for 8–10 months of the year, naturally rodeo became their life and any jobs they had fitted in and around the rodeos. The Bushies were and are still referred to as the amateur associations — not necessarily because they were not as good at the Pros but because they fitted the local carnivals and shows in around their lives and jobs, not the other way around.

There are claims that class distinctions played a role in why the ABC and the roughriders often didn't see eye to eye. Jack's son, John Stanton, who was there at the beginning of the Northern New South Wales BCA in 1946 and is still winning campdrafts today, sees things differently: 'No snobbery between one and another ... All the same fellas, all good mates, all the rest is a heap of garbage ... They would all sit down and share whatever they had. Still do.'

There were some excellent roughriders among the Bushies. John Stanton and Stumpy Timmins, who 'often did the impossible', being two of the leading exponents of this generation. Jimmy Jupp and Tom Smyth, who went to the USA in 1949 with Johnny Roberts, Zella Quinlan and Johnny Moyland, both stayed ABC riders, as did Kinga Knight and Kevin Lather. Lather was a great rope ring rider; he travelled with buckjump showman, Jack Gill. Jack Wakeman was a good bulldogger but an even better bareknuckle fighter. And then there were the

Purcells — the youngest of whom, Johnny, hit his stride in the 1960s and became a superb saddle bronc rider.

Riders' allegiances were not necessarily fixed. In the late 1940s most of the 'star' roughriders of the ARRA rodeos had ridden in the rope rings and in bushmen's carnivals and agricultural shows all their lives and they all knew each other. Most of the subsequent ARRA riders cut their teeth in the 'Bushies' and then moved on to the ARRA. Gib Bloxsome and Jack Stanton stayed ARRA-aligned only a short time then went back to the bushmen's carnivals for the campdrafting. Stumpy Timmins did the same in the late 50s. But the ARRA were the 'Pros' and there were more good roughriders among them. In a competition between the top 25 roughriders from each association held at the Sydney Royal in 1957, the ARRA boys won every event.

From 1950–53 the two associations had an agreement whereby their members could compete at each other's shows. Then a high-profile ARRA rider was accused of cheating while he was the chute boss at Gloucester rodeo and the battlelines were re-drawn. Eventually the two associations settled down into an amicable non-competitive relationship. They have always collaborated on important matters like establishing guidelines for the welfare of horses and livestock in rodeos.

Running a tight ship

Bushmen's carnivals remained much the same as they had always been, characterised by tradition and community spirit. ARRA rodeo competitors consolidated 'rodeo' into five or six events. Out of the agricultural shows, bushmen's carnivals and gymkhanas they brought the buckjumping and bullock ride and added the bareback buckjumping. Then there were the two American sports, bulldogging and roping — generally wild cow milking or sometimes steer roping. Plenty of smaller shows and carnivals that affiliated with the ARRA still ran only buckjumping and a bullock ride. Most always ran a campdraft, too, but it wasn't generally incorporated into 'the rodeo' and was run the day or morning before. By the end of the 1950s most of the big rodeos had these five standard events and if a committee was to host the ARRA national championships they had to guarantee all five would be on the program.

Annual general meetings were held at the championship rodeos each year. Minutes of the ARRA meeting in Prospect in October 1945 show that they basically adopted slightly adapted American rodeo rules and regulations for each event. As of 1 January 1946 all riders in ARRA-affiliated rodeos had to be members of the association. Committees had to pay 10/6 to affiliate with the association. Members who competed at a 'black' show were automatically disqualified for 12 months. The provident fund for the riders' insurance policy was made up entirely of a percentage of entry fees and already had a healthy £124. 96.

All rodeo horses had to be registered. The following year at Warwick a list of approved judges and a rule book were drawn up. Membership fees went up to £1.10 and an injured rider could expect £50 pounds for hospital and general expenses and £1.10 a week for a maximum of 12 weeks after that in compensation. The ARRA also regulated the conduct of contestants and the show committees. They imposed fines for cheating and larrikinism and issued a black-list of recalcitrant riders, who could not nominate at any ARRA rodeos. Anyone found guilty of any sort of animal cruelty was disqualified for life.

The association decided the standard buckjumping saddle was to be a Davidson and Smith-designed poley saddle, nicknamed the flat saddle, the postage stamp, ole slippery dip and the self-emptier. It had a 15-inch tree and a crupper fitted with a sliding dock. It had 2 ¼ inch kneepads — nothing to speak of — and nothing much behind. It was held loosely in place by the girth and crupper. Now everyone rode in the same saddles. The association owned all the saddles, which were held at various centres in sets of six and sent to the rodeos by train as they were required. The saddles for New South Wales and Queensland were made by roughrider and saddler Robin Yates in Sydney and R.M. Williams' company manufactured them for Victoria and South Australia. By all accounts it was a terrific saddle but 'very bloody small'.

In 1946 roughriding contestants rode for 10 seconds. The rules were straightforward — it was one-handed riding, the other not touching down, and in all three roughriding events disqualifications for not spurring enough were applied. Losing an iron cost 10 points and 20 for losing both irons. Bulldogging time limits started at two minutes and came down to 90 seconds. In the steer decorating, calf roping, single steer tying and team roping events there were American rules and time limits of two minutes or 90 seconds applied. In the roping they had to throw the rope at least nine feet from the animal's head. For the wild horse race and wild cow milking, the original 1930s ABCA rules were adopted. Novelty events like pony speed races and Roman races were often included. Dan and Buddy Crotty gave roping and trick-riding exhibitions at most of the southern rodeos as well.

Lindsay Black joined the ARRA in 1949:

The older ones, like Kevin McTaggart and Noel Bottom, they fashioned the ARRA. They came up with the rules and we'd all vote at the annual general meetings ... They'd experiment with the rules all the time. Once they had it you had to spur the horse in the break of the shoulder the first three bucks out of the chute. You'd have to count as well as ride. Well, that didn't last long. They tried all different things; every year there'd be something different.

Last but not least the ARRA increased the roughriders' prize money. By the 1950s at the bigger ARRA affiliated shows, the buckjump riders were winning £50 and £100 and the campdrafters £10 and £20. As one of the oldest continually running rodeos, Warwick retained its prestige. It had one of the richest purses and a great string of buckjumpers. In 1948 the Warwick Gold Cup Rodeo events consisted of campdrafting, buckjumping, ladies' buckjumping, bullock riding, bulldogging, calf roping, wild cow milking, a consolation bareback ride, a Roman ride, pony speed test and a flag relay race. Popular pre-war rodeo contestant and ex-POW, Les McNamara from Moree, won the Gold Cup Camp-drafting Championship with his horse, Flashlight. He pocketed £40. But when up and coming ARRA star rider, Johnny Roberts from Goondiwindi, rode Chained Lightning and then Woodpecker to clinch the Gold Cup Buckjump Championship he took home £100. The roughriders had turned the stakes around completely.

In August 1955 the tiny dusty town of Richmond in western Queensland, hosted its first ARRA rodeo with £1000 in prize money. The open campdraft was worth £135 and the ladies' campdraft £30, but the prize for the open buckjumping was £300. There was £150 for the bullock ride and £100 for the novice buckjumping and bulldogging. Within a few short years the roughriders' vision for the future of rodeo as a sport, not just as an exhibition of bushmen's skills, had been achieved. A write-up in the *Longreach Leader* a couple of weeks beforehand claimed proudly that the 'heavy' nominations for Richmond 'included all the top rodeo riders who have been riding at Mareeba and Townsville rodeos ... including that of the Open Buckjump Champion of Australia', who at the time was Ray Crawford.

Thanks to *Hoofs and Horns* magazine, the ARRA riders were creating good publicity for the rodeos. It ran profiles on the stars and lauded their conquests.

The young stars like Allan Woods and Kevin McTaggart found themselves being hero-worshipped. It listed where and when the rodeos were and who won what, and young ringers all over Australia and New Zealand subscribed. More and more towns began to have proper rodeos proper. By the early 50s in Queensland alone there was a rodeo practically every weekend. As the events grew in number and popularity, so did the numbers of competitors. With more rodeos and better prize money, more roughriders could afford to travel a growing circuit full-time.

By the end of 1945 there were over 200 competing members of the ARRA. When Angus Frame joined in 1946 he was badge number 413. Wally Woods and Lindsay Black joined the ARRA in 1949 with badge numbers 1168 and 1956 respectively, at least 800 new members joined in that one year. When Jim Dix joined the association in 1959, his was badge number 5858. Dix was the beginning of a new generation but many of the original competitors were still in the game. There have been over 17 000 members of the ARRA since its inception and many many more than that with the Bushmen's Carnival Association.

Lady roughriders

Women had always excelled in all horse events at bushmen's carnivals, sports days, gymkhanas and agricultural shows. They were also great trick riders and performers, and of course had always been wonderful equestrians and rosin-back riders with the circuses and Wild West shows. Over the years many women had ridden buckjumpers, bullocks and steers in the travelling shows and big arenas but they were outnumbered 100 to one. Trailblazers like Miss Kemp, Violet Skuthorpe (Snr and Jnr), Dorrie Phillips, Audrey Croasdale, Beryl Riley and Kitty and Gladys Gill were riding in competitions and exhibitions at Warwick, Sydney Royal, the Brisbane Exhibition and the few other big rodeos that held ladies' buckjumping. Stories abound of women riding in the open buckjumping against the men in the 1930s and 40s. Justine Gollan competed with the men at Tamworth Police Boy's Club Rodeo in 1944. Norma Jory rode in the open bullock ride at Lang Lang in 1948. She didn't win but they gave her a special prize anyway. No-one knew what to do with women if they did win. Don Johnson writes of his aunts, Eileen and Deane White, who rode in the travelling buckjump shows for the likes of Curley Bell, Ken Huntley, the Skuthorpes and Thorpe McConville in the 1930s:

> *Eileen was a champion buckjump rider ... When she competed at Rockhampton for the Australian Buckjumping Championship, she equally scored with the winner,*

> *Joe Atkinson. The trophy, ribbon and prize were given to Joe Atkinson. My aunt Eileen was given a wallet of notes and a special sash. A bit chauvinistic, but that's the way it was.*[4]

Beryl Riley estimates there were 20–25 women who competed regularly in her day (1944–51); not many compared to the hundreds of men. But as rodeo proliferated in the late 1940s and early 50s, more women joined in the fun. Most had mastered roughriding in the rope rings.

Betty Urquhart, now Betty Good, grew up on a farm and was always horse mad. At 14 she made jaws drop when she rode Frank McFarlane's horse, Stormy, at his circus and rodeo. As she recounted to Andrea Lemon:

> *The man in charge said, 'You wouldn't be able to ride it,' and Mum said, 'Yes, she would!' Anyhow, I made him let me have a go. I had no stirrups, just the saddle and a head rein, no bit or anything. It was one hand up, not even hanging on to the saddle. I had to ride him for 10 seconds, and I did.*

Many others had tried and failed. Later Betty toured with Frank McFarlane for a couple of years (1949–51) as a roughrider and trick-rider. The Le Garde Twins were with him, too. She had to take extra jobs to support her buckjumping as there were not enough ladies' buckjumping competitions at rodeos, or decent enough prize money to make a living. After she married, her husband didn't approve: 'It took me a long time to settle down in one place. I sort of had to fight myself you know.'

Sis Atkinson was another gifted lady roughrider. She rode open and she was with Jack Gill's Wild West Show before she married Victorian champion roughrider Kevin Lather. Their son Errol Lather became one of the classiest bronc riders of all time. Pat Elder (now Pat Peters) says: 'Sis Atkinson rode against the boys and she came second in a novice buckjump without her irons tied. And they stopped that then — they weren't allowed to ride against the men.'

Sis Atkinson had a sister, Margaret, who also started riding in Jack Gill's travelling show. She took up riding in rodeos just as ladies' buckjumping was being phased out in the ARRA arenas and came second at Lang Lang's last ladies' bronc ride in 1961. Like many of the women roughriders, Margaret also married a roughrider — Jack Gill's son, John Jnr (Happy). She continued to ride buckjumpers in the Gill Brothers shows and gave exhibition rides at rodeos. Margaret was one of the women who formed the Girls Rodeo Association in 1967. She was a great barrel racer and went on to win a national title in that event and the all-round cowgirl title in 1974. Other early ARRA lady roughriders included Eunice Bougoure from Stanthorpe, Dawn Shirmer and Marge Bratby. In the mid–40s there were Beryl Riley, Bessie Blundell and the gang from the Girls' Rodeo Club in Sydney.

Women roughriders were members of the ARRA until they formed their own Girls' Rodeo Association in 1967. Most of these early women have life memberships with the ARRA. Despite this there has never been a woman on the committee or the board of the ARRA. It has always been an association run for and by men.

At the Annual Meeting at Kyabram in March 1947 Johnny Pierce moved the motion that the lady roughriders be contacted and a vote taken in regard to using the association saddles and riding rules. It was decided they would have the same rules as the men except they'd have their stirrups tied.

This meant there was no spurring in the women's buckjumping because they hobbled the women's stirrups together with a leather strap underneath the horse. Buckjump showmen had used the trick for years; they had also used the string girths to tuck their spurs in. It was supposed to make it easier for the girls and certainly it was an advantage to most as you were more or less tied on (if you kept your feet in your stirrups) and you could hang on with brute strength. But to others it was a hindrance.

Buckjump riding is more than clinging on. If a woman was really riding she'd be using her feet to counterbalance the horse's moves. Betty Urquhart was a balance rider. As she told Andrea Lemon: 'It didn't help me at all. I think they thought we weren't very good riders, but the women were just as good as the men. The men wouldn't let us compete with them in case we beat them. They were in control.'

Emily Lock agrees with Betty. She started off in the late 50s with a season in the Bakers' Snowy River Stampede and won the ladies' buckjump at the World Championships in Winton in 1958: 'I had mine right out loose, I didn't want it to stop me getting my balance. The others might have had theirs tighter, but actually I didn't find it helped at all.' It could also be dangerous. If a horse fell on you and you didn't get your feet out of the stirrups quickly enough, you could be pinned down or wind up with a broken leg.

At the ARRA's Annual General Meeting at Rockhampton in October 1949, it was decided to ban women from competing with men in steer riding and buckjumping, or anything else for that matter. They could only compete in ladies' buckjumping.

Even though the women had never been equal to the men in numbers, there were several who could ride buckjumpers better than a lot of the blokes during the 50s. First and foremost were the three tent show professionals, Kitty and Gladys Gill and Beryl Riley. Three other terrific all-round horsewomen were Gwen Duncan, who married roughrider Arthur Winter and was tragically killed while competing in the campdraft at Walcha in the mid–1950s; Norma Jory, who married roughrider Billy McDonald, and Pat Kenneally, who won the ladies' championship at Lang Lang in 1949. Two more talented girls were Enid Bennett from Stanhope, Victoria, who married roughrider Ken Healey, and Norah Vickers from Townsville, who married roughrider Dally Holden. Betty Urquhart was also a very good rider. All these women could have given the boys a run for their money. Phyllis Mayne from Springsure didn't ride often but was very talented, and there was June Mossiter, who married roughrider Bram Toohey. In the words of Col McTaggart, 'Now *she* could ride'.

Mostly the ladies' horses were selected more carefully than the mens' — exhibition horses, that were known quantities and not wild or unduly aggressive. But they didn't always pick the easier horses for the women, as Norah Holden well knows:

> *My toughest ride was at Mareeba and I bucked off. It makes me angry every time I think about that little horse in Mareeba. I dunno whether Ray Crawford topped scored on him and Chilla Seeney bucked off or vice versa. And they ran him up in the finals, and I got him ... He just came out of the chute that fast, and I just got a bit behind him. And I thought I'd caught up but he just whacked one into me and I was gone, ha ha ... At Lang Lang in 53 or 54 I rode a horse that was pretty tough — actually it was written up in Hoofs and Horns that Norah Holden rode the toughest horse at Lang Lang!*

Pat Elder (now Pat Peters) declares she was never much good but she had 70 rides from 1949–57 and was only bucked off four times, so she couldn't have been too bad. Pat was a nurse and she, too, had always been horse-mad. Not being able to afford a horse as a youngster, being a cowgirl was a way of getting among horses and horsy people. Pat estimated there were 20 or 30 women who regularly rode in buckjumping competitions in the early 50s. Among those not already mentioned were Rosemary Armstrong, Beryl Collins, Phyllis Brereton and Colleen McLaughlin from Springsure. Jessie Jenkins, Brenda Quale and Kim Mahoney, 'who used to laugh when she rode and she didn't know she was doing it', were all from New South Wales. South Australia had Mrs S. Daunt, who won the Ladies'

Championship at Hahndorf in 1944, and Margaret Noack. There were plenty of Victorians thanks to Lang Lang Rodeo holding a ladies' buckjump competition every year from 1949–61 (except 1957 and 60) — Audrey Croasdale, Barbara Robertson, Iris and Eileen McFarlane, Beryl Jones, the beautiful Buddy James and the dramatic Ray Mattei, who rode as Texas Lil.

Although the ARRA recorded lady buckjumping champions from 1944–1958 it was not taken seriously as a standard event. There was no official championship circuit — or points award champion — for the women because it was an optional event for committees. At best ladies' roughriding competitions were held at a third of the circuit rodeos and then a particular rodeo would hold the annual championships where the winner on that day would be named Australian Champion. The Sydney Royal and Warwick Rodeo continued to hold ladies' buckjumping every year and they, too, were deemed Australian Championships. Lang Lang ran the annual Victorian Championships. Rockhampton, Townsville, Winton, Longreach, Brewarrina, Walgett, Narrandera, Berry Berry, Kyabram and Houghton also held ladies Australian Championships. There were never more than 10 or 12 girls competing at any one rodeo, often only three or four.

At rodeos with no ladies' competition, the women on the circuit would give buckjumping exhibitions — it was actually more lucrative than riding in the competitions. They were invited to do so and were either paid by the committee or else the roughriders would take up a blanket collection and the spectators would all pitch in. Norah Holden says: 'You'd pick up a fixed £50 or £60, which was a lot of money ... Mostly the cowboys would be winning £20 or £30 or something like that, more at the big rodeos. Girls didn't get much ... probably about £10 if you were lucky.'

Women's prize money was never half what the men got, but they got at least twice the fanfare and drew the crowds like nothing else. The fact that so few ladies competed made them a novelty. The committees used women extensively in their promotions and newspaper journalists saw them as a good angle to their stories. Lady roughriders did steal the limelight.

Kitty Gill said that although there were a lot of good men about who helped them there were a few who resented the attention women received. Ned Portley at Warwick knew the girls were good for publicity; he always invited the Gill gals along and would 'bill us like anything. Out of sight of the men, you know'... Pat Elder agrees that the women riders probably got too much publicity because: 'The boys were there all the time, they were riding everything and better than we could and all this sort of thing.' The men had mixed opinions about the girls riding. Equality wasn't an issue because they didn't ride against them and the girls rode under different conditions.

Like the men, women never showed anger, disappointment or pain in front of the crowd. There was no collapsing in tears when you were hurt. Pat Elder: 'Ohh, no, no, no, no. Goodness me, you couldn't do that! If you wanted to have a cry you'd have it later. No, you'd try and get up as soon as possible ... get up and walk off. Well, you had to, you couldn't let yourself down, let the side down.'

Some thought the gals were pretty good. Allan Woods: 'Yes, they had pretty solid horses. I used to take an interest in it and help them get on.'

Dally Holden's reaction to women buckjump riders is amusing, considering he married one of the best of them: 'Ohhh, bloody sheilas. Nobody used to worry about it much. Sheilas riding, a waste of time. Mucking about. Of course, if you could get a quid out of it, well, ahh. I didn't mind saddling up for Norah ... it was part and parcel of the show.'

Pat Elder again:

I think they treated us as a bit of a novelty, too, really. But in a very kind sort of way and a very protective sort of way. You know they always made sure that our horses were right and did anything they could to help us and were there whenever anything went wrong and they'd sing out to you when you were riding ... No, I think the boys probably thought we were a bit of a pain in the neck, too.

By the end of the 1950s most of the buckjump shows ceased — that's where a lot of women had learnt to ride buckjumpers — the majority of the lady riders had married and had families. Girls' rides were getting hard to get. The last ARRA ladies buckjump championship on record was won by Margaret Noack in Longreach in 1958 with Emily Lock of Charleville second. The year 1961 saw the last Ladies' Victorian State Championships at Lang Lang — Mrs K. Cross won with Mrs Margaret Gill runner-up. That was about the end of the roughriding competitions for the ARRA women, although they continued to give exhibitions occasionally in the 1960s.

At some point the ARRA officially stopped women's roughriding. Theories why are many and varied: 'It just wasn't lady-like,' is one. Women riders just 'got married and faded away' and there were 'no new riders coming on'. Apparently there was a rodeo out of Melbourne where a lot of city girls entered and got injured, so the sport was deemed too dangerous. Kitty Gill had retired but says: 'It got very rough. A lot of ladies got very hurt off buckjumpers, so they cut it out.' It wasn't that more women got hurt than men, but 'It was bad public image ... that's what they came at at the meeting,' and Kitty agreed. The fact that women stole the limelight might have been a problem. Emily Lock thought the men 'just didn't want women showing them up'. She also suspected that girls getting the better (exhibition) horses to ride went against them. Margaret Gill was philosophical when she spoke to Andrea Lemon:

> The ARRA thought it was too dangerous for women. I mean you had the odd horse roll over women, or stuff like that, but no more than the men. We didn't like the decision, but there wasn't anything we could do about it. There weren't any women on the board and the men weren't listening to us. You know what men are like. They thought they were doing the right thing.[6]

Women now had no rodeo events to compete in. They went in the campdraft if there was one at a rodeo.

Commercial cowboys

Unlike the lady roughriders, who only had a few opponents to beat, the men had hundreds. According to Lindsay Black:

> In those days there'd be 30–40 boys just travelling from rodeo to rodeo and then you'd get to towns like Hughenden and there'd be 50 ringers and they'd all be nominating in the buckjumping and the bullock riding ... there were hundreds of blokes that could ride from around the central west. The stations in the central west had 15–20 stockmen on them in the 1950s, and they all nominated in the rodeos, and this is what made the rodeos. And all their horses, because they walked them into the rodeos ... There were good riders in the bush. There was hundreds of good stockmen and they only did the one rodeo a year.

And these numbers were not just for the towns teeming with ringers in Queensland either. It was because there were so many competitors nationwide that the ARRA introduced a novice buckjump and a novice steer ride. This stopped the novice riders drawing all the good horses, which is a terrible waste of a good buckjumper and first and second division in those two events were introduced by the end of the 60s.

Most of the famous Aboriginal roughriders of the 30s and 40s, the likes of Fred Lawton and Alec Haydon, had finished competing by the time the ARRA was formed. Billy Bargo turned up to the occasional Queensland Championships in the late 40s. Surprisingly, although there were thousands of Aboriginal stockmen and ringers in Australia in the 1950s, few took to the ARRA rodeo scene. Johnny Cadell in South Australia was one ARRA celebrity, a good all-round horseman and roughrider, but he never travelled the national circuit. Numerous others rode now and then, when rodeos came to them, but of this generation only two Aboriginal roughriders really embraced the lifestyle full-time, for any length of time, and they were Queenslanders Wally Mailman and Lindsay Black. Wally's brother Lenny and Lindsay's brothers Gordon and Frank also rode a fair bit and later the brothers, Ritchie and Donald 'Ducko' Fraser. Most Aboriginal stockmen were happy to ride the rough ones at work and compete at their local rodeos. Herb Wharton is of the opinion that chasing around the countryside after titles was not their style. The ARRA didn't reach into the Northern Territory or Western Australia — the Kimberley — the hotbeds of Aboriginal stockmen, until much later. They mostly ran local unaffiliated rodeos up that way. Lindsay Black:

> *They always called you a bloody blackfella but you'd ignore it. It was never bad. Fair. We were accepted as much as any. Well, we were really accepted more than the European, that's the way I felt. After I got going, well, people took to me and they gave me a good time. And that came from all different sorts of places, different quarters. There was Wally Mailman and myself, we were well liked by everybody, we had some real good friends ... We had a great time. Jesus, there were some good people around.*

During the 1950s rodeos proliferated all over the country. By the end of the decade there would hardly have been a bush town that didn't have an annual rodeo. Now that they were organised, the founders of the ARRA, with a lot of help from rodeo committees and Australian townships, redefined themselves, moving from a family- and community-based sport to a quasi-professional one with a big public profile. Bushmen's carnivals, gymkhanas and sports days continued to run as community events but rodeo was entertainment for the people. As Lindsay Black says: 'You put a rodeo on for the public, not for the cowboys.'

To the media- and publicity-minded committees, roughriders came to be cowboys and cowgirls, and they became the stars and heroes of the bush. This extract from the program for the 1952 Lang Lang rodeo in Victoria exemplifies this change in image from Australian stockmen and women competing in the sporting arena to Australian cowboys and cowgirls competing in the performance arena:

> *In the Northern States of Australia, Rodeo, Camp drafting and Round-Ups are looked upon as Australia's National Sport, and rightly so, because everything and everybody connected with this sport is in every sense truly Australian.*
>
> *... Rodeo is taking its place in Southern States, and is being wholeheartedly accepted by the public as an exhibition of the unquestionable grit, determination, fortitude and skill that stamps the Australian people as a hardy, sport loving race. A people who have shown their worth in battle, their worth on the land in face of bad seasons, drought and such like, and yet can always come up smiling and ready to face their task again. Such is the spirit shown by Australia's outback cowboys for whom no horse or beast holds any terrors ...*
>
> *There is no diversion that has a stronger appeal for Australians than the Rodeo, and for thrilling and fascinating entertainment the modern show ring does not stage a programme of amusement which meets so much with the approval of its patrons ...*
>
> *... Its cultural influence in Australia has been to revive and immortalise the stirring deeds of the horsebreaker and cattle-musterer, who have given so much colour and background to Australian literature.*
>
> *It is these boys we so loudly acclaim as they stage the exhibition of which every minute is crammed full of dangerous spills and thrills, but possessed of an almost superhuman strength and endurance, the Australian Cowboy faces his task with a happy, carefree mood that wins for him a place in the hearts of an ever admiring public. 'Fellows, you are tops.'*

This a fine example of bush heritage myth-making and also marks the tentative emergence of the term, 'Australian cowboy'. Probably 90 per cent of working stockmen never went near a rodeo arena, they got enough dust and danger at work every day and preferred fishing or tinkering in the shed on their days off. Those who opted for rodeo were becoming cowboys who earned a living as sportsmen but presented themselves as entertainment. In the eyes of the general public, the Australian stockman's identity was dividing — one stayed at work and the other became a cowboy on the rodeo trail.

Cowboys had continued to gallop out of Hollywood Gene Autrey, Roy Rogers and the fictional character made famous by actor William Boyd — Hopalong Cassidy — became well-known cowboy heroes to most Australians. All over the western world children were running around their backyards dressed up in cowboy gear, learning the 'cowboy's ten commandments'. With the introduction of television all three cowboy heroes made the successful transition to television and were joined in lounge rooms by the likes of the Lone Ranger, the Cisco Kid and Annie Oakley.

A lot of this latest cowboy resurgence was driven by a new consumerism. It was the 50s when cowboy heroes of screen and radio got into merchandising and advertising, endorsing everything from watches to breakfast cereal. The original Marlboro Man was created in 1954 by the Leo Burnett advertising agency for Philip Morris in order to sell filter-tipped cigarettes to tough guys as well as women. By the early 1960s Philip Morris dropped all their other campaigns and 'made the cowboy the lone master of Marlboro Country'.[7]

Australia's urban and regional public knew all about cowboys. Rodeo as we know it today grew in popularity because of these identifiable cowboy heroes. We had our own Country and Western stars, like Tex Morton, Buddy Williams and Smoky Dawson. The Skuthorpes and Kitty Gill were also big stars. Travelling buckjump showmen were plentiful through to the mid–50s and they were definitely styling themselves as Wild West shows starring cowboys and cowgirls. Where Hollywood couldn't reach, in the outback, the popularity of rodeos was because roughriders represented Australian heritage and because bush carnivals and rodeos had become the sport of the bush people. This was particularly so for the battlers and for those in cattle country.

Dressing the part

Paradoxically, most of the 50s western pop culture and advertising escaped Australian roughriders themselves. They were in the bush, on the road or in the arena, they weren't in the marketplace. Money was tight; food, entry fees, vehicles and fuel were the priority. Fancy clothes were fine if they were on a winning streak, and most of them were pretty 'flash'. The backblocks had only a few cinemas and no television for a long time, but the roughriders knew and sang the songs. They pored over imported American rodeo magazines and aspired to the standards the Americans set in the rodeo arena. Among themselves and in the backblocks the riders were still considered Australian 'roughriders' right up until about 1960. 'Cowboys' and 'cowgirl' took over after that. But they couldn't resist the American marketing and merchandise completely.

Roughriders were image-conscious — a showman is a showman and should have style. They only wore rodeo clothes, hats and boots in the arena. They travelled in civvies and always dressed up in suits and ties if they were going out to the movies or a dance. Lindsay Black looks back: 'Ask anyone and they'll say I was a pretty flash sort of bloke ... I had 50-odd tailor-made shirts.'

Baggy jodhpurs and tall boots or concertina leggings over moleskin trousers and shirts and ties in the arena went out with the war. From then on and right through the 1950s the ARRA roughriders, men and women, all wore R.M. Williams outfits, all made-to-measure gaberdine trousers and matching jackets. 'They called us the gaberdine boys,' says Lindsay Black 'You didn't have to iron them too much and they never lost their creases, 18-inch knees and 20-inch bottoms, cross pockets, had a bit of style about 'em.'

Unfortunately the trousers were as slippery as silk on a smooth leather saddle. Rosin was banned for any use so the roughriders all wore leather chaps for a bit of grip and they gave the illusion of better spurring. Jeans were less slippery. In fact the early jeans were as stiff as a board. Although jeans were coming in, the only denim trousers available in Australia at the time were dungarees — shearer's pants, reinforced at the knee and baggy, and roughriders need tight-fitting pants.

The thing to do was to send off to America for jeans — Lee and Lee Riders, Levis and later Wranglers. Buckjumper extraordinaire, Allan Woods, said he was the first. He organised an American contact to send him jeans and jean jackets for £2/10 each, just a few at a time, sent over as presents. Allan would add 10 bob for postage then sell them here for £3 — no profit. Many others followed his example.

Chilla Seeney had a different approach. In towns like Rockhampton and Mackay he'd hang around the pub waiting for Americans to get off the ships, follow them around — usually into a pub — and buy their jeans. American jeans were being finally legally imported by the end of the 50s.

A few individuals resisted the changes. 'Coolibah' Jack Sullivan was a traditionalist in his attire, along with his great mate, R.M. Williams. But being 'the bushman's outfitter', business considerations prevailed with R.M. By the end of the 50s his range included American Western-styles and designs in shirts, plus jeans and tall cowboy boots. He advertised his gear in *Hoofs and Horns* and his catalogues contained illustrations of cowboys against desert mesa and butte backdrops — Hollywood Western landscapes. And his most popular style of boot was called the Santa Fe.

From the beginning R.M. made roughriders' boots, the famous short boot with low heel, green-hide bottom, red-hide upper, elastic sides, and Cuban heel if you thought you were snappy. Allan Woods was about 14 when he bought his first pair: '28 bob 29 shillings, with the highest fake heel you could get. The bigger the heel the bigger the lout, but I soon woke up to that — enough spraining of the ankles. I was never real tall so I used to think these high heels were good.'

Akubra made the felt hats, mainly in fawn and grey. There were all sorts of styles — each man's hat reflected his character — but they were smaller-brimmed than the cowboy hats of today. Lindsay Black had a little brown pork-pie hat: 'Allan Woods had one and Noel Bottom he had one ... From about 1956 onwards we started to get into the cowboy-hat style, a few fellas had before. But I stuck with my brown hat until 1956, then I went to a black hat.' Lindsay maintains that he and Doogie Bourke were the first under black: 'Well, I liked black, but anyone that wore a black hat wasn't much good, they reckon. "Never employ a bloke with a black hat." That's what they used to say.' This was probably from watching too many Hollywood Westerns with the good guys in white hats and the bad guys in black.

The queens of the cowgirls, Violet Skuthorpe and Kitty and Gladys Gill, always dressed in Western cowgirl gear — fringed and coordinated outfits, shirts with piping, either two-tone or with Western motifs. Violet wore split skirts, as did Texas Lil, who went all out with her cowgirl costume. The rest of the circuit girls dressed like the boys, in R.M. Williams gaberdine trousers, a Western or normal shirt, and boots. Pat Elder described it as, 'ordinary sort of clobber. You couldn't carry much ... we were dressed adequately but nobody had a lot of money.' The girls borrowed the boys' chaps.

Chilla Seeney brought straw cowboy hats back from America in 1959. By the end of the 1960s all Australian cowboys and cowgirls were wearing American jeans, boots and hats, and trophy belt buckles had become the champion roughrider's number one accessory.

During the 1950s rodeo and its stars received a lot of media attention. *Hoofs and Horns* spread the word and radio, newspapers and magazines did stories on them. The full-time champion roughriders became household names. They were strong and athletic, practically all good-looking, debonair, and devil may care. And they excelled at the toughest of bushmen's sports.

The 1950s also saw the invention of the teenager. Just as James Dean and Marlon Brando were jeans-wearing icons for the rebel hearts of urban youth, cowboys became heros for rural teenagers. Teenage girls adored them and chased them from town to town but cowboys were popular with all ages. Rodeo has always been family entertainment — the oldies love it as much as their grandchildren. Lindsay Black recalls: 'The kids would come up and say, "Mum wants you to — you've gotta come round to our camp and have lunch with us".' They were invited into homes for breakfast, lunch and dinner. Fan mail poured in; autograph-seekers lined up behind the chutes; they were celebrities.

The star roughriders were recognised everywhere they went. Lindsay Black remembers:

You'd walk into the drycleaners or the laundry in Rockhampton and they'd be lining up their daughters to go out with you and all that sort of thing. It was unbelievable ... The whole lot of us had a following of people, young and old people. They'd be there. They'd want to see their roughrider ... You'd come home and you'd get letters from girls. A big pile of letters when I got home, mostly from girls ...

Chilla Seeney has a trunk full of cards and letters, collected by his remarkably good-natured wife, from adoring girls all over Australia. Accompanying the *billets doux* was usually a photograph of the writer in a groovy 1950s bikini.

Women roughriders had more publicity than the men but they kept a lower profile. They didn't socialise much. Money was tight and by law they weren't allowed in pubs — not that many of them drank. Those who were travelling the circuit kept to themselves and camped at the showgrounds with the couples and families. They were asked to dances but they rarely went, either for want of a decent frock or because they couldn't dance. As a single girl on the circuit, Pat Elder had to chase men out of her tent occasionally: 'The boys would play tricks and turn up or crawl in and you'd say, "Now away you go, there's a good boy".'

Covering the map

Coordinated by the ARRA 'runs' of rodeos, or circuits, developed in different parts of the country. These were based mostly on the seasons — up north in winter, down south for summer and everywhere in New South Wales in between. There was a rodeo every weekend in Queensland from early March to the end of October, starting in the towns of Taringa, Dingo, Bluff, Emerald — at Easter — Alpha and Jericho. Then the roughriders would go down and do the Rockhampton Show followed by Bowen, Proserpine then back to Wowan, Springsure, Home Hill and Townsville. In July Mareeba Rodeo set off a western run.

According to ARRA cowboy and historian, Peter Poole: 'The Western Run always held a special aura of its own. There was more of a Frontier atmosphere about it all.'⁸ It was one of the most popular and lucrative runs — big country, cattle country with enormous stations. The rodeos had plenty of spectators with hundreds ringers nominating each year. Perhaps most importantly the committees had plenty of rogue station horses in their strings. The western run included Hughenden, Winton, Longreach, Richmond, Cloncurry, Blackall and, from 1959, Mt Isa.

After the western run, the ARRA circuit riders could either head south to the New South Wales rodeos through August–September (the likes of Walgett, Bourke, Moree, Brewarrina, Collarenebri, Cobar, Wilcannia, Coonamble, Gravesend, Narrabri, Gilgandra and Warren). Or there were the border towns where the cattle came down through the stock routes from Queensland and the Northern Territory to markets in the south by foot, train and now by truck. Those were places like Texas, Goondiwindi, Boggabilla, Mungindi, Cunnamulla and Moree, where all the roughriding drovers were. The ARRA riders could then head down to South Australia in October and November via Marrabel, Carrieton, Coobowie, Spalding, Hawker, Wanilla and Penola. The South Australian committees had good strings of bucking horses — rogues from the cattle stations in the pastoral zones of the centre. Then they could stay for the Victorian and southern New South Wales rodeos over Christmas and New Year. This included Myrtleford every Boxing Day, Tumbarumba on New Year's Day and Lang Lang or Sydney at Easter; they could fly to Tasmania from Melbourne if they wanted to.

There were plenty of rodeos around Victoria and plenty of good roughriders. Unlike the Queenslanders they could rodeo from home because there wasn't so far to travel. Consequently rodeo was less a way of life and more of a weekend sport in the smallest of the mainland states. In 1954 Melbourne's Moomba Festival was launched. The official opening ceremony was a rodeo at the Royal Melbourne Showgrounds which started at 11 am and continued under lights until 11 pm:

> *Events were held simultaneously on all parts of the arena ... the showground stands were packed to capacity ... at six p.m. the gates were thrown open to try and relieve the congestion ... no one knows how many attended as they were jammed into every conceivable space, including the arena itself ... Official estimates were 40 000, and it was a Friday.*⁹

If they didn't head down south the roughriders would stay in Queensland and compete in the annual Rocky Round Up in September then head back across to the rodeos at Miriam Vale, Eidsvold, Monto, Mundubbera, Gayndah, Theodore, Taroom, Wandoan, Condamine, Chinchilla and down to Warwick in the last week of October.

The core group of ARRA roughriders now competed all over the eastern states practically all year round. They did it collectively, sharing everything and living in each other's pockets, cars and caravans. They became their own gipsy tribe, friends of the highest order, a family. Lindsay Black: 'You were all mates. You all travelled together and nobody would go without a feed.'

Hitting the road

The hardest thing about rodeo was the travelling. In Queensland in particular, Lindsay Black says: 'You had to travel by train, mail train. There was no here today, gone tomorrow. You went down to Rocky on the mail train and you had to stay there until the mail train came back.' With private vehicles it was still excruciatingly slow going. Distances between each rodeo were huge, especially in Queensland, and decent roads were few. Wally Woods adds: 'Some of those roads in Queensland, there were no roads, just a two-wheeled track ... when we drove to Mareeba there was no road north of Rockhampton, just a track.' They'd cram into someone's car. There'd be no air-conditioning. Chilla Seeney and Lindsay Black travelled together in the early 50s in an old mini minor sedan. Utes were popular, occasionally carrying a horse balancing precariously among the swags and ports, all tied together with ropes. Those with families bought caravans. They trundled along and much to everyone's amusement they often flipped over. Dally and Norah Holden started off with a ute and a tent while they saved for a caravan. Dally remembers: 'Sometimes we'd never speak all day. She'd sit there and I'd drive, and the only thing we'd say was, "Roll us a smoke, Norah".' Bad weather would disrupt everything. Vic Gough says:

> You'd be halfway between Mackay and Rockhampton and there would be a storm and a creek would come up. And you might be two or three days in between creeks waiting for the creeks to go down ... The roads were shocking. You'd go out west and I'd be sometimes travelling with a truck of horses and a van and I'd sometimes leave the road and go through the grass to see if it was any better. And that's no exaggeration.

Pat Elder travelled most extensively in 1952 and 53, either alone or with Enid Bennett. They went by train or occasionally hitchhiked. 'If we did hitchhike we always tried to dress up as well as we could, so we didn't look like swaggies.' Sometimes they travelled with the boys:

> *They were always very good the travelling boys, you know. You'd travel with them and pay part petrol. And I never had any romantic attachments so it was a lot easier for me to do whatever I did. They treated me as another one of the fellas really. But they were very good, always very good and they looked after you at a rodeo, always kept an eye out for you when you camped on the grounds.*

The single blokes used to go careering about in cars with 'about ten blokes hanging off it'. As time went on they got married and either quit or bought caravans and took the children along. Norah Holden has fond memories of her and Dally travelling with Tom and Eileen Willoughby, Ray and June Crawford, Allan and Barbara Woods, Wally and Lexie Woods and Vic and Frances Gough: 'They used to come and have cups of tea and coffee and sit in the van and talk to all hours ... go from town to town and everybody would pull in and set up camp and talk and play cards and whatever until the rodeo started.'

They began to cart time-event horses, bulldogging first then roping horses. Vic Gough even carted a hazing horse that doubled as a campdraft horse. Allan and Barb Woods married in 1953 when Barbara was 20. By the time she was 25 they had four children and a caravan and were a travelling menagerie. Their son, Robert, was allergic to cow's milk, so they carted a goat, which sat in the back seat next to Robert in his bassinette, his sister, Kay, and the chooks who supplied them with fresh eggs. Barbara also carried around a huge bucket of silverbeet as greens for the kids were often hard to come by. When they got to the showgrounds, Allan would be off so Barbara would tether the goat, the chooks and her disgruntled children so she could set-up camp and cook dinner without losing any of them.

Generally they all camped together at the showgrounds and cooked for themselves. The showgrounds either had sheds, stables or pavilions to roll out your swags in. Among the families there was usually a race to the next town to get the best spot — one with shade that was handy to water and other amenities. If they had money they would stay in pubs and eat there.

Sometimes townspeople would go down to the showgrounds and 'pal up' with the roughriders, and maybe take them home to camp there. There were roughriders and their families in or near most towns. After a year or two on the circuit the roughriders knew people they could stay with in most parts of the country — a mate whose verandah would be covered in swags; whose yard would hum with all kinds of dogs chained to dusty vehicles with men tinkering underneath them; whose Hills hoist would be laden with washing; and whose kettle was always on the boil for the storytellers around the kitchen table.

In Winton the whole community laid it on for the roughriders. The first year Lindsay Black and the travelling crew went there they stayed at a boarding house, the next year the committee had rented them a house:

They brought in all the beds from the shearing quarters and they brought in all this meat. Too much meat, it went rotten, so next year we could go to the butcher shop and the butcher gave us the meat. People gave us groceries. They looked after us ... Then Winton built a big pavilion and that's where we stayed and they gave us meat and bread and vegetables.

Winton was especially hospitable but in most towns local graziers would bring in fresh meat and distribute it among the camps in the showground. The roughriders really appreciated the community's generosity, and in turn they would pitch in and help. They generally got to town a week before the rodeo and helped get the show up and running. They mustered and brought in the bucking stock, repaired posts and rails and gates or worked for the local graziers around the area. They mixed in with the townies, hung out in the pubs and cafes, flirted with the barmaids and fought about it with the local lads. The rodeo might have been over for two days and there'd still be an outfit or two in town, holed up somewhere having a party. Headly and Cecil Parter and cohorts loved singing and playing guitar around the fire. In Winton and Longreach the Fraser brothers were the entertainers.

Col McTaggart:

You very seldom struck anybody that wouldn't give you a meal or supply something for the cowboys often travelling. Because there wasn't much prize money about and you know it did cost money to go. While I was younger and travelling all in one car it wasn't too bad, but when you got older and got a family and trucks and caravans and that, well it was a bit harder travelling then.

Lindsay Black:

There was money in it if you were good enough ... In the 50s the basic wage was £6 a week ... the cost of living was cheap ... so if you won £100 it was a lot of money ... You could go and stay at a hotel for a week for 30 bob. You could go and buy a three-course meal in a cafe for 4 bob, you could go and buy sixpence of stewing steak and you'd have a hard time carrying it out.

The average ARRA rodeo was £15–£30 to win the buckjump. Mareeba rodeo had a £100 bronc ride; Bowen had a £50 bronc ride; Rockhampton, Warwick and Kyabram in Victoria also paid £100 to win. Winton, Marrabel and, from 1959, Mt Isa, were also all worth winning.

The ones who weren't winning survived because everyone borrowed, lent and shared everything. Bludging and scamming became a fine art. Everyone has a spell when their luck runs down and they're drawing bad stock or getting injured. Lester Cain reckons he rodeoed around Australia twice and 'all I ever learned was to live on one meal a day'. A lot of the time they were broke. Lindsay Black states: 'Well, we made a living out of it but sometimes we were pretty slack. We lived off people's eggs and chickens and fish traps along the Thomson.' Hungry roughriders have also been known to help themselves to the occasional sheep off the side of the road. Dally Holden: Norah was my bank. She used to keep it in her bag because we'd seen a lot more dinner times than dinners ... It was a tough life, a very tough life ... We lived off the smell of an oily rag. But it never hurt us. Stopped us getting big pot guts.'

There was, of course, always paid employment. Most ARRA roughriders worked at least a couple of months a year. There was hay-carting and fruit-picking down south in the summertime, and up north over winter there were meatworks at Bowen and Townsville. Everywhere in between there was stock and station work, mustering, branding, horsebreaking, droving, fencing, or in the sheds, sheep shearing or crutching. Being mostly bush-bred boys the roughriders could turn their hands to most things, if they had to. Graziers were very supportive in finding them something to do.

The making of legends

Of all the legendary rides in the history of rodeo, two have remained at the forefront of folklore. This has as much to do with publicity as prowess because when *the* gun horse is beaten by *the* gun rider you can get a lot of mileage out of it. The first of these was in 1906 when Lance Skuthorpe rode Martini's star horse, Bobs, in Sydney. The second took place in 1953 when Allan Woods rode Curio of Marrabel.

A scruffy, flea-bitten grey, Curio was a true star. She became the feature horse at Marrabel in 1947 — only Australian title-holders were invited to try her and she only bucked once a year. By 1953 Curio had pelted a whole string of excellent roughriders to remain unconquered.

Allan Woods was the Australian Bronc Riding Champion in 1953. He rode Curio in front of 10 000 people. Woods takes up the story:

She was only about 14 hands high, a little clumper thing, her father was a draughthorse, mother was a pony. They tried to break her in as a 2-year-old and they put a pack saddle on her and she bucked the pack saddle off, bucked into the fence and hurt her neck, so they didn't go on with breaking her. R.M. Williams went up there and bought 8 or 10 buckjumpers. And the manager said, 'Take that roan thing. She'll buck, don't worry about that.' ... In 53 I held the title, so I got the ride on her. They said to me, 'Do you accept the challenge to ride Curio?' I said, 'Definitely'. ... I rode her in 53. So I finished the ride, straight up to the microphone they take me. They say, 'We think Allan fluked the little mare today,' and handed me the microphone. Well, it looked like I'd been in a bit of trouble there the third buck. See, what she'd do, she'd go one, two, boom! And then suck back from me to you and throw her head to you. So it was like driving a car down the road and you haven't got hold of the wheel. You get a hold of it, you don't know which way it's going to go. See, while you've got the message coming through your arm and your leg you're right, but when they throw their head to you, then you've got to lift {your arm} and she nearly lifted me, too. But what I always said was that everyone that got on her tried to sit down tight on her, and she used to bust them out ... I said there's only one way to ride her and that's to go out after her — go up, get in rhythm with her. If you sit in tight she'll bust you out. And I was right. So when they handed me the microphone, I said, 'Well, never worry about the fluke. Get me back next year under the same conditions and I'll show you whether it was a fluke or not. Thank you.' And I went back and rode her again in 54.

They call them the 'old legends' now, the star roughriders of the 50s. And Allan Woods is widely regarded as the greatest buckjump rider of them all. In his day (1946–60) Allan named Stumpy Timmins as the best, then named Kevin McTaggart the best bareback rider, Allan Bennett the best bulldogger, Dan Crotty the star roper, Tom Willoughby 'a terribly good bullock rider', and his brother Wally Woods as the best all-rounder. Few would argue with that. Together with 10 or 20 others who were on the road as full-time roughriders, they outshone the rest.

To some, Brian Gill was 'the best bareback rider Australia's ever seen'. Dally Holden was 'as good a cowboy as was ever in the game'. Ray 'the Fox' Crawford and his brother Barry 'Bo' Crawford were 'always in the money'. Chilla Seeney and Vic Gough were two of the toughest bronc riders going. Vic Gough was considered by many to be one of the best all-round horseman in the country and Chilla was way ahead of the game in the time events. Norman, the third Woods brother, was a natural but was forced to retire because of injury. It was also hard to beat the McTaggart brothers, Kevin, Max, Malcolm, Colin and Bruce. Kevin and Colin, in particular, excelled at the sport. Kevin was a great all-rounder and the bareback king until he, too, was badly injured in his prime. Colin kept rodeoing — he was an exceptionally good bronc rider — until 1979. He quit at Shepperton rodeo after he won the bulldogging and came second in the bronc ride; he was 45: 'It was enough for me.'

Up there with them were Lindsay, Gordon and Frankie Black, Ken Perrett, Tom Cannon, Alwyn Torenbeeck, Bob Weick, Les Whyte, whose nickname was 'the Brahman Kid' for obvious reasons, Joe Napier — 'Ole 'avachat' — a wild man both in the ring and in the bush, 'Jimbo' Hawkins a good bullock rider, Bram Toohey and Noel Toomey, Dick Hawkins, John Huey 'the Kynuna Kid', who used to drink gin in defiance of the rum crowd, Pat Clarke, Ron Richards, 'a good and fearless' roughrider who also did a fair bit of picking-up. Frank Stockholm the shearer, Jack Powell, Colin Meek, Bob Glover and Robin Yates from Sydney was 'a good class of saddle rider'. Doyle Gill rode the rough ones in the big ring and the small, and Fred Fuller, Bluey Potts, Ken and Max Healey, Dick White were also around. Buddy and Brian Gravener were hard to beat, but their younger brother Barry was going to be harder. Neville Shields was a very good bronc rider, as were Danny Baldwin from New Zealand and Les Cowan from South Australia 'who used to ride with their tongues out, never bit them, which was quite incredible'. Queenslander Keith Lindley was 'one hell of a bullrider'. There are too many good riders to name them all.

For every champ there were thousands of ringers, stockmen, bushmen, townies and city folk who rode against them. These were the ones who didn't win all the time, the ones who only did the circuit for a year or so or who only rode at their local rodeo every year. Plenty of knockabout and part-time roughriders came and went. Some were only in it for the lifestyle, the girls, the booze, the parties, the travel and the image. Few of these became champions. Competition was too stiff, and the money too hard to win. The champions were either naturally brilliant athletes and/or they were seriously determined to win.

By the end of the 1950s the ARRA had over 6000 members, a healthy provident fund and each big rodeo would generate another four or five hundred dollars in nomination fees. There were more than 40 annual ARRA rodeos in Queensland alone. The ARRA had defined and consolidated Australian rodeo as a sport and a culture. It lifted the standards of the sport and became the elite rodeo association. As Lindsay Black put it: 'Every Tom, Dick and Harry who wore a pair of cowboys boots wanted to be a member of the ARRA.' The circuit riders were not rich but they were famous. The bigger established rodeos were attracting crowds of 10 to 12 thousand people and many more for the championships. The sport was organised and official, the lifestyle tough but terrific. Although the sport has evolved and factionalised considerably over the last 50 years, the ARRA will always be the core of it.

Col McTaggart sums it up:

It was a good life and I'm pleased that we rodeoed in that era because although the conditions were not real good, the mateship we had and the friends we made over those years were. I'm sure the boys today won't have the friendship that we made over those days. People don't value friendship as much as we did you know in those days. It was probably as good a mob of people in any organisation as you would ever see, as what we had ... It was just a good, clean, open sport and you just had to win on your own merit, you just had to excel and do things. And everybody helped each other in those days, you didn't try and do things to stop other blokes from winning. You just helped them, you know. You didn't care if he beat you or not. If he beat you, good on him, and we'd all go and have a party or something when it was finished. That's the way it was, it was a good spirit.

6

THE SWINGING 60s

If you're handling a rough one

There's bound to be perched on the rails

Of the Stockyard some grizzled old tough one

Whose flow of advice never fails;

There are plenty, of course, who aspire

To make plain that you're only a dunce,

But the most insupportable liar

Is the man who has ridden 'em once.

Via America to the world stage

THE 60S SAW MAJOR changes in the bush. Wool prices dropped and beef markets expanded. Upgraded roads in the north, west and interior made those places accessible for trucks and eventually road trains to take over from drovers on horseback moving cattle to market. First the motorcycle then the aeroplane and later still the helicopter began to replace stockmen for mustering. A mineral boom generated new wealth for Australia. A lot of ex-ringers found jobs in mines or on town councils building better roads. Throughout the 1960s horses and horsemen were still a large part of bush culture, and the cattle industry still depended on them, but their role declined and their demise had begun.

The rodeo scene continued to grow. It was in the 1960s that Western Australia, Tasmania and the Northern Territory got their rodeo circuits going. Prior to that they had been spasmodic, independent affairs. The eastern and southern states had their own circuits and individual championships and the ARRA roughriders travelled the whole eastern half of Australia, Tasmania and New Zealand each year.

For rodeo the outstanding feature of the decade was the wholehearted adoption of American rodeo methods and style. It had started in the 1890s with audiences enjoying US performers and Wild West shows. By the 1940s promoters and journalists were tentatively calling roughriders Australian cowboys and cowgirls and using the terms stampede and round-up instead of rush and muster. In the 1950s American jeans and shirts with Western designs and motifs had become all the rage. The trickle of 'cowboy' influence became a flood and by the end of the 60s American language, clothes and customs, once rare and coveted or shyly copied, became *de rigueur*. Australian cowboys and cowgirls now rode broncs not buckjumpers. They travelled in rigs with their outfit, not a truck with their mates. A good man became a good hand. The ARRA promoted and developed roping as an event with all its idioms and paraphernalia. It was American gear from top to toe — straw or Resistol felt hats, Justin boots and Wrangler jeans, in particular, became the uniform. Trophy belt buckles, saddles, bareback riggings, ropes and chaps were either imported or made locally from American designs.

Australian showmen and professional roughriders such as Thorpe McConville and Jack Morrissey had worked and ridden in America (pre-World War I). In the 1930s Alan McPhee had been there, as had Lance and Violet Skuthorpe with Art Creasy and Jack Watson, who had even made headlines — 'Beating the Yanks!' — in a bulldogging contest in Chicago. All of them had implemented what they had seen and learnt. American cowboys had been here before and during the war and the ARRA had modelled itself on their Cowboy's Turtle Association. Australian roughriders read American *Hoofs and Horns* and other cowboy magazines when they could get their hands on them, but there were still very few who had been overseas. Colin McTaggart: 'It was unheard of for anybody, any working-class people, to go — just the odd one that really set his mind to it and had the opportunity of getting away. Not too many went in those days. You didn't know what was over there, it was so far away.' In 1949 roughriders Tom Smyth, Johnny Morlan, Jimmy Jupp and Johnny Roberts competed in the USA but without much success. Johnny Roberts returned with a bit of a reputation, perhaps because he came back 'cowboyfied'.

The Americans and Canadians were roughly 50 years ahead of us in developing rodeo as professional sport and entertainment. They had so many rodeos and contestants that there was a very high standard of competition. They had professional stock contractors so the bucking stock were bigger, better and tougher. Rodeos were more professionally organised and run; they had big, fancy grand entry parades and ran much slicker, faster shows. There was no sitting around waiting for someone to tighten a girth. If you weren't ready they'd just open the gate and off went your horse. It was more entrepreneurial and business-like and rodeo's huge popularity made it extremely lucrative. All in all America was — and is — the Mecca for cowboys from all over the world. Only in America do they have international competition of the highest calibre — providing the real prestige.

In 1959 four of the top ARRA roughriders went to the United States for a few months. They were Bob Holder (26), Chilla Seeney (27), Ray Crawford (31) and Robin Yates (24). They were touted around as celebrity 'Australian cowboys', they signed lots of autographs but to their dismay they competed virtually without success. Chilla Seeney remembers:

American cowboys, I'll tell you now they could never run tracks with the Australian bushmen and cattlemen. But not in that ring. Once you got in that arena those Americans would beat the hell out of us. Because they were professionals and they went every bit way that made it easier for them ... Man, you know, they rode a lot different to how we did. We had these little bits of leather that they used to call saddles that we had to ride in. And we got over there and they had Western saddles and the bareback riders, they were good, man they were good. And we'd never seen anything like this in our lives.

Let's get internationally competitive

They took it as a challenge and upon their return the ARRA decided to bring Australian rodeos up to international standards so that we could compete over there and win. This meant bringing our rules and regulations — and our bronc riding saddles — into line with the Americans.

Prior to 1959 the ARRA head office had been run voluntarily by two highly capable secretaries, first R.M. Williams (1945–56), then fellow South Australian Martin Quinlivan (1956–59). All new ideas, rules and regulations were discussed and voted on by all members at the AGMs at each year's national finals.

In 1959 they held a special meeting at Brewarrina National Finals. It was agreed that they needed to strengthen their association so they formed their first board of directors. Wally Woods was President, Vice-presidents were Joe Gray, Sid Long and Allan Bennett. The first *salaried* secretary/treasurer became Peter Poole, who had emigrated from England in the early 50s and has the distinction of being the 'only bloody Pom to ever win a title' (for bulldogging in 1957). Assistant secretary was R.M. Williams. Each rodeo event had a representative director. They were 'Coolibah' Jack Sullivan (saddle bronc), Vic Gough (bulls), Kevin McTaggart (bareback), Neville Shields (bulldogging), and Dan Crotty (roping) — all great contesting cowboys.

The changes began immediately. Lindsay Black: 'They went out to it with open arms, Peter Poole and all them fellas, when Crawford and Chilla and all those fellas came back from America ... Well, America wouldn't come our way, no money over here. We had to go their way ... Crawford, Holder, Yates, Seeney, it was their idea. They started to live and breathe America.' As Chilla saw it, 'If somebody's doing something and he's doing better than you, you go and see what he's doing. And then do what he's doing to improve yourself.'

In retrospect it seems obvious that a professional sport should be conducted under international conditions and rules, but at the end of the 1950s rodeo in Australia was only quasi-professional at best — a great sport, a great lifestyle and very much part of our bush heritage and culture. It was controversial to Americanise it and the traditionalists, who were mainly on the committees, resisted the changes all the way.

In Australia riding conditions continued to be fairly rough and ready. Only a few of the major centres had anything like a proper rodeo ground. Most rodeos were held at showgrounds, sportsgrounds or racecourses on unploughed grass that was slippery and rock hard. Many were also encircled by the notorious bicycle tracks which came in front of the chutes and were harder than cement. Bike tracks and hard ground caused more injury and death to roughriders in the 50s than any other factors. The arenas were also so big 'you'd need a cut lunch to get around 'em'. Spectators often needed field glasses to watch the action. Peter Poole wrote of Blackall Rodeo that the 'heat waves used to shimmer, and man and beast on the far reaches of the arena used to fade away in the constant mirages.'[1]

Spectators would certainly know what was going on when a horse and rider landed on them, which happened a lot because there were no fences to speak of. At best showground fences were 4 feet 6 inches high, which is fine for a gymkhana but not suitable for a rodeo. Some grounds were just sectioned off with wooden posts and hessian or calico strung between them. At Condamine you bucked straight out in an open clearing of 100 yards. There were six chutes with a wing out each side; the pick-up men sat between the chutes and the brigalow. Bowen River's rodeo was at the racetrack with the audience standing all down the straight. Lindsay Black recalls, 'You bucked straight out and went bush'.

During the 1960s, professionalism, safety, fairness and respectability were at the forefront of the ARRA's agenda. A stack of changes were introduced. Committees were encouraged to plough their arenas and upgrade their facilities.

They put in better yards, chutes and fences and built time-event boxes so they no longer just backed their horses up into open bucking chutes and drew a line in the dirt with a heel. Committees had to provide roping and dogging steers that were roughly the same size and condition to even out the competition. Further animal welfare guildelines were drawn up in 1961. Stock for time events had to be above a certain age and the roughstock were run through before the rodeo so that they knew what they were supposed to be doing. Taped-up spurs were replaced with spurs with running rowels. Many committees and individuals were openly hostile. But they came around, and nowadays you wouldn't dream of running a rodeo on unfenced or unploughed grounds.

Judging remained an issue. Many judges were from the committees and were either biased or had never contested in the events they were judging. At Cloncurry one year Lindsay Black's horse went over the fence and 'left me hanging in a prickly bush. When I came back the judge had disqualified me for deliberately riding the horse over the fence. I couldn't believe it.' Chute bosses were also local committee men and despite the draw card system they often managed to put the star cowboys on the rankest horses in the hope they'd buck off. Chilla Seeney always struck the same horse in his home town of Monto: 'I think he was the toughest horse I ever got onto in my life because five times I went to Monto Rodeo and five times I drew him. They had him there waiting, like. Harrimi Bill. He threw me five times and that's something that never happened to me in my life.' Things improved once ARRA cowboys took over the judging, chute bossing, announcing and so on. The cowboys joined their hometown rodeo committees and got involved in running the shows. They also started promoting and running their own independent rodeos. Cowboys were not necessarily above cheating, but there was generally honour among thieves. Eventually all loopholes were ironed out by the introduction of computer draws and judges' scoreboards.

The ARRA implemented more control over its members. They brought in a strict dress code — a proper 'Western style' of dress, including a cowboy hat — and behaviour regulations — there was no more grog around the chutes. The stiff penalties and expulsion for bad behaviour drew mixed results. The prize money was also evened up. Where it might have been £50 to win a bronc ride and £10 for everything else, as they professionalised the time events they also equalised the prize money.

Perhaps the biggest catalyst for professional uniformity was the setting up of an approved rodeo system. The ARRA would affiliate any rodeo but to be part of their championship circuit a committee had to meet their new conditions. Until 1962 the ARRA national titles had been awarded to the winners at a designated National Titles Rodeo. Under the new system the Australian title belonged to the cowboy who won the most point *all year*, including the final. Within the first year about 50 committees had taken to the scheme — they had to if they wanted the star cowboys to compete at their rodeos.

The pain of parting with tradition

The two most controversial changes that the ARRA cowboys brought in were mandatory added entries and the adoption of the American bronc riding saddle as Australian standard. Mandatory added entries obligated a rodeo committee to put a large percentage of the cowboys' nominations (entry fees) into the posted prize money. Up until then a committee might put up £100 to be split first to fifth for a bronc ride, and the cowboys' entry fees went into committee coffers. Added entries meant the prize was the £100 *plus* a large percentage of the entry money.

On one hand, the committees needed to make money to pay the contractors, chute bosses, arena judges, rodeo secretaries, announcers, clowns, bullfighters, entertainers, photographers, council workers — to plough and water the grounds — and all the rest *and* make money for their charities. The 1968 ruling meant they now had to do this from takings at the gate, the bar and the barbeque. Smaller, battling committees who couldn't afford it and the riled-up ones who wouldn't left the ARRA and affiliated with the Bushmen's Carnival Association or ran their rodeos unaffiliated. On the other hand, cowboys had never been able to live entirely off their winnings. The majority of them were broke most of the time. Yet they were the stars of the shows; they were doing the miles and taking the risks; and they wanted to be paid accordingly.

The saddle saga was even more controversial because, unusually, the cowboys were not in agreement. The older generation regarded the poley saddle as part of our tradition and heritage; it had become a roughriding icon. As it was also hard to ride in, they thought it made for better riders. The younger generation, with their eyes on America, was unanimously for the saddle change. The New Zealanders adopted the American/International saddle as their standard in 1965. Now everyone except the Australians was competing in the same saddles. That year the ARRA introduced the new saddle on a voluntary basis. By 1970 no-one in the ARRA was using the poley so the international saddle was officially made our new standard. The ARRA no longer provided communal saddles, each bronc rider carried his own.

Changing to the American saddle was a quantum leap for our bronc riders, who had to learn a completely different style of riding. In the poley saddle, according to Herb Wharton, 'Your feet had to be in front of the girth or you'd be gone'. This was perfect for the wild bucking horses of the time which bucked up front and high in the air, plunged, lurched and threw themselves about, spun, sucked back — everything and anything they could to shed their rider. And because the poley saddle was shallow and loose, if you came up and out of it you'd have half a chance of getting back in. The American saddles are big and deep with large pads up front and tied down stirrups. It's designed for more consistent and extravagant spurring motions. The bronc rider sits further back with a longer head rein and in rhythm with a horse's bucking motion, he sweeps his heels from in front of the horse's shoulders up to the cantle (back) of the saddle. This action is known as a full lick.

Beauty in the beast

Just as the rider's style had to change, so did the horses. The new saddle was designed for seasoned professional horses that bucked straight ahead, rhythmically and consistently, in what is termed the 'jump–kick' style. It wasn't any good with the unruly reprobates we had been riding. Stock contracting, which had traditionally been more akin to a hobby, was about to become a serious business.

Luck of the draw had always played a huge part in the roughriding contests because half of each score is for the animal's performance and half for the rider's. Most committees had strings of buckjumpers — unbroken horses and recalcitrants, discards from pony clubs and big stations. Some horses are born to buck, some learn to buck and some never buck at all. Old Lance Skuthorpe's theory was that bucking is a horse's natural instinct to rid itself of its predators. Jack Stanton said of Rocky Ned: 'He had his ancestors' fear of the cougar still with him.' Some horses resent the indignity of bit, saddle and dominating rider; for others it's just the saddle — ride them bareback and they're fine. Horses are intelligent and every one is different. When they're being tamed or broken in, some might just hop around nervously a bit whereas others will go berserk, squealing in anger and throwing themselves on the ground. It all depends on the horse's background and age, its character and disposition, and most of all the way it is approached and handled. Most horses, being noble and magnanimous creatures, soon learn what is expected of them and work with it. Often a perfectly reasonable horse has a sudden scare which sends it bucking and it's unrideable from that day on. There's always been the nasty horse, the one that will kick or bite you if you're unwary; the ratbag horse, who won't be caught until it's good and ready and you're puffing and swearing; the rogue horse, who will attack, and maybe even kill; and there's always been the buckjumper, who just likes to buck. On cattle stations and properties the buckjumper's fate could be a bullet or a trip to the meatworks, or to be ignored in the horse paddock for the rest of its life. The lucky ones had their bad habits turned into their profession. They might be driven to local rodeos for the roughriding competitions, sold to buckjump showmen or given to rodeo committees.

'Outlawed' station horses from the rugged pastoral zones of the north, west and centre seemed to make the best buckjumpers. Tough country breeds tough flora and fauna; and there were thousands of horses to choose from. Western Queensland's rodeo committees had great bucking horses. Lindsay Black: 'Longreach and Winton would run them in, all unbroken horses, last time they saw a man it was when they were branded.' They were cunning, powerful and hard to handle by the time they were back in the yards. Mareeba and Rockhampton, both big cattle towns surrounded by cattle stations and a lot of stock trade, also had tough horses. The ones from around the central ranges that were supplied to the rodeos of smaller cattle towns like Springsure and Taroom were also wily. According to Chilla Seeney a station might have 400–500 horses and they'd just draft off 70 big wild ones and say, 'Here y'are. These are yours.'

There were plenty of stars among them, horses that looked good, made you look good, the judges liked them, and if you could ride them you could win. Winton's good 'money horses' were Windermere Whirlwind, Blazing Bird Bob, Olympic Star, Blue Gillette and Shotgun, who was perhaps the greatest of the western Queensland bucking horses. He was a big unbroken thoroughbred, 16–17 hands high, that jumped and kicked as though born to do nothing else. Carandotta had a big reputation. There was Touch and Go, Tickle Me Gentle, the Doctor, Quandong, Gentle Annie and Devil's Own. Sonoma Rose and Tokyo Rose were from Bowen River and Wombi bucked at Rocky. In the late 60s Springsure rodeo committee had the big grey mare, Consuella Curio, who was owned by Jack Powell and travelled by Frankie Black. Sam Fuller had Sugar. And years before that there was the one and only Curio of Marrabel.

South Australian rodeo committees also had the riffraff of the big stations' horses at their disposal. Many top-class buckjumpers came from the cattle stations in the pastoral centre, particularly Kidman's station horses — tough, older unbroken station rogues, desert-bred, resilient and big-hearted. And a lot of them were only bucked once a year.

As in Banjo Paterson's epic poem, 'The Man From Snowy River', brumby running was a profession in many towns along the Great Dividing Range. Towns like Tumbarumba bucked brumbies at their annual rodeo. The day before men would go up into the mountains and muster up a mob of brumbies. Everyone in town would hear them coming. The shops and pubs would close their doors and windows, and children would be hustled inside to watch as they thundered down the hill and galloped straight through the main street to the showgrounds.

There were plenty of brumbies in the semi-arid or desert country, too. Ken Coleman remembers, 'They were mad, they'd eat you'. At Alice Springs every year the brumbies were wild and crazy. They'd wreck chutes, gear and everything in their path, especially the stallions that they'd draft out for the finals.

It was time-consuming getting untamed horses through the chutes. The crowd had to wait while they fought the whole way, throwing themselves down, over and into the fences. They could hurt themselves and the cowboys struggling with them. Some would turn savage and attack a fallen rider with flailing hooves and snapping jaws or roll on them if they couldn't buck them off. Some would buck, some wouldn't and some did sometimes, which was unfair on the cowboys.

At the end of the 50s most committees had gathered a decent string of consistent finals horses, or knew where to get them. The horses in the go rounds could still be anything.

Generations of stock contractors

There was a fledgling contracting industry consisting mostly of horsemen who collected bucking horses for their local rodeos because it interested them — local stock added to the community spirit of the sport. In central Queensland Jim McGhee had a good string of bucking horses; Bonshaw Bob Campbell used to send horses by train to rodeos in northern New South Wales and the Sydney Royal; Grosvenor McDonald used to buck his at Clermont Rodeo; and ex-roughrider and showman Sam Fuller used to buck his droving plant horses.

Lofty Kennard was a great bush character who used to run surplus horses off old Kidman stations and drove them down to markets in Melbourne and Adelaide. He'd keep the buckjumpers and supplied show and rodeo committees in New South Wales and Victoria as well as Wild West shows, such as Tex Morton and St Leon's Circus and Rodeo, in the 50s and 60s.

Arthur Mottershead was perhaps the first to collect buckjumpers on a grand scale. He was an ex-Skuthorpe (Snr) roughrider turned ringer who settled as a saddler in Hughenden. He ran rodeos there during and after World War II, collecting a large string of notorious ex-station rogues. Lindsay Black: 'They came off the tablelands and they all had a good story about them. They'd frighten the bloody hell out of you, the stories they'd tell you about them.' Mottershead contracted his horses to rodeos in north and central western Queensland in the early 1950s, sending them by train to places like Bowen, Townsville, Charters Towers and Richmond.

Horse-dealer Norm Cakebread, from Footscray, Melbourne, operated on an even larger scale. He'd buy up in the summer when horses were cheaper and agist them with rodeo committees. Some would buck, many wouldn't. He'd sell them off in winter, often sending a thousand head of horses per week to Sydney by rail. He supplied most of the Victorian rodeos throughout the 1950s. Norm was the forerunner for professional stock contracting, which evolved in the 1960s. His string of finals horses, led by the famous and powerful chestnut, Eldorado, included Big Thrill, who was rarely ridden, Murray Downs, Murray Queen, Black Track, Silver and Sundowner. The latter two were excellent 'money horses' that Gary McPhee later obtained.

Buckjump showmen were the first rodeo stock contractors as we know them today. They often leased their buckjumpers to rodeos. Tom Handley provided the set-up for the Australian titles at Merriwa in 1929 and Thorpe McConville ran Wild West shows for Albury Show in the 1930s, to name just two. Most showmen worked in with agricultural show and rodeo committees on and off.

It was a natural progression for people like roughrider and then entertainer Ron Anderson and his buckjump showman partner, Frank McFarlane, to move from their rope rings and canvas side walls to producing independent 'paddock shows' and organising rodeos for show societies. Anderson produced and contracted rodeos with hefty but portable chutes borrowed from the Melbourne Showgrounds in the late 1950s.

Stuart Lear also used to borrow the portables from the Melbourne Royal and he first contracted and produced a rodeo with them in 1963. He was the first to have a string of bucking bulls in Victoria and became a complete roughstock contractor/rodeo producer when he built a demountable full-sized arena and chutes in 1964. From then on he was producing, contracting and performing as a trick rider for rodeos such as Myrtleford, Kilmore, Maryborough and others around Victoria.

Yet for much of the 60s horses at rodeos were largely local and either untried or unreliable — Wally Woods was the only one who could remember them all from one year to the next. To even the odds and enable the riders to master the American saddle, professional full-time contractors were needed to supply consistent bucking stock *all* the time.

Gills at the forefront

Jack Gill and sons pioneered stock contracting as we know it today. Happy, Brian and Peter were serious contenders on the ARRA circuit from the mid-fifties. Happy, according to his peers, was a good, tough bull and bronc rider, pretty handy all around, and a great rodeo clown. Brian was a fantastic bareback rider — a death or glory rider — he went for broke every trip and never played it safe. All three brothers won plenty of state titles, but it was Peter — who went harder at it than his brothers — who succeeded the most. A three roughstock-event man, Peter rodeoed full-time in the 60s and 70s, qualifying for the ARRA National Finals every year from 1961 to 1975. He won the title for the bullock ride in 1961 and the bareback in 1967 and quit in 1976.

In the early 1960s Gill Brothers Circus and Rodeo was on the road and the boys were competing in ARRA rodeos as they went. In 1965 they combined the two. Inspired by a trip to America in 1961 where he travelled with champion cowboy and now stock contractor, Casey Tibbs, Happy Gill designed and built a fully demountable rodeo arena and chutes and the Gill Brothers rodeo tent show was from then on also Gill Brothers rodeo producers and stock contractors. They were on the road full-time and could supply stock and/or arena to other rodeos, as well as producing their own rodeos. They were still putting on the odd tent show right through to the end of the 1970s.

The Gills' first full-scale ARRA rodeo was at Warrnambool in 1964 followed by Port Fairy and Mudgeeraba on the Gold Coast in 1965. By 1967 they were producing roughly 30 shows a year, most of them in conjunction with Apex and Rotary clubs. They were staunch ARRA rodeos and always ahead of the changes. The ARRA cowboys backed the Gills 100 per cent with moral support and manpower. They had the professionals helping them with every aspect of the show, from setting up, to judges, announcers and chute bosses, to clowns, bullfighters and stock. The Gills also invented the maxim 'a good rodeo is a fast rodeo'. Performance rodeos 'for the people' — short and sweet at three or four hours maximum.

Professional bucking stock — horses and bulls that know their job and do it — have done more to improve rodeo in Australia than anything else. Tame in the yards and paddocks, they turn it on and off on cue. They learn to travel, stand quiet while in the chute and buck out clean so there are no broken kneecaps for the cowboys. They consistently give their best before returning to the holding yards without fuss or delay after each trip. In the 1960s the Gills won bucking horse of the year awards with Gravesend, Limbo Rock and Satan and two bucking bull of the year awards with Red Ned two years in a row and fourth with 007 from 1970–1974. Gravesend, named after the north-western New South Wales town near where he was bred, was special because he bucked well in both the rope ring and the big arena. Peter Gill says: 'We bucked him every day of the week for over 20 years and that's a lot of bucking. He was as fit as a fiddle. Our horses were corn-fed three times a day and at the end of the week they'd be better off than we were.'

From bullocks to bulls

Steer or bullock riding, after buckjumping and horseracing, is the oldest bush sport in Australia. It was the only event that they *always* had at bushmen's carnivals, sports days, gymkhanas and rodeos. Local graziers lent the committees their stock and everyone had a go. It was always the crowd favourite. When rodeo kicked in, teamsters' bullocks were often used, as they were tame and easier to handle. Whisky, Mareeba's black-and-white feature bullock, was well known in the 50s. He weighed 1000 pounds, stood about 15 hands high, and 'was about as wide as that table'. The only person who ever rode him was Keith Lindley. Barry Gravener remembers the bullocks were just as tricky to ride as the bulls: 'You had to be terribly quick because their moves are a lot quicker. They don't make the full circle, they go there, there, there, there, there [chop from side to side]. And if you were spurring all the time, which you should have been [rules were to spur every jump] you had to be very strong in the arm to keep in tow with them.' Nevertheless bulls, especially now that they are bred for the job, are more agile and have 10 times the power. A number of showmen had bucked bulls over the years but it was around 1960 that they arrived in the rodeo arena.

Bonny Young was the bullriding director on the ARRA board during the change from steers to bulls: 'All the rule changes at the time were what brought rodeo out of the Wild West into what we've got today ... We had been riding steers and bringing bulls into the finals. That's how it started off and then, sort of gradually, the bulls came in.' By the end of the 1960s the steers and bullocks were gone from the roughstock riding in ARRA rodeos — bulls had taken over.

Plenty of rodeos make the claim of bucking bulls first but in Queensland they first made an issue of bucking bulls at Home Hill in 1954. It was in fact a World Championship Brahman Bullriding Contest but the first round was on bullocks, because there were not enough bulls to go around. It was probably the first time bulls had been openly promoted as roughstock outside of the tent shows. The 'world' competitors were New Zealanders, but Australian Brian Young won the day with Wally Woods as runner-up. They were riding bulls from Rocky Ponds Station and Fred Purdie ran the show.

It is generally agreed that Vic Gough's first ever proper ARRA National Finals Rodeo at Dude Ranch in 1959 was the first ARRA rodeo to use bulls from start to finish. The notorious Tar Baby, owned by Merv and Lindsay Payne from Eidsvold, scored eight out of eight victories that week and their bull Matador had seven out of eight victories. The only one to ride him was Doug Flanagan. Jack Frame's great bull Chute Boss, 'the arena cleaner' was also there and remained unridden. Chute Boss was also a good fighting bull. 'He'd play all day with you,' says Stuart Lear, who was bullfighting there with Bluey Bostock.

The 1960s was when contractors started collecting, quietening, training and breeding professional bucking bulls. Jack Frame of Chinchilla, Queensland, is generally regarded as the first. He provided a fearsome gang for Vic Gough's rodeo at the end of 1959 and in 1962 most of the 11 bulls nominated for the first-ever bucking bull of the year award were from Jack's string. Blackman Jacky Jacky, whom he owned with Stan Bischoff, won and Condamine rodeo committee's Matador was runner-up.

In 1962 after the Warwick Rodeo, stock contractor Pat Clarke bought Blackman Jacky Jacky and several other prominent bulls from Jack Frame. Along with Kevin McTaggart, Wally Gunn and Ken Mackay, Clarke belonged to the Border Bronco Trust, which contracted horses as well as bulls to rodeos in that area. At one stage they provided the bulls to the Sydney Royal, where they so outclassed the riders that the qualified ride time had to be cut back to five seconds. The bulls have never looked back, and the high-quality professional bucking stock impacted on roughriding times, which have moved from 10 to 8 seconds.

Up north in Darwin American ex-pat Ray Townsend got together a string for his Circle-T rodeos. Down south Bert Hall added bulls to his horses. At Geelong, in Victoria, Bill McCann and Jock Lincoln also put together a string of bulls. Bulls have gone from strength to strength.

Roping

Bronco branding (with paint brushes, not hot irons) has been a sport in cattle country since the late 1980s. Contrary to popular belief, years ago Australian stockmen often used ropes when they branded — 30-foot green-hide ropes. They used to drop them over a beast's head, haul it up to a post in the yard, rope its fore- and hind legs, then brand it. Lindsay Black says: 'Some of those old blackfellas up in the Territory, they were the greatest bronco ropers I've ever seen in my life. They would never miss. They would just flick the rope over, over the backs of cows, out backwards, left- and right-handed.' 'Bronco Branding' as a method died out as yards fell down and new ones were built with crushes and cradles.

In the ARRA rodeo arenas of the 1950s roping was the fifth standard event — either wild horse racing, steer roping or wild cow milking. Most of the 50s cowboys could swing a rope but the Crottys were peerless. Steer, calf and team roping, as we know it today, was not properly introduced into our rodeo arenas until the 1960s. By the end of the decade they were standard events. ARRA cowboys gave exhibitions to promote these American roping events to try and popularise them. Vic Gough remembers: '...we had a job getting it going... Once Bonny and I were in Tasmania; Bonny was heading and I was heeling. We did a good run and the announcer said, "Well, ladies and gentlemen, that was a really good exhibition. Just a pity the other guy missed his head." That's what we were up against.'

Early time-event stock was even more motley than the bucking stock. They often used to ride the same bullocks that they bulldogged. Sometimes they were straight out of the scrub, had never been in a rodeo ring and would hardly notice a cowboy hanging off their horns.

The greatest stars of the ARRA rodeo arenas in the 60s were Bonny Young, Barry Gravener and Jim McGuire. Tough as these men were, roping was tricky. Barry Gravener recalls an embarrassing moment at Warrnambool in Jack Gill's portable rodeo arena.

I was on a horse with a mind of its own. I couldn't ride much, and I went out and I rode. And I was going round over my head with the rope and I let it go and I caught the arena post. And I pulled the arena down. True. Pulled all one side of the arena down. So that's how good a roper I was. Jack Gill was going to shoot me.

With time events — steer wrestling (bulldogging), roping and barrel racing — no matter how talented you are or how hard you practise, you're only as good as the horse under you. As time events grew, so did the need for well-trained, fast horses. In the 1950s and 60s most cowboys still only travelled one horse that did everything — dogged, hazed, roped and picked up if need be. If there was a campdraft on, well, they might have a go at that, too. Most people of his generation name Vic Gough as the first cowboy to transport a bulldogging pony around the circuit. In 1956 he bought Trumpet, so-called because he was a 'very snorty little horse', but apparently there were other bulldogging horses on the circuit before then. Noel Bottom had a horse called Panther and Allan Woods and Allan Bennett had Mick. These horses became part of the family and were stars of the arena. Chilla Seeney had Baby Doll for roping and dogging and Chico for campdrafting and lairising. Wally Woods had Toots, Ray Crawford had Pal the Palomino and Buck, Bonny Young and Bo Crawford had Joker, then Bonny had Jake, and Darcy Twohill shared Tim with Norm Woods. The cowboys all tended to share each other's horses and paid a third of any winnings to the owner who fed and travelled them.

The calf, steer and team ropers didn't really hit their strides until the 1970s and 80s. Those records are now held by Shane Kenny with 7.8 seconds for the rope and tie at Narrandera in 1999 and Guy McPhee and Jamie Knox with 5.0 seconds for the team roping at Kyabrama in 1999. With specialised horses, time-events boxes and lots of practice, long-held bulldogging records started to get broken. In 1967 Barry Gravener broke through the four-second mark with a 3.4 performance at Port Augusta. Barry Jones then smashed that with a 2.4, equalling the then world record, at Wandoan in 1971. That record was set before the introduction of the barrier start so it cannot be broken in Australia now. But since the barrier start the ARRA record for bulldogging (which is now called steer wrestling) is 2.8 seconds set by Danny McGuire at Tumbarumba in 1986.

A thousand miles behind you, a thousand more to go

Despite the radical changes to the rules of the sport, the lifestyle of the ARRA circuit cowboys in the 1960s stayed much the same as in the 50s except that there were more of them. There were also more rodeos, more prize money and the added incentive that to be Australian Champion you had to win the most points all year. Cowboys still needed to be able to pick up casual work here and there. Many were butchers and boners and could get good money at the meatworks. Some broke in, bought, sold and trained horses, like the talented Crawfords and Jim McGuire.

Bonny Young looks back on his itinerant working life:

We had our seasonal work. When we went north we worked in the meatworks. When we went out west I used to get a job in the sheds ... roustabouting. I was always too sore to shear ... you always seemed to have knees that hurt and ankles that hurt and arms that hurt. Shearing was a bit out for me. Then we went south and we used to go fruit picking and we'd do all the Victorian rodeos down there ... Go into the Riverina and break in horses ... We always had work where we went in those days. It was a lot different. You'd go to Clermont rodeo and you'd pull in on a Monday or Tuesday and there'd be a couple of station owners come in, and 'You guys want a few days work?' And they'd take you out to their place and you'd do a few days work. Well, that's not around any more. You know we always worked. We had to work to support our habit — rodeoing — it was a good life.

Des 'Yogi' and Lyn Steffensen were among the happy band of full-time rodeo travellers in the 60s. Des won the Australian bareback title in 1968 and was pretty handy in all the time events. They travelled with their daughter and hauled a horse and a pet kangaroo. Des says: 'Jeez, you can fit a lot in a caravan. Ray Crawford designed it for us. You gotta live in a caravan before you can build your own.' Lyn's heart's desire was a wardrobe that hung shirts properly, not squished in sideways. She used to press trousers by folding them carefully under the mattress for a day.

Vehicles were getting better but roads were still dreadful. Reg Gale states: 'No-one ever made it anywhere without bloody car trouble.' There were always delays,

178

mechanical or climatic, or someone's horse or cat or kids got away and had to be tracked down. Someone else would be in hospital so they'd wait for them. Families set up bases so their children could go to school for a few months. Otherwise they had to study by correspondence, which was difficult on the road. The Victorian rodeos could all be done on weekends and they often flew to Tasmania for weekend rodeos from Melbourne. In Queensland they could do all the coastal and central rodeos from a base in Townsville and then head out for the western run.

Once on a run they often didn't work between rodeos. It became one long cross-country gambling session. Even for the champs money remained tight. Marg McGuire and her husband Jim were down to £6 one time at Mt Isa. They'd packed up and were going to Winton Rodeo from where, if they had no luck, they could just make it home. Jim suddenly decided to go to Darwin Rodeo and jumped in with some of the others:

So I gave Jimmy £3 and I kept £3, and if he didn't win anything that's all the money we'd have for fuel to get going and get home. I had food in the caravan ready to go ... So June Crawford and I, for entertainment, we'd walk up to the mines. They'd have free movies on, and we sat in the stand with the kids and watched the movies. I think they were gone for about a week and they came back and he had won £80. Oh, ho. Rich!

In every town from one end of Australia to the other, you had to know where the best places were to stay, eat, wash, shop on the cheap, get stock feed and mechanical parts, fuel up and borrow tools. Wally Woods and 'Crawfy' (Ray Crawford) were the two to beat for the best spot to camp at showgrounds. You needed to know where the next fuel was, the state of the road and the whereabouts of the creeks and rivers so you didn't get caught by them. Stock contractors had even more constraints. They couldn't drive for 24 hours non-stop. They had to know where they could unload their stock every now and then to feed, water and stretch their legs and where the stockyards were in each town so they could unload and camp overnight. It helped to be a farrier, a vet and a mechanic or at least to be a whiz at changing tyres. It was also handy to know what the police were like in every town, who the feisty locals were and which of the local girls had lots of big brothers.

The rodeo contingent were expected everywhere they went but belonged nowhere, which is why they stuck together like glue. Years ago when the showmen came through town, there was a saying, 'Lock up your chooks and your daughters'. To a certain extent the rodeo tribe were similar, but generally they were a bonus to every community. The cowboys got involved and worked with local people to put on the show; they entertained them; and they filled the town to overflowing once a year, which was good for business. They also broke in the horses and worked at whatever needed doing. They were predominantly country people — down-to-earth, well-mannered and principled. Unless desperate or drunk they stayed within the law. They enjoyed good old-fashioned fun and weren't shy of a fight or even an all-out brawl, if that's what the locals wanted. The cowboys numbered a lot of good boxers. The most famous, of course, was Chilla Seeney, but he preferred to avoid most fights unless they were in a tent and involved a deal.

Joe Napier has a story from Winton:

Man, {they} just took to cowboys at a general pace — twenty-five black eyes; me, one, and twenty-four other cowboys all had black eyes. It was humorous. Bloke hit Charlie Newton in the mouth. He was smoking a big cigar. Sparks went everywhere. Charlie yells, 'Get him, get him!' and I start laughing. I thought it was funny. Bloke hit him fair in the mouth and this big cigar went pphhhtt!

Cowgirls

Although cowboys' girlfriends and wives couldn't ride in the rodeos, they didn't sit around all day. Marg McGuire:

By the time you finished travelling you had two kids to catch up on a week's {correspondence} school each. And then you had your rodeos on the weekend. And then you worked your horses during the week. The washing and ironing and cooking and everything, you'd catch up on, so you didn't have a lot of time to yourself. It was a pretty tough life if you weren't used to roughing it a bit. A lot of people used to think, 'Oh, it's real romantic. Oh, gee, it'd be great,' you know. But, see, I think you've sort of got to be a certain breed to handle it, got to be able to do without and rough it and not have the comforts like you do at home.

But above all it was the constant travelling that took its toll. It was a long time before air-conditioning, pumping car stereos, truck stops with everything a body could need, fast-food chains in every second town and mobile phones became commonplace.

Marg McGuire continues:

When I quit rodeoing all I needed was some smart bugger to come along and say let's have a caravan holiday. I said I'd drop 'em. After 18 years living in a caravan I reckoned that was all I needed, a caravan holiday.

With all the charging around the countryside keeping itinerant house and home for their husbands, children, horses, ponies, cats, dogs and various hangers-on, it's amazing the rodeo wives had time for anything else. Yet in 1967 they formed the Girl's Rodeo Association (GRA) at Myrtleford Rodeo in Victoria. Mrs Remfrey recalls: 'It was in a little old tin shed. Norma and Lou McTaggart and Jo Griffith and myself and daughter ... Before that girls did have barrel races, but there was no committee, just the open barrel race.' Other founding members were Marg McGuire, Margaret Gill, Cheryl McTaggart, Carol Height and Anne Crawford, who became the first president. There were five directors and Elsa McMartin came on as secretary. Although Elsa had never ridden a horse in her life, her daughter Tracey became one of the most successful cowgirls of the 70s.

Initially the GRA's aims were to promote barrel racing, in which each contestant gallops around three strategically placed barrels — in a cloverleaf pattern — and back to the finish line. The fastest horse wins. Once barrel racing had been established they introduced goat tying, steer undecorating and breakaway roping — all ladies-only events. They didn't reintroduce roughriding. Margaret Gill told Andrea Lemon: 'We spoke about getting it back in but there wasn't enough women interested, even in our association, to warrant trying to get it back in as a spectator sport.' Women now team-rope with the men as well.

1968 was the GRA's first year of competition. Pam Schiller won the national title for the barrel race and she won it the following year as well. The Schillers are now one of those families whose names are synonymous with rodeo in Australia. Pam was married to Des Schiller's cousin, Paul. Des Schiller was a good cowboy who became a highly respected horseman, breeder, trainer and pick-up man. His two daughters, Tania and Vicki Schiller, are two of the best cowgirls in the country today.

So the late 1960s saw the return of women to the rodeo ring, and they have never looked back. The women have maintained their own independent association while working in conjunction with the ARRA. There is a high level of dedication and competition, the horses are extremely skilled and valuable, and although the prize money is never as much as the men's events, the satisfaction of winning is. Women add class and style to the rodeo arena, as well as dynamic action, and barrel racing remains one of the most popular events on the rodeo program with the spectators.

Bushies

During the 40s and 50s the bushmen's carnivals grew rapidly in size and number. The Northern New South Wales Bushman's Carnival Association eventually grew to become The Australian Bushman's Carnival and Rodeo Association.

In the 1960s bushmen's carnivals outnumbered ARRA rodeos. The carnivals had changed little. Some had embraced new rodeo events, such as the bareback, the bulldogging and roping, but they still ran flag and bending races, hacking classes, stockhorse classes and a bullock ride and perhaps a bronc ride. Their only standard event, albeit unofficially, was campdrafting, which the ARRA did not run during their rodeos any more. The smaller carnivals might just have a steer ride but the bigger ones in the north-west drovers' towns, like Brewarrina, Moree and Walgett, would run a full-scale rodeo. Most ARRA stars, including Ken Coleman and Errol Lather, started with the Bushies. It was for many years considered to be the training ground for the Pros.

Barry Gravener recalls:

Years ago if you went outside the ARRA you were called a scab, like the wharfies now. Very few did it because, well, you only had the Bushmen's Carnival and the Pros . . . There was a damn lot of difference between the ability of the ARRA and the Bushmen's Carnival, they were not in the same class . . . They didn't have to mark out, they didn't have to spur, that sort of thing. They were just a bushmen's turnout, which was great. That was what it was all about, you know, for the ringer on the station.

In November 1963 Wally Woods, the then president of the ARRA, instigated a high-level meeting with key ABCA figures, including Arthur Winter and Vivian Sharpe and riders' representatives John Stanton and Aubrey Tribe. They wanted more active collaboration. Many issues were canvassed, including saddles, insurance and fees. There was a friendly atmosphere at the meeting. Wally Woods even admitted that the ARRA had been in the wrong when the previous working relationship had broken down a decade earlier.

But the essential differences between the two associations were cultural, ideological and philisophical. The ABCA felt that in many ways the ARRA membership rules 'destroyed the Australian spirit of "anyone have a go"', and they were strongly opposed to added entries, which denied charities money, and to overt American influence. The ARRA wanted to be full-time professionals. They believed in their elitism as they felt it was important for cowboys to have something to aspire to, which would in turn lift the sport. Campdrafting was also a sticking point. The ARRA were not interested in running anything not classed as rodeo, whereas the ABCA 'catered for all events, including children's' and furthermore campdrafting was 'essentially Australian, and amateur, and must be encouraged and maintained'. They saw the ARRA rules as 'hard and fast, irrespective of venue' while ABCA rules were 'elastic ... to provide for certain slight modifications as applicable to local conditions'. And the bottom line for the ABC was: 'Camp-drafting events were of considerably more importance than rodeo events.' It was an amicable meeting but at the end of it the impasses remained.[2]

Despite digging their heels in against nearly every new idea and condition advocated by the ARRA, slowly the Bushies have adopted all the changes. In 1969, with their backs against the wall financially, the ABCA finally introduced membership fees. John Stanton holds badge number 1. They also changed from the poley saddle to the international saddle in 1975. With contractors supplying both associations with the same quality bucking stock for the last 20 years, roughstock riders from the Pros and the Bushies are on a reasonably even par these days.

Back in the 1960s rodeo riders among the ABCA champions included all-rounder Aub Tribe, John Stanton — who had his last bronc ride in 1968 at Sydney's Easter Show, Graham Amos, Mick Ward, David Weekly — a stylish bronc rider, and Les Buckingham — a great athlete who 'could ride a bareback horse inside out'. Then there were the Caban boys, led by elder brother, Lionel.

In the firmament

The ARRA's strategies to make Australians internationally competitive worked. Australians started competing in New Zealand, America, Canada and Brazil. Queensland's Doug Flanagan was the first Australian to win a major world-renowned title when he won the bareback riding at the famous Calgary Stampede in Canada in 1964. In 1969 West Australian bareback whiz, Jim 'Digger' Dix, became the first Australian to qualify for the ultimate, the Professional Rodeo Cowboy's Association (PRCA) national finals in the United States. He was followed by Darryl Kong, who qualified for the saddle bronc in 1972. With aeroplanes frequently crossing the Pacific, the international rodeo scene was now at our doorstep.

The early 1960s saw the end of a decade-long domination of ARRA rodeo by the Woods brothers, Kevin and Col McTaggart, Dally Holden, Allan Bennett, Vic Gough and their peers. They retired and moved on, with occasional comebacks when they couldn't resist. Plenty, like Lindsay Black, Chilla Seeney and Buddy Gravener, kept going. The legendary Ray Crawford certainly kept going and his younger brother Bo's career took off. Jack Gill's three boys, Happy, Brian and Peter were out and about and Robin Yates and Dick White were still putting in appearances.

Like the stars of the 30s, 40s and 50s most rodeo stars of the 60s had also polished their skills in the showmen's buckjump and Wild West shows in the late 50s and early 60s. Allan Hicks, Bonny Young, Errol Lather and Barry Gravener were just four of these. But theirs was the last generation to do so as the travelling showmen, apart from the singers, the circuses and the Gills, were dead and buried by the end of the decade.

Happy Gill went on to be the pre-eminent stock contractor and rodeo producer in Australia. He and his sons, John, Jason and Jarrad, are still on the road from one end of the country to the other, practically 365 days a year. Peter Gill and his sons, Peter, Denna and Clay (he also has a daughter, Jane), are also among the leading contractors. And, of course, there are Malcolm and Eddie Gill — Brian's sons. There are currently close to fifty professional stock contractors, subcontractors and bucking stock breeders in Australia. They include Gary McPhee — who is up there at the top with Happy, Ron Woodall and sons, Brian Fish, Noel Fraser and sons, the Remfrey family, Kevin Kasper, Kerry Hall, Frank Biddle and George Hempenstall, with Campbell Frame and the Johnson brothers for bulls.

The incredible Bonny Young, Barry Gravener and Jim McGuire are the greats of the 60s. For the first half of the decade Barry and Bonny were ridiculously out in front. Barry Gravener said:

> *Bonny Young is the best all-round rider I have ever seen ... he could go out and look pretty, didn't matter what he did. If he rode a saddle horse, a bareback horse, even riding bulls, he always looked part of the animal. Bonny could rope, he could steer wrestle. He wasn't a very big man but, oh, he was solid. He was just unique. Everything he did was good to watch.*

John Skinner remembers: 'Bonny Young. When I was a kid, I don't know if he was above God or below God, but he was right up there with him.' In 1964 Barry won the all-round from Bonny by $1.80 (dollars equalled points). On occasions Bonny beat Barry by about the same. Then the phenomenally tough Jim McGuire, 'the Iron Man', came along and beat them both. As Mrs Remfrey said: 'Toes-in-Jim: he was a sticking plaster.' Barry Gravener was the first king of the bulls. According to photographer Mike Kenyon, he simply looked like he was made of steel. He dominated bullriding, with Bonny, Maurie Height and Barry Jones his main contenders.

Allan Hicks was the star of the bareback along with riders like Headly Parter, Peter Gill, Des Steffensen, Richie Fraser, Jim Dix and later Ross Piper. Don Hafemeister did the three roughstock events and won the national title for bareback in 1966. Brian McPherson and Bob Hocking were two great cowboys who did all three roughstock events and steer wrestled. Darcy Twohill and Max McTaggart were both capable all-rounders who could also throw a rope. Darby McMartin threw them and made them. Trevor Christensen, who won his first open bullock ride at 13 at Gympie, won the steer wrestling title in 1963, was another all-rounder — 'handy' as they say. His thick black-rimmed glasses only added to his considerable character. His son Tom, now one of our best saddle bronc riders, won Warwick rodeo in 1998. But no-one won anything until Jim McGuire had had his turn. No-one underestimated him — he was 'The Toughest Man'.

There was also the contingent from Footscray, a colourful, inner-western Melbourne suburb that was also home to the cattle and horse saleyards and to Norm Cakebread. Footscray youngsters would head to Norm's stables every Sunday to muck around and get bucked off. In the late 1940s and 1950s these local lads included Norm's two sons, Norm Jnr and Graham; Ron Boardman, first president of the ARRA; Ron Anderson, president of the ARRA from 1983–87; Les Turner, who now trains trotting horses; Norm 'Smoky' Dawson, nicknamed after the singer, who won the ARRA bullock riding championship in 1948; Peter Armstrong, who became a stuntman; Joe Raynor, who became a good bronc rider and pick-up man; and Stuart Lear, who became a trick-rider.

In the 60s the city cowboys, led by the Footscray lads, became quite a force. Over time Ron Anderson became known to the next generation of Footscray youngsters as 'the Cowboy'. 'They used to come to my place as kids,' he says. He took a group of them to Romsey Rodeo in the mid–50s and, without telling them, entered them all in the steer ride. Allan Hicks and Johnny Lax were two of these. There were also Reg McNair, who lived across the road from Ron Anderson, Kenny Hargreaves and Keith 'Doogie' Bourke, a much-loved character. Keith later became a racehorse trainer. Brian Swift, Phil Guest, Wally Dalton and Kerry Jacobsen were also from the neighbourhood. The latter went to the USA with Allan Hicks and Graham Mathrick in 1964.

Brian Gill, Tom Cannon and Bo Crawford were all favourites with the fans. Doug 'Dougie' Spann was another good cowboy, one of the A-Team who competed in the Ampol-sponsored World Series in 1967.³ There was Dallas Powell from Springsure, Reg Wiles, Noel Toomey from Julia Creek, Les White from South Australia and Victorian Ken Lloyd, who won far more than his fair share. Brian Woodhouse, Ossie Cottam and West Australian Ron Lacey were 1960s contenders.

A couple of excellent cowboys left Australia for good. Myrtleford's Bob Hocking won three state titles and the national title for the saddle bronc in 1963. He went to Canada in the mid–1960s, where he competed successfully (and in the USA), married and settled. Queenslander Doug Flanagan did likewise. He won the bareback at Mt Isa's first invitation rodeo in 1959 and took out the national titles in the bareback and steer wrestling in 1961 before going to Canada.

Then there was the likes of Queensland's Garney Beresford and Sydney's Des Dessaix, who both joined the ARRA in 1961 but made more of an impact in the 1970s. Beresford started off as an all-rounder, but hit his stride with the roughstock events, particularly the saddle bronc in the 1970s and then the roping in the 1980s. Des Dessaix was the same. He won his first title for steer wrestling in 1973. Johnny Raaen, who won the first-ever Rookie title in 1967, became a good bullrider in the 70s, and Tom Kenny, who was Rookie of the Year in 1969 and a great athlete, also rode plenty of bulls. Billy Nichols was a great talent, as were John Brearley and Ross Piper, not to mention the next decade's two biggest stars, Ken Coleman and Gary McPhee, who both joined the ARRA in 1965. 'Coley' had rodeoed with the Bushies and Gary had already won what there was to be won in New Zealand before he moved across the Tasman. They were both in the money in the late 60s and started winning ARRA national titles in 1969 and 1971 respectively.

It was during the 1960s and early 70s that Australian rodeo completed its journey from the cattle camps and showmen's rope rings to the international sporting arena. They were professionals in performance and principle, if not entirely in pocket. The ARRA led the way and was prepared to lose committees and their rodeos over their demands — which they did. But they got away with their progressive yet controversial changes because they had the stars who drew the crowds. The Crawfords, McTaggarts, Bonny Young, Barry Gravener, the Gills,

Chilla Seeney and Jim McGuire all had a following and people would come from far and wide to see them ride.

The early presidents of the ARRA were Tom Willoughby (1957–59), Wally Woods (1960–64) and then the superb negotiator, Ray 'the Fox' Crawford (1965–77). They were also three of the most respected and accomplished rodeo competitors Australia has ever had. Together with their teams of directors, also all successful competing cowboys, they set about to improve the sport of rodeo, make things safer, fairer, faster, bigger, better and more entertaining. And with the stock contractors, who also got rolling in the 1960s, rodeo became more humane. These cowboys did more to improve the sport of rodeo, upgrade its standards, performance, prize money and its image than at any other time before or since.

Jim and Margaret McGuire

Poster recording a piece of Australian rodeo history

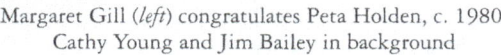

Margaret Gill (*left*) congratulates Peta Holden, c. 1980. Cathy Young and Jim Bailey in background

The legends! Brian Gill, Bonny Young and Colin McTaggart at the McTaggarts' 'Flying M' Old Timers Rodeo, early 1980s

Ken Coleman on 'Funny Face', Bundaberg Rodeo, early 1980s

Allan and Mavryn Remfrey

Ray Hermann

John 'Happy' Gill (*left*) and Gary McPhee, 1985

Brian Fish, Tasmanian all-round champion and stock contractor

Steve McCarthy presents buckle to Steve Thorn (*left*) for 1980 ARRA Bullriding Champion

Steve Gibson rides 'Miss Bouncer', 1987

Guy McPhee with the 1987 Bareback Bronc buckle for 'Toss Up', presented by Dave Johnson

Bernie Smyth Jnr on 'Rose Marie' at Warwick, 1980s

ARRA National Finals Rodeo at Warwick, mid-1980s
Left to right: (*on gates*) John Wigley, Robbie Woods, Warwick Turner and Wayne Judge; (*standing*) John Bowtell, Errol Lather, Jim Pierce, Ron Wilson, Bernie Smyth Jnr, Ray Hermann and Rick Norris; (*squatting*) Ken Coleman, Bruce Watkins and Norm Hilton

Billy Hughes roping a calf at Willomurra in the early 1980s

Tony Hecksher riding 'Buckskin Billy', Cloncurry, 1998

Scott Bloxsome, Gold Coast Rodeo, early 1980s

Vicki Gough barrel racing at the
Brisbane Exhibition Rodeo, 1990

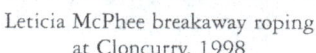

Leticia McPhee breakaway roping
at Cloncurry, 1998

Vicki Schiller barrel racing at the Adelaide Invitational Rodeo, 1997

John Osborne Jnr and Jeff Miller team roping at Warwick, 1999

1998 Hi Point WPRA champions.
Left to right: Tania Schiller (all-round), Kerry Johnson (breakaway roping) and Jaime Cottam (barrel race)

Roughstock champions, 1998.
Left to right: Scott Fraser, Simon Burke and Troy Dunn

Shane Kenny, time-event champion, at the APRA National Finals Rodeo Tamworth, 1997

Dean Pace takes on 'Bambi', Tumbarumba, 1996

Darren Brandenburg atop 'Chainsaw', ARRA National Finals, 1987

Champion all-round cowboy, Robert McPhee, picking up champion roughstock rider Gavin 'Jack' Woodall

Dave Back, 1998 APRA Bullfighter of the Year

Three of the best protection clowns in the business. *From left:* Darrel Diefenbach, Graham Borghero and Clint 'Wombles' Dolan

Graham Borghero

7

RODEO TODAY

K is the Kick that is rather un-nerving,

When it happens to come between bucking and swerving

L is the Lurch when you almost come over,

And also the Laugh when by Luck you recover.

A land in crisis

THE DAYS WHEN THE horse was king, and 'great horseman' or woman was the highest compliment a person could get, are now long gone. The gradual demise of horses, horsemen, stockmen and drovers began in the 1960s. The mechanisation of the cattle industry saw motorbikes, then planes and choppers replace the horse for stockwork, and road trains began their takeover from drovers and rail to move cattle to market.

It depended on individual methods, location and finances but in general — in open country — horses were redundant by the end of the 1970s. The men went to town — to the pubs or mines, or they worked for councils building better roads for road trains. Hundreds of thousands of horses went to the slaughterhouses — and became pet food. There is no ducking the fact that mechanisation and advances in technology are job-takers, but other factors were involved.

In the 1960s wool prices dropped and more graziers turned to cattle. Large multinational companies invested in the industry and from 1965–73 Australian cattle numbers rose from roughly 14 million to 32 million. The glut in the market caused cattle prices to crash in 1974. World markets closed, exports plummeted, and it wreaked havoc on Australian cattlemen. Calves were being sold for $1 and cows for $10; people couldn't even afford to muster their cattle. Many families were forced off the land and several years of economic disaster followed. The full sociological impact of the crash has never been assessed but

Australian horse and stockmanship skills, tradition and culture were among the casualties; stockmen's wages were the first go.

In the 1960s and 70s the vast open-range pastoral holdings of the inland, north and north-west had plenty of wild cattle. The development of the high-protein, low-fat US hamburger industry provided a market for bulls. It was time to clean the scrubbers out of the rough country. Large-scale musters of wild cattle were ideally suited to the speed and accessibility of small planes and helicopters. A man in the air can see and get to places where no man on the ground can. Wild cattle are cunning and are experts at camouflage so mustering them — particularly bulls — is dangerous on horseback. It's also dangerous for horses to gallop in rough country — hidden gullies and logs have caused more injury to man and horse than hell-bent bulls ever will. Choppers were faster, safer and more productive — where horses and 'bull men' might catch 20 scrub bulls a day, choppers caught hundreds.

Then there was the enormous and enormously successful brucellosis and tuberculosis eradication campaign (BTEC). During the 1970s and 80s the Federal government committed hundreds of millions of dollars to testing and immunising every single beast in Australia. The clean sweeps of stations required by government testers were impossible without choppers. Portable stockyards also arrived with BTEC. They signalled the end of many labour-intensive 'open range' methods of stock handling, as had the introduction of cradles for branding.

Over the last thirty years millions more acres have been cleared for grazing. It's been out with trees and scrub and in with grass and motorbikes.

Droughts, floods and plagues always have and always will batter the rural community, but the odds of surviving them financially have been practically annihilated by the short-sighted policies of successive governments. The realities behind the catchcries of 'economic rationalism' and 'global economy' have hit the rural sector hard. With too few voters, the rural sector has been sidelined by urban political agendas. Constant fluctuations in commodity prices have always been part of the grazier's gamble. Increasing foreign ownership and control of our beef industry — from station gate to consumer plate — has also increased the odds against them.

In 1999 the cattle market has 'picked up'! But the cattlemen are only getting 20 cents more per head than they were 20 years ago. This hardly reflects the increases in their expenses. As the cattlemen see it, in 1979 it took 29 steers to buy a Toyota Landcruiser and six to buy a motorbike; in 1999 it takes 103 and 20.[1] Labour costs have risen and rural fuel prices continue to spiral ever upwards.

In 40 years Australia's population has jumped from 10 to 18 million. However, the population in the bush has roughly halved. In 1995 there were 100 000 less people employed on the land than in 1950. In the pastoral zones the number of individual stations has dropped from 6000 to 4000 in the last 20 years. Independent stations are run by husbands and wives and families, employing only as they need for seasonal work. Only the big corporate stations employ full-time workers these days.

Youth unemployment in some rural towns and cities runs as high as 40 per cent; and alcoholism is epidemic. Australia's (white Anglo-Celtic) rural men have among the highest suicide rates in the world. Graziers' sons and daughters are opting for lives in towns and cities and young people in general are leaving the back country in droves. These are hard cold facts but the spirit in the bush is, surprisingly, alive and well. Rodeo's cultural and historical context may have disappeared along with the stockmen and drovers, but as a sport it now keeps those traditions alive, and helps keep horses out of zoos.

A long time coming

Rodeo is intrinsic to the cattle industry; historically the two have borne the trials and tribulations of wars, droughts, depressions and recessions together. But contemporary rodeo has not only survived the industries struggles over the past 25 years, it has prospered. This is because it has cut its reliance on the cattle stations and community and become a sport for everyone.

As the Wild and Western breeding grounds of great bucking horses and the riders to ride them changed their methods, rodeo was already moving away from tradition and transforming itself in two ways. Firstly stock contractors proliferated, collected, bred, trained and travelled professional bucking stock. This also resulted in quality not quantity. Secondly a new breed of contestants emerged, not bushmen, or stockmen, or even horsemen — but rodeo cowboys and cowgirls — athletes — from all walks of life.

By the end of the 1960s the ARRA (the Pros) had taken rodeo out of the 'Wild West' and created the sport of rodeo as we know it today. The 1970s proved successful years for rodeo, with plenty of contestants, spectators and good prize money. Television coverage and profiles in popular magazines helped to attract people to the sport from everywhere. The majority of contestants still came from rural towns, properties and stations but a good number hailed from the cities as well. Contestants whose families had been in the sport for years found themselves mixing with all sorts. A 'rodeo cowboy' or cowgirl became where your head and your heart are, not your experience or background.

Rodeo schools facilitated this progression when they started to appear in the 1970s. Darryl Kong, Garney Beresford, Peter Gill and Jim Dix were among the first to run bronc riding schools. By the 1980s everyone was running them and now most rodeo contestants start off by attending schools. Gib Bloxsome's son Scott started in the Bushies in the mid–60s, joined the ARRA in 1968 and became a major star in the 1970s. A saddle-bronc and all three time-event hand, he says:

> I came in just on the turn. When I started there wasn't many practice arenas around, wasn't many good (time-event) horses but during that time that's when things started to get going. Now these young kids grow up, mate they've got it made. They can just waltz in to somebody's school, see techniques have changed, people have been to the states and there's videos out, blokes can learn in bloody six months, it used to take us six years, ten years, that's a change. A young kid now, he can be tough, some of these kids, they're tough.

During the 70s there were around 50 or 60 full-time ARRA contestants on the road at any one time, including families. Like those who had gone before them they supplemented their winnings with itinerant work. Cowboys could now fly to rodeos, enabling them to do two or three per weekend, although cowgirls and time-event hands still had to truck it with their horses. Roping really took off in the 70s and 80s and standards improved tremendously.

Rodeo in Australia has become a serious and highly competitive sport. Most contestants now specialise in only one or two events — either timed events or roughriding events. Many roughstock riders move on to roping as they get older but plenty of time-event rodeo cowboys have never been near the bucking chutes. Today's 'All-Round Champion' only has to do two events to be eligible for the title. Entry fees have risen which also accounts for specialisation. Gone are the five-event men — those all-round bushmen — who hedged their bets across the events in the hope of winning something.

As the kind of rodeo contestants changed, so did their priorities. The ARRA was a national association, to be the champion you had to do some serious miles. You had to dedicate your life to it. This ensured it was the elite association with the highest standard of competition. The new breed included plenty of people who didn't want to travel full time, they wanted to work and rodeo on weekends. Committees were also looking for alternatives to the strict demands dictated and imposed by the ARRA, particularly after the added entry rule was enforced in 1968. The ABCA provided for casual cowboys and conditions and were flexible with committees but it was not enough. This was the impetus for the rise of factions which changed Australian rodeo dramatically.

Diversification

Many new regional and amateur associations and splinter groups have sprung up over the past 30 years. None have the cultural and historical roots of the Bushmen's Carnival or Rough Rider's Associations, nor do they share the same idealism or principles.

The first new rodeo association, the South East Queensland Rodeo Rider's Association (SEQRRA), was established in 1966 by a breakaway group of cowboys, those with jobs and family commitments. Among them were Jim Greenaway, Des Gilbey, Kerry Hall, Buddy McLaughlin, Barry Brandenburg and John Osborne Snr. The SEQRRA absorbed a lot of the smaller shows initially, unaffiliated agricultural shows that might have had a bullock ride or a bronc ride, but they gradually gained other rodeo committees over the years. They provided more junior events and a less competitive field for up-and-coming talent. Their rules and regulations were more flexible and standards and conditions negotiable to give struggling or stubborn committees a break. The new association affiliated so many rodeos from all over Queensland, New South Wales and even Western Australia that they changed their name to the National Rodeo Association (NRA). Still based in south-east Queensland the NRA run about 50 rodeos a year and adding another 50 run under the other associations, that region has the highest concentration of rodeos in Australia.

Frank Green is the most legendary NRA cowboy, winning no less than six NRA all-round titles during the 1980s. Like the ABC contestants before them, NRA cowboys and cowgirls tended to rise through the ranks of their association and then join up with the pros. Frank Green did exactly that and won the ARRA bareback and all-round titles in 1987 before moving on.

In 1982 the even more committee-friendly Queensland Amateur Rodeo Circuit (QARC) was formed. By 1997 they had 60 rodeos spread over a vast area of central and western Queensland. QARC members are committees not the competitors and they set minimal conditions — the antithesis of the ARRA. Billy Johnson has been the QARC all-round champion cowboy for the last eight years.

Numerous other regional rodeo associations are dotted around the country. A few isolated communities run their annual rodeos with no association at all but most affiliate with someone for the insurance they provide. Among the smaller groups are the Central Rodeo Cowboy's Association (central and northern Queensland), the Northern Cowboy's Association (Northern Territory) and the West Coast Rodeo Circuit (Western Australia). In the 1970s the United Tasmanian Rodeo Committees ran 16 ARRA rodeos a year, and they still run plenty of their rodeos in Tasmania — the 'Island Rodeo Circuit'.

Then there's Colin McTaggart — one of the few 'old legends' still in the game — who runs Rodeo Administrative Services, which produces roughstock competitions. The bullriders have at least two associations — Steve Thorn's Australian Professional Bull Riders Association and Championship Bull Rider's Association, whose principals include Troy Dunn and Peter Blackall. The ropers, headed by Gary and Stuart McPhee, Jeff Miller and John Osborne Jnr, have formed the Australian Team Roper's Association, which fosters talent and runs jackpots. There is also the Aboriginal and Torres Strait Islanders Corp for Rodeo Riders, Workers and Sport. The National Rodeo Council (NRC) is an umbrella organisation attempting to unify all the different groups. The bigger associations have now initiated state circuits so that their members can win championship buckles without having to travel nationally. But of course they still run their national pro rodeo tour and national championships, which are the buckles to win. Over and above all the associations there are scores of independent promoters and producers, who affiliate with someone for an event but more or less do their own thing. It's certainly a far cry from rodeo's first official 20 years when it was simply 'the Pros' or 'the Bushies'

The ARRA definitely lost some of its power base with the rise of these smaller associations but it staunchly continues to promote A-grade competitions and high standards of professionalism. Wherever possible it remains true to the concept of 'performance rodeos', streamlined down to three or four hours. Excess contestants and junior events, which are being introduced, are generally run in the 'slack' — before the gates open — so that the ticket-buying public sees only the best action from the best riders and the best stock. Pro rodeos must run at least the six standard men's events and they usually run two for women. The entry fees are higher than other associations but their added back entry fee is also the highest. Judges, contractors and rodeo clowns must be approved and they maintain a full rodeo policy and do not (officially) condone or affiliate bullrides, roughstock-only events and roping jackpots.

Forging ahead

Meanwhile the Bushies have gone from strength to strength. Always a big association, the ABCRA has nearly 5000 members, 3000 of whom currently compete in over 200 rodeos and campdraft competitions a year. During the 1960s and 70s the ABC were reluctant to use stock contractors and the judging remained dodgy. There were even strikes and fights about the judging. Mike Kenyon recalls he once saw a rider at Taralga miss his mark-out, lose an oxbow and still score the highest. The rest of the cowboys went on strike for the rest of the rodeo. Another time he says: 'I heard one judge crack a guy off and they said, "Why'd you crack him off?" and he said, "Well, they told me I missed him last week so I got him this week".' Scott Bloxsome concurs: 'Everyone who wanted to better themselves hooked up with the ARRA because there was more competition ... they had runs, they had rules, the ABC was pretty slaphappy and they never kicked into gear until the late 70s.'

The Bushies have lifted the standards of their rodeo competition immensely over the last 20 years. Stock contractors have been providing them with high-quality, consistent challengers which has improved their riders — as they have benefited all associations. Many ABC roughriders are currently at the top of the sport internationally; they move up through the ABC then head straight overseas. Those returning from competing in the professional circuits of Canada and the USA have been keen to implement what they've seen.

Perhaps more importantly, because of the overwhelming numbers of contestants in the 70s and 80s ABC rodeo and campdrafting contests are now rarely staged together at bushmen's carnivals. Committees run either one or other or both as separate occasions. The 1998 ABCRA calendar shows a 50:50 split between campdrafts and rodeos and about 10 per cent — including a huge annual turnout at Coonamble — run both together. Rodeo events therefore no longer have to compete with campdrafting for time and resources.

As stock contractors made rodeo more expensive to run, many ABC committees dropped rodeo altogether. But although tall grass grows in bucking chutes all over

New South Wales, the committees that have stuck with rodeo now produce good-quality events and as Bushie contestants have become more professional, ABCRA rodeo has grown stronger and better every year.

An exception to the final separation of rodeo from campdraft is the Warwick rodeo. It is Australia's oldest continually running rodeo and one of its most distinguished. Warwick has always been an ARRA rodeo, their most prestigious, and the association's head office is there and yet Warwick has always run both rodeo and campdraft events together. Practically every October for 70 years campdrafters and roughriders have headed to Warwick from all over Australia to compete in the Warwick Gold Cup rodeo and campdraft competitions and the Canning Downs Camp Draft. The Warwick Gold Cup is regarded as the 'Melbourne Cup' of campdrafts. Warwick is also one of the most coveted saddle bronc wins of the year. With between 700 and 800 horses in the grounds over the weekend it is possibly the grandest assembly of Western horses, horsemen and women in Australia. In 1998, prize money for Warwick's camp draft and rodeo totalled $120 000, and over 30 000 people passed though the gates over three days.

The backlash against the ARRA was particularly noticeable in north Queensland — cattle country, which would have felt the full brunt of the beef crash in the 70s and put rodeo committees on the back foot. During the 1970s and 80s a lot of stalwart ARRA rodeo committees went ABCRA, including the famous old rodeo towns of Home Hill, Bowen, Charters Towers and Mareeba. The ABCRA now have a north Queensland circuit and the mighty Mareeba rodeo is becoming the ABC's answer to the Pros' gigantic Mt Isa Rodeo.

Mareeba and Mt Isa are among the biggest and most lucrative rodeos in Australia — in fact Mareeba promotes itself as the biggest rodeo in the Southern Hemisphere. In both towns the whole community gets behind the show with a Rodeo Queen Quest, a big street parade and a carnival with sideshows. Tourists arrive from around the world and all accommodation is booked out weeks in advance. In 1999 Mareeba boasted $50 000 in prize money and mega-champ Kevin Cooper won the all-round. In Mt Isa the same year over 800 rodeo contestants vied for $200 000 in prize money and Tania Schiller and Heath Kimber won the all-round titles, Tania for the fourth time in a row.

Kevin Cooper is one of many great cowboys and cowgirls who started in the Bushies, joined the Pros, won the title and then went back to the Bushies. Others who stayed with the Bushies include Lionel and John Caban, Les Buckingham,

Mick Ward, Graham Amos, Ron Raynor, Tom Stanton and Paul Farley. Legend has it Paul Farley rode 87 bulls straight without being bucked off. Glenn Morgan, now one of Australia's top rodeo announcers, rode in the Bushies in the 70s and 80s and won just about everything there was to be won. Peter Mills was a champion bull-dogger and bronc rider. Greg Gibson, Mark Gibb and Steve Parkinson are all Bushie greats, and some of their more notable cowgirls are Mary Morgan, Anne Stanborough, April Hanby and Dianne Parkinson. Jeff Miller, the Pros 1998 All-round Champion came up through the ABC, as did the likes of Ken 'Coley' Coleman, Errol 'the Hoon' Lather, Dudley 'Spud' Kearney and Dave 'Johno' Johnson — everyone in rodeo has a nickname.

As Bushie and Pro rodeos are not much different these days, neither is the demarcation in the capabilities of their contestants. Ex-pat ABC bronc riders Glen O'Neill and Scott Johnson are proving this time and again — both are currently killing it in the USA and Canada.

Despite all the different factions the ARRA has remained the leading body in the sport of rodeo in Australia. In 1978 big changes swept through head office when Ray Crawford, who had been president for 12 years, was not re-elected and Peter Poole, secretary for 18 years, quit. Luckily he continued to write for their newssheet and remained the organisation's official historian — Poole's thorough records are the backbone of ARRA history today. Apart from R.M. Williams, who remains as Patron, it was the end of the 'old boys' era. Cowboy Jim Bailey headed up a swankier organisation with Jim Stuart as secretary. From then on the Pros took a more businesslike, media-savvy approach. Chasing a higher profile they pursued the urban audience, courted corporate sponsorship and sought more publicity. Magazine, newspaper and television journalists obliged. Jim McGuire, Ken Coleman, Ross Piper, Tom Kenny, Gary and Cheryl McPhee, Tracey McMartin, Scott Bloxsome, Neville, Yasmin and Sharon McCarthy and Billy Hughes were their stars at the time and Ray Hermann and Bernie Smyth Jnr were about to become legends. The ARRA ran a series of hugely successful international rodeos including John Singleton's extravaganza in Sydney in 1978, another at Kooralbyn in 1979 and at Rockhampton in 1981. Crowds of between 30 000 and 60 000 roared for more.

But the bubble burst over Xmas and New Year, 1981–82, with the debacle of the World Cup rodeos held in Melbourne and Sydney. Firstly the promoters skipped the country with the takings. Then animal liberationists seized the moment, supported by an eager press. The public didn't notice the media's flagrant disregard for fact during this affair because by 1981 no-one outside the pastoral community knew anything about horses and livestock. Headlines fuelled the popular imagination and the resultant public outcry shocked the rodeo community. There had always been strict codes of practice enforced for animal welfare within the rodeo association but they were irrelevant as a defence when dealing with a misguided public. It was hard to discover that sensible talk and even proof against animal cruelty allegations were not enough when up against the media's appetite for sensationalism and the 'never let the facts spoil a good story' school of journalism.

The World Cup fiasco was an unmitigated disaster for the ARRA. Everyone lost money, particularly Australian contestants. The animal rights issue was suddenly a problem with serious long-term ramifications. But as the gurus say, out of all bad things comes good. The ARRA and the ABCRA immediately got together and worked out a plan to involve government and animal welfare bodies in drafting and sanctioning 'official' guidelines for the use of animals in their sport. This provided much needed credibility and insurance against future misunderstandings. These two rodeo associations have maintained a proactive approach in their strong, ongoing commitment to educating the public, their accountability to the RSPCA and their collaboration with various government bodies. It costs them hundreds of thousands of dollars a year but it's worth it. Rodeo's valuable livestock gained official and objective watchdogs; and the public was reassured.

Changing fortunes

Another setback was looming for the ARRA. This time the antagonist was one of its own, namely Neville McCarthy, one of the greatest time-event cowboys Australia has ever had. From Tottenham, New South Wales, he won 17 ARRA national titles during the 1970s and 80s. He also competed successfully in the USA and was the first Australian cowboy to take his horses with him. Neville's wife, Yasmin, won the GRA all-round title in 1979 and 1980.

In 1987 Neville McCarthy took the ARRA to court to challenge its policy of not allowing members to compete at any rodeos that were not affiliated with the ARRA. Over time other rodeo associations had raised their standards and their prize money to a reasonable level. Neville resented that on his way to and from

ARRA rodeos he often had to drive by the amateur rodeos — rodeos where he would undoubtably win. It was simple — his right to earn a living was the issue.

Backed by fellow members and some of the other associations, who stood to benefit from the prestige of ARRA stars competing in their events, McCarthy had been negotiating with the ARRA about an open card policy for a while. The board of the ARRA had initially refused, citing their role as the elite association (whose solidarity had got them to where they were) was to set the yardsticks, with the toughest competition and provide a goal for every Australian cowboy and cowgirl. This in turn, it was argued, was good for the sport of rodeo. But McCarthy had a strong case for freedom of trade, proven by former captain of the Australian Cricket team, Kim Hughes, who had recently won a similar case against the West Australian Cricket Association after he defied an international boycott and played in South Africa. The ARRA lost the case and were consequently required to let their members ride anywhere they pleased.

Interestingly, the Girls Rodeo Association had allowed their members to ride in all associations and vice versa way back in the 1970s. With fewer events and inferior prize money, economics had demanded it.

Once 'compulsory' was lifted the cowboys scattered to the winds. Only the old-timers showed any allegiance and they've mostly moved on now. By the 1990s any cowboy or cowgirl could be a member of all or any rodeo association and compete in their rodeos or simply turn up and pay day membership. The Neville McCarthy case effectively killed the union and destroyed the exclusivity that had made the ARRA so prestigious.

In 1988 the Australian Rough Rider's Association changed its name to the Australian Professional Rodeo Association. The organisation's aim was to accentuate the professional nature of modern rodeo and to distinguish itself from the other 'amateur' associations. The APRA felt the term 'roughriders' did not represent the time-event competitors of the sport (it did in the old days), and it had become an antiquated if not actually extinct term, which had long since been replaced by 'cowboys' or 'roughstock riders' or 'bronc riders'. And, as Steve Hilton added, the Rough Rider's Association: 'had a bit of a union stigma about it' — union being another antiquated, if not actually extinct, concept. For many old-timers, bushies and roughriders, it was seen as the last nail in the coffin for the traditions and heritage of Australian rodeo. The GRA became the women's professional rodeo association, WPRA.

The APRA will always be Australia's premier rodeo association — Australian 'rodeo' was their invention, after all — but without the undivided loyalty of the star cowboys it has lost its glamorous edge. They retain most of the biggest and most prestigious rodeos in the country and count the majority of the best riders, ropers and wrestlers in their ranks. APRA rules, regulations, standards, conditions, judges and prize money are still out in front, but the other associations are narrowing the gap. More importantly, the public don't know the difference any more, which makes Pro rodeo harder to promote.

To be fair, the Neville McCarthy case was simply a reflection of the times. Society was changing, priorities and values were changing. It was the 1980s after all and money and materialism were becoming the major factors in life. Increases in rodeo prize money were not covering the rising cost of living, let alone travelling, and by the end of the decade money was harder to get and easier to spend than ever before.

But the main problem was work. With the economic decline of the bush and rising unemployment levels in general, the casual jobs that supported the rodeo lifestyle had dried up. Scott Bloxsome tells it straight:

... back in our days {1970s}, a lot of people just rodeoed for the lifestyle, too, don't worry — socialised, chased women, drank. A lot of blokes did that. They couldn't care less; they worked, that's how it was. Money wasn't a problem in those days, get a job anywhere, pull up for a couple of months, get a heap of money go again, a lot of blokes did that. Same in the States — fellas that live hard, work hard. But that's all gone now, I'd say. No-one can afford to do it; people just set their marks and go — might do a run, but no-one can do it full-time. You've got to make a lot of money these days to survive; back then you could survive on nothing.

Rodeo's popularity levelled off in the 80s but remained perfectly respectable, however the number of full-time rodeo contestants had shrunk to maybe 15 or 20 when the recession hit at the end of the decade. It only lasted a couple of years but it was enough to take the last of the full-time cowboys and cowgirls off the road. As the quest for the elusive dollar became more urgent, the next major change to professional rodeo was also based on economic rationalism.

Now that members could ride at any local rodeos and they didn't have to travel the distance to the APRA ones, the next question was, why then should they have to travel the thousands of miles to win the most money for the national title? In 1991 the APRA recognised that increased travelling costs and living expenses had made it impossible for full-time rodeo competitors to make ends meet financially, not to mention the stock contractors, judges, announcers, pick-up men, timers, photographers, secretaries, comedy clowns and bullfighters who were all putting in big miles for virtually peanuts. Champion and former full-time APRA cowboy, Robert McPhee, agreed:

> *It's just not feasible, you can't make money out of it. I rodeo'd for, what, 14 years, lived on the road. And if I wasn't picking up I was judging, and if I wasn't judging I was picking up. And I was buying and selling horses and making a living out of it like that. And I was having trouble surviving, so how much trouble was the guy having surviving that just turned up, that wasn't being paid to be there? There's no money for them to make, there's no money at all for them ...*

The controversial solution of the boards of the APRA and WPRA was to return to the pre-1962 'sudden death' finals for their national titles. The top 15 money-earners for the year in each event were invited to an annual championship and the winners at the finals were the APRA Australian Champions. They also awarded a 'Pro Tour Champion' title for most dollars won in each event throughout the year, but they were not considered *the* champions. Gone was the hallmark of the APRA Australian Champion — the gruelling endurance test of travelling nationally to as many rodeos as possible. Gone, too, was the fact that the Australian Champion had therefore been winning consistently all year. Sudden-death finals enabled contestants to do their local rodeos and a couple of big paying ones, make the top 15 and then have a shot at the national title. The APRA had gone a full circle; their rodeos went back to being a weekend sport. As Robert McPhee says:

> *The sudden death finals are the working-man's finals and it actually works pretty good because you've got a life. You've got a life other than just being stuck on the road, rodeoing and killing yourself on the road, because I can tell you right now, it ain't the rodeos that hurt you, it's the miles that you travel getting to them. That's what wears you out.*

In 1999 after ten years of debate the APRA have changed back again. Rank-and-file members felt that lady luck played too strong a part in deciding the champion over only five or six rounds. Professional stock are pretty consistent but they can still have a bad day and worse, if you're injured in the first round and sidelined for the rest, you're out. The ABCRA and NRA have maintained their national champion as the winner of the most points (in their case not dollars) all year. But these are not national associations. The APRA contestants are now going to have to figure out how to cover their expenses.

Ray Hermann won his record seven APRA bronc riding titles in the 1980s. He had to travel hard to do it — four rodeos some weekends, six over Easter — in 1987 he rode in 96 rodeos. Ray flew everywhere back then but he says:

You wouldn't now, dammit. Even if I won the same amount of things I could never do that now because it's too dear to travel. You can't travel as hard; it's altogether different now. Some young fella starting off now, he'd want to be real real good to travel hard ... the prize money has only gone up a little bit. Back in the early 80s it was $400 or $500 to win and you don't get much more than that now.

Making a living

No cowboy has ever been accused of doing it for the money, but in the 1990s, they don't travel any more because they simply can't afford to. Entry fees can be anywhere between $50 and $130 but average at about $70 per event. Add fuel, food and 'entertainment' costs and you're talking an expensive weekend for one person in one event.

In 1998 the APRA Pro Tour all-round champion was Victorian roper, Jamie Knox — 'Pro Tour' meaning he had won the most money that year — just under $24 000, not including the national finals. That $24 000 doesn't go very far in a year especially when you have to travel thousands of miles, pay entry fees — in Knox's case in two events — and provide for and transport horses. Add a family to support, rent or a mortgage and you've got Buckley's. In 1998 the average winnings for the top 20 APRA cowboys (at APRA rodeos) was about $10 000; only the top nine APRA cowboys won more than that, excluding the finals.

It's even worse for the women. The WPRA Pro Tour all-round champion in 1998 was Victorian barrel racer and roper, Tania Schiller. She won $16 500 at APRA rodeos (not including the finals) and that was a record. Only two women won more than $10 000 that year and the average for the top 20 women was $5000. Because of the nature of their events all cowgirls have to cart and care for their horses along the way. The average annual winnings of Vicki and Tania Schiller, two supreme cowgirl talents, are between $10 000 and $15 000 each, with a few thousand more from ABCRA rodeos depending on how many they do.

For Robert McPhee, who's been a rodeo cowboy for 35 years, the main change to rodeo is that nowadays 'it's a business not a lifestyle'. Interestingly this reflects what is happening in the pastoral industry where graziers are grappling with the same economic realism. What was once a way of life, hard yakka but in your own time, now has to be run as a serious business or else you'll go under. Says Robert McPhee:

> *You've got to look at the feasibilities, how much money you can win, how far to go, what you can do, what you can't do. But when you get like me, you just love it. It doesn't matter what it costs, you just go and do it.*

The glamour of bulls

Since the early 1990s bullriders have been promoting their sport independently of rodeo. Bullrides, 'bulloramas' and 'bullmanias' are hugely popular with the public, and hence the sponsors, simply because bulls are magnificent and awesome in action. Australia's oldest roughrider, Dan Edwards, says horses are for him and bulls were made to eat not ride, but he adds: 'I love the bullriding, I love it as a spectacle — it's beautiful. They're a mighty spectacle you've gotta give it to them and some of those young fellows that are riding them are definitely mad.' Bullriding has become the glamour event of rodeo because it's the gladiator event. As Lester Cain says, 'When I was rodeoing (in the 60s) the saddle bronc riders got all the girls, now it's the bullriders.' For bullriders it's not *if* you are going to get hurt, it's *when* and how bad. The general public can be ghoulish, especially children who are the first up on the fence to gawk when someone gets badly injured. Stock contractor Allan Remfrey remembers a conversation he had after professional bucking bulls were first used at Mt Isa Rodeo:

> *I was up at Mt Isa a few weeks later, I was getting my tax done and the office girl said to me, she said, 'I didn't like the bullride, Allan'. I said 'Didn't you?' She said, 'Nuh, because those bulls only jump out there, buck, throw the rider off and just walk back. They've got no kill in them'. That's what she said. You know, you hear that everywhere. People like to see blood and guts.*

Roughstock specialist and World Champion bullrider, Troy Dunn, agrees: 'It's like the people who go and watch Formula One racing for the car wrecks'. Bulls have been called 'hell on hooves', 'terminators', 'eliminators' and 'annihilators'; they can weigh up to 1500 pounds, are powerful, aggressive and very fast. Bullriding, according to a *Time Magazine* survey a few years ago, is the world's most dangerous sport. Like parachuting and bungee jumping it's a great adrenalin hit, which goes most of the way towards explaining why it is now one of Australia's fastest-growing sports.

Bullrides are also easily accessible. They were first tried out in the beer garden of a pub in Darwin in the early 1990s. You only need a small ring because bulls are as agile as cats and can buck and spin virtually on the spot. As bull contractor Campbell Frame likes to say, his bulls 'will buck in the back of a ute'. Portable chutes can be set up practically anywhere and bullrides are run at pubs and clubs all over Australia as well as rodeo, sports and entertainment arenas.

Bullrides pay often and well, currently around $10 000 plus added entries to be split among the winners. Uncommitted, talented and lucky bullriders are the only ones who can still freewheel it around the countryside and (packing into cars) still cover their expenses. They don't need to cart more than a gear bag and if they keep winning they can even save for that ticket to Texas.

New ways

Corporate sponsorship is the only avenue for talented athletes to be professional in both senses of the word. But there's stiff competition from the mainstream sports like cricket and football not to mention all the Olympic sportsmen and women who need money too. Our cowboys and cowgirls have never been the world's greatest entrepreneurs or self-promoters but as one independent rodeo producer in Australia lamented: 'Getting sponsorship money is like trying to get teeth out of a chicken'. Nevertheless over the years sponsorship from the likes of the tobacco giants, before cigarette advertising was banned, airlines, fuel and car companies has been good to rodeo. Like the footie, a lot of rodeo sponsorship comes from alcohol companies, breweries in particular. The old 'How do ya' feel' image of the hard-working, hard-playing, sweaty masculine type slaking his thirst after a tough day is an Australian classic. Cowboys fit right in. Still, the lion's share of rodeo sponsorship comes from the local businesses in each rodeo town, not the large corporate head offices in major cities.

Initiatives like the open-card policy and sudden-death finals changed the face and the fabric of Pro rodeo completely. To a certain extent the camaraderie among riders has been lost. Certainly the folklore and tales of road trips and adventures are fewer. Cowboys and cowgirls are also less in the public eye and their close relationships with local communities have ended. Colin McTaggart remembers the days of welcoming committees at the railway station and invitations to homes for lunch and dinner, when cowboys were involved in the town. 'But', he says, 'today they blow in, a carload of them blow in, run to the chutes and get on something and then they take off straight after she's over. or they'll watch the go round and party on that night, but God help them, just in and out and gone again.' Well, they've got to be back at work on Monday.

The 1980s saw the last of the APRA's star system — stars as in fame, not just talent — the last heroes with the public. Firstly, because contestants now arrive, ride and leave and they only do one or two events, their names are not being heard all day. And secondly, now that the stars ride everywhere and often there is no obvious hierarchy or elite. There are now far more contestants in far more associations, which also muddies the waters. Star potential is now fulfilled overseas.

Scott Bloxsome reluctantly admits that he and many others *were* household names in the 1970s. But even then it was nothing like the adulation of a couple of decades before:

People used to sign autographs, but it was more that people would go to rodeos to see blokes ride. People used to go to rodeos to talk to blokes, you know. I know people would drive miles to a rodeo to see you ride, talk to you, drink with you. I bet you now a lot of people wouldn't even know who's riding.

Nowadays, it's true, it's usually only the hometown cowboys and cowgirls whom the audience barrack for.

The exceptions are those like Glen O'Neill and Troy Dunn, who excel overseas and come home heroes. They give Australian rodeo back some good old-fashioned star quality. The cowgirls are luckier. For a start there are fewer of them, which makes them special, they can't head overseas to become stars without the proverbial silver spoon, and thirdly there are cowgirls whose talent sticks out a mile, such as Brigett Brandenburg (aka Terri Lillyman), Kerry Johnson, Lulu Lundholm (now Dianne Parkinson), Vicki and Judy Gough (Vic's daughters), Leanne Ryder (now Leanne Caban), Shona Tribe and of course the remarkable Schiller sisters, Vicki and Tania, to name a few. Tania and her famous barrel horse, Rambo, have won so much over the years the public have simply had their names drummed into them.

The biggest star in rodeo in the 1990s was a bull called Chainsaw. The bulls, it seems, are pretty much promoted over the cowboys these days. Dr Jeckyl, 007, Fireball, Eagle, Silver City, Point Danger, Honey, Cream Puff, Easy Come Easy Go, Top Gun, Vibrator, Crime Time, Undertaker and Bambi are some of the notorious hard cases the public has loved in years gone by, more recently Desperado, Tornado, Jungle Juice, Earthquake and Akubra Insanity are the infamous names. Bulls, strangely ... have huge egos. When they are admired and feted and paraded around they swagger. When they're top dog in the pen and pelting cowboys left right and centre they positively gloat.

Stock contractor Peter Gill says the star bulls are easy to pick: 'It's in their personality, they're a bit flash about themselves. Bambi, the way he looked at you, the way he came off the truck, always looking around waiting for someone to take a photo of him.' This sort of cockiness and strutting about gets people's attention and Chainsaw was the best advertisement for rodeo since Curio, the grey mare from Marrabel. Discovered by George Hempenstall, then owned by John Condon but travelled by stock contractor, Gary McPhee, Chainsaw was special. Plenty of bulls, especially of late, go unridden for years. Chainsaw was rideable, just, if you could survive his high jump and belly roll but more important — like Bambi — he had attitude. He was a natural showman and relished the attention. Chainsaw always did a victory lap after each performance, which, Gary McPhee says:

he sort of figured out himself as he went along. He was always a spectacular bull, when he bucked them off, he'd have his head up and trot around the arena and he really looked the part. He had the personality that you could promote, everyone liked him ... People would come up and say 'Oh, can you get Chainsaw to stand on this piece of paper so we can have his hoof print?' or 'Can you stick this piece of paper on his horn?' — anything to get something of Chainsaw's. They just loved him.

Especially the bullriders.

Under Gary's guidance Chainsaw's wild and crazy 'angry young man' days (he got his name after what he did to George's chutes) mellowed into consummate professionalism. He featured in countless television and print stories, starred in his own documentary film, endorsed products such as the beer XXXX in television and print advertisements and became a household name. When Chainsaw died in 1996 there was a minute's silence in his honour at rodeos all over the country.

Committing — body and mind

Rodeo, as with all sports, particularly individual sports, is as much about mental discipline as it is about physical prowess. General physical fitness, strength and agility are important but mental discipline is harder to come by. A positive attitude is essential. Darren Brandenburg, bull and bareback champion and team roper, says:

It was a bit natural for me when I started. {He won the mutton busting at the Brisbane Exhibition when he was 4.} I just did it and it worked. Now I've started to learn. I understand the basics a lot more ... I really think you've got to be mentally strong to be a good competitor, you know. That's why you see those same guys that win all the big ones — it's because they are so mentally strong.

There is an additional mental challenge with rodeo in that it's dangerous. Ropers can lose fingers; steer wrestlers and un-decorators can have neck-breaking wrecks; and you will get seriously hurt roughstock riding, particularly the bulls. You have to be fearless or at least master fear — fear of certain injury and possible death. For all the physical, mental and tactical preparation, when the gate opens it's an almost blinding adrenalin rush. Then you rely on survival instinct, reflexes and a killer competitive streak — an all-consuming determination to win.

Barry Gravener, the first real king of the bulls, says he was always on edge:

... not frightened but just tensed. It doesn't matter who you speak to, even Greg Norman said it, if you're not tensed you won't win ... As soon as you nod your head for any beast, whether it be a bulldogging steer or whatever, it all goes out the back door. You'd be thinking, 'Ohh, this bloody bull,' you know. 'He threw so and so last week, he threw so and so the week before and he jumped on Jim McGuire and hooked him.' And then as soon as that gate opens it's, 'You're mine now.'

New techniques continue to improve the odds of surviving — cowboys now take the time to stretch and loosen up before each ride, for example. Schools teach roughstock riders how to get on, get off and get out of trouble. Protective vests for the bullriders are almost standard these days, helmets are also being worn and the bullfighting (protection) clowns are better trained than ever. But still you've got to be lucky. Very few bullriders, or bareback riders for that matter, make it through a year without being sidelined through injury.

Roughriding is a young man's sport. Youth's bravado, recklessness and seeming invincibility all help. Injuries heal fast and nerves and imagination are a lot steadier. Few cowboys ride bulls and bareback horses past their mid–30s, saddle bronc riders last a bit longer as it is not quite as physically punishing, although Ray Hermann has 'broken every bone in his body at least once'. Ropers can go on forever. Ex-bareback whizz, Headly Parter was 61 when he qualified for the APRA National Finals Rodeo in the team-roping in 1997. And he's still in the game.

Troy Dunn has said what makes a champion cowboy is 'heart, dedication and commitment'. Add nerves of steel, mind control, focus, fortitude, strength, agility, split-second timing, fast reflexes, coordination, horsemanship for the timed events, balance and aggression for the roughstock riding — schools, gyms, training and lots of practice. Talent is not enough because rodeo is too physically demanding and competitive to succeed without all of the above — and more. Tenacity, perseverance, guts and determination in rodeo are summed up as 'try' (as hard as you can). Barry Gravener again:

> *It's like anyone that does any sort of sport, if they really want to win and they've got any ability at all, they win all right. Whereas the bloke that's got twice as much ability and hasn't got near the try that they've got, he won't beat them. That's why Jim McGuire was so good, he just never gave up.*

Last but not least, cowboys and cowgirls need luck. Luck of the draw is the brutal equaliser. Luck against injuries and accidents which put you out of the running or worse. Roughriders need a good draw to score, if the animal doesn't buck there's nothing they can do but hope for a re ride. In the timed events if your calf or steer run straight and true, you can rope, wrestle or un-decorate it, but if it ducks off left and right, it's going to take more time. And if it ducks off the split-second after you've thrown your rope, well you're history. Scott Bloxsome speculated that to win in the time events it's 70 per cent horseflesh, 10 per cent ability and 20 per cent luck. 'But I'd rather have a lot more luck than ability, you can be the best in the world but if you don't draw, what are you going to do?'

Everyone has runs of luck, good and bad. When you're on a roll no-one can beat you, then sometimes for weeks things just can't go right. That's another test of mental discipline, to keep going when your luck is down.

Roping horses

In all time events you need a great horse. Robert McPhee, who breeds, trains and competes them, says the horse also has to be an athlete:

> *You need a good mind in a horse and it takes a special horse to be a great horse ... Your bulldogging horse has got to be very fast, got to be really good in the box — solid, square, stand straight, stand dead-still like a statue. When you nod it's got to be like a trigger on the gun ... And the same trigger applies on all your time-event horses ... They've got to be able to break and run from a standstill to flat, as quick as they can leave. Your bulldogging horse does not have to stop, he's just got to run his heart out to the other end ... He's got to run you by, run you right by. Can't run wide, he's got to run true to the beast ... The roping horse, he's got to be a bit more of an athlete than a bulldogging horse because he's got to run as hard, but he's got to be able to stop and go backwards ... Way it is today it's just automatic for him to do it ... I rope the calf and I pull my slack and I'm starting to get off. As I'm roping and*

pulling my slack he's starting to stop. As I get off, he's got to start going backwards. When I flank the calf he's got to keep the rope tight, he's got to work the rope. When I finish tying him, he's got to stop working, stand there. I got to be able to get on him and walk him forward. That's the end of it ... I believe it takes me two years to start a horse from scratch and be able to take him and put him on the road and have a successful road horse.

Risk factors

Rodeo is a tough sport anyway you look at it — lots of miles, no money, the luck factor and there's the injuries. Part of the allure of the sport is its danger. The chance a competitor is going to get hurt, perhaps killed, ups the stakes and heightens the tension. Broken bones are an everyday occurrence, as are ripped, torn, popped and shredded muscles, ligaments and cartilage. Riders who sustain wrenched groins, dislocated shoulders and whiplash are also getting off lightly. The strain on a bareback rider's arm is the fast route to wrecked wrists, elbows and shoulders; repeated bashings in the chutes and rough landings ruin knees and ankles.

Generally it's the roughstock riders who cop most of the serious injuries in rodeos. A fair few have been killed over the years, flung from a horse or a bull onto hard ground, or crushed, stomped, trampled, head-bashed or gored. Many have ended up with broken backs or necks and are confined to wheelchairs forever. More still have suffered head injuries — diagnosis is vague and recovery is uncertain. At the very least, everyone knows that so and so was never really the same after he had that bad buster.

Countless cowboys have had knees, faces and other body parts reconstructed. Even if they're not held together with nuts and bolts, most have the classic 'rodeo limp'. Years of abuse pay back with arthritis and rheumatism, stiffening, aching, grinding joints and bones with chunks missing out of them. A lot of old-timers hobble around deceptively, still as quick as cats if they have to be. Apart from steer wrestlers — who cop their fair share of pummelling — timeys, as time event hands are known, and cowgirls don't often get seriously injured. But there have been freak accidents, generally the result of an errant steer tripping a horse or a horse slipping and falling on a bad surface.

Bucking horses rarely turn on a fallen rider; professional horses almost never. Nor will a horse tread on a person if they can help it. The bulls, thanks to breeding and training, are far more civilised than they used to be, but they're still bulls and are aggressive in contest by nature. Unlike the more or less predictable 'jump and kick' bucking horses, bulls will dislodge a rider any which way and loose, and the longer they've been at it, the more tricks they'll have. Once you're off, a lot of bulls will have another go at you, if they can catch you. Bulls will run you down like a freight train, hook and hurl you in the air, drill you into the dirt with their horns or stomp on you instead. This is where the clowns come in.

Clowns came to rodeo via the circus and the travelling showmen. In the 1920s and 30s most agricultural shows and rodeos hired various performers to entertain the crowds between events. Clowns also helped manage the bullocks in the arena, and as they were not cleared until the end of each round, the bullocks gave the clowns plenty of opportunity to ham it up. In the 1930s American clown 'Jasbo' and his performing pony were a huge hit at the Sydney Royal. Dan Edwards used to clown at Newcastle in the 30s and 'hang on behind the bloomin' trotting blokes and be dragged around the arena and all those silly lookin' things'. Cousins John Sutton and John Kelly were exceptionally good horsemen, gentlemen riders, campdrafters, roughriders, showjumpers, comedy and bullock-wrangling clowns, who worked the Sydney and Melbourne shows through the 1940s and 50s.

With their painted smiles, funny hats and baggy trousers clowns became a fixture in rodeo arenas. They invented all sorts of specialty acts and gags with performing ponies and dogs, taunted the children (and paid for it), taunted the bullocks (and paid for that, too), sawed people in half, blew things up, fell off the fence — landing on the family jewels, got in the way, acted drunk, told jokes, teased the announcer, tripped, swaggered, staggered, danced, sang and generally played the fool.

In the 1960s when bulls began to replace bucking bullocks, the clowns' job took on another dimension — that of life saver. These days there are two types of rodeo clown — the comedy clown, or joker, and the bullfighting clown, who is there to protect the cowboys. Rodeo bullfighting has nothing in common with the Spanish version besides the name, which wasn't used until the 1980s. Underneath the lairy outfit is a trained professional athlete in lycra and sprint shoes.

Bullfighters work in pairs. When the eight seconds is up, they get the bull's attention — they whistle, shout, tap him on the nose — and when the rider hits the dirt, they put themselves between the bull and the cowboy and lure the bull away. When a bullrider finds himself in the harrowing, horrifying predicament of being 'hung up' — meaning his hand is locked in his bull rope and he is being spun and flung around like a rag doll — the bullfighting clowns get the rider to his feet and his elbow up high enough to release the rope. Bullfighting's really about playing or dancing with bulls — clowns try to get the bulls to chase them. Today's bullfighting clowns have only one prop, a specially made barrel, which they put between themselves and the bull and occasionally jump into. The bull tries to mow down or hook the clown, who keeps just ahead of him, touching him on the nose, stepping lightly out of the way, sometimes even jumping over the top of him. The closer the bull comes to wiping out the clown, the more the crowds love it.

Happy and Brian Gill and Bluey Bostock were among the first of the modern-day rodeo clowns, and Bluey clowned for 33 years, starting in 1959. Like all of them he did comedy and bullfighting. Roughriders Allan Bennett and Stuart Lear were also clowning in the 1960s. Pat Speedy came along shortly afterwards and became a great bullfighting clown; he has since been responsible for breeding and unleashing some of the wildest bucking bulls in the country. Angus Frame's son, Russell — better-known as 'Rusty', joined Pat. 'Rusty' is also a naturally brilliant comic who sets the audience rollicking the minute he steps foot in the ring.

Bullfighting really took off as a profession in the early 1980s. Graham and Lance Borghero started 'Bullfighting Enterprises' a sort of agency for bullfighters and Graham started running schools. Ahead of his time, he spent ten years in and out of Canada and the USA, learning his trade. A bullfighter has to be fearless, assertive and fast. They have to be clear-headed in an emergency and know bulls — what they can and can't, will and won't do — preferably individually. Graham says:

> *It's like dancing with a partner and if the person's standing on your toes, it's a little rough until you get it worked out ... if you move in on the shoulder, which we call a 'pocket', you're safe. It's only a small area but the bull can't get to you; if you're outside the pocket, you're in trouble ... They learn what happens; it's a habit, they're very smart animals. People don't think they're smart, but they are. You've got to be on the job and take control of the situation. You can't let the bull take control; you're dancing with him, reading the bull rather than letting him stop and then zero in on someone ... Sometimes you make the right decisions, sometimes you don't. And when you don't, you pay for it.*

Australia has some great bullfighters at the moment — it seems to be more of a buzz to be on the ground face to face with them than it is to be sitting on top of them. Clint 'Wombles' Dolan proved his abilities by winning APRA Bullfighter of the Year from 1990–95 inclusive. Darrel Diefenbach won it in 1996 and is currently in the USA working the pro circuit with his sights set on the Wrangler Bullfighting Championships (the world title). Denis Johnson is bullfighting for the Professional Bull Riders Association in America. 1998 APRA Bullfighter of the Year, Dave Back, is excellent at his job, and the Champion Bull Riders in Australia draw on the talents of Peter Blackall and Brett Wilson.

International prestige

Rodeo in Australia is an old-fashioned, provincial subculture pushing hard to embrace the age of commercialism. It is a country sport seeking recognition and credibility in the predominantly urban, professional sporting arena. For contemporary cowboys and cowgirls it has come to the point where rodeo is no longer financially feasible, and besides nowadays no-one wants to become a rodeo relic with nothing to show for their life but belt buckle trophies. To seriously pursue their sport and to be able to make a real living out of it, they have to head to Canada and America.

The lure of rodeoing in the United States is irresistible. It's not just the money, it's the challenge of the toughest competition — because of sheer numbers — both with contestants and bucking stock and, of course, the ultimate prestige of the World Championships.

Rodeo as a sport and cowboy culture in general are big business in America. There are 240 million Americans and cowboys are one of their most enduring icons. All Americans are taught their frontier history as a matter of course and most are well versed in and proud of it. Many Americans might never have seen a horse but they have absorbed their Western heritage and mythology, and millions of them affiliate with the spirit and style of Western/cowboy culture.

Rodeo is one of America's most popular sports. Americans have big-paying rodeos on every day of the week, often running a full week to get through the nominations. There is little britches rodeo, high school rodeo and college rodeo. Talented youngsters can go to college on a rodeo scholarship. They have amateur and pro rodeo circuits, and an enormous number of independent producers and entrepreneurial types who run 'all black' (African-American) rodeos, gay rodeos, all women's rodeos and celebrity rodeos. The American professional bullrider's association (PBR) alone have a Bud Light Cup series worth $5.2 million that's watched by a cable television audience of 72 million people. And that's only one of their sponsors.

Australia has a distinguished history of great sportsmen and women and our cowboys are steadily adding to our growing list of international achievements. In the 1990s at any one time there are between 50 and 100 Australians competing on the American and Canadian rodeo circuits; they also compete in the arenas of New Zealand, Argentina, Brazil and Mexico. The professional rodeo associations of Australia, Canada, New Zealand and the United States have formed an alliance called the World Rodeo Association (WRC), which promotes cooperation and standardisation between countries. There is also a World Indigenous Rodeo Association, bringing together the Australian Aborigines, New Zealand Maoris and American and Canadian Indians.

Our overseas success stories have been predominantly roughstock riders. Time-event contestants rely on the talent of their horses and it is very expensive and complicated to take horses overseas and more so to bring them home. Once there the horses have to acclimatise to different altitudes and climates, which may take up to a year. Some never do. Neville McCarthy's Danny, arguably Australia's greatest bulldogging horse ever, became ill when taken to the US and died. It's expensive to buy top trained horses overseas. An average time event horse starts at US$20 000, a champion can be up to US$70 000. (In Australia we are trading top barrel horses for AUS$10 000.) The option of buying a cheap horse and training it requires a few years, during which you have to live on something. The horse less can lease or borrow roping and barrel horses for jackpots and small rodeos, but no-one is going to lend you a great horse, because you'll beat them. Our ropers, wrestlers and barrel racers go to the USA for the schools and the experience. Contractors supply all roughstock so all those riders need is a gear bag and maybe a saddle.

Throughout the 1970s and 80s there was a constant trickle of ARRA National Champions testing themselves in the USA and Canada. Ken Coleman, Gary McPhee, Scott Bloxsome and Neville McCarthy were all serious contenders there. They won plenty and had a great time doing it but they were still outsiders. Scott Bloxsome remembers, '...it was harder to get accepted over there, now they've broken through'. Steve Hilton remarks: 'When I first went there in 1981 you could count the people who'd been there on two hands.' Dave Appleton says, 'People who had been there [the USA] painted American cowboys like they were gods, and the horses like they were dinosaurs — they'd swat you off their backs and stomp on you and eat you. Lots of guys said, "They'll kill you over there".'[2]

But Appleton went anyway and by the time he was through Australian contestants in American rodeos were no longer a novelty.

Brought up on a cattle station near Clermont, Queensland, Appleton went to the USA in 1980, spent two years studying and competing in college rodeos and went pro from there. Somewhere along the way he picked up the nickname, 'the Lone Roo'. Dave qualified for PRCA NFR on countless occasions in the bareback and saddle-bronc events, won the average for the bareback and the saddle bronc in 1984, and in 1988 Appleton became the PRCA's World Championship All-round Cowboy. It is the highest award in professional rodeo in the world and he was the first-ever non-American to win it. Dave Appleton now lives permanently in Texas, USA.

Hot on his tail was another great Australian success story, Bernie Smyth Jnr. His father, Bernie Smyth Snr, was the ARRA all-round champion in 1948. Bernie completed a rodeo *tour de force* in Australia in the mid–1980s, winning a record five consecutive ARRA Australian All-round Champion titles (Jim McGuire and Shane Kenny have also won five and Wally Woods, Bonny Young and Gary McPhee have each won four). In Canada, which he now calls home, Bernie won the prestigious PRCA Linderman Award in 1990 and 1992 and also the Canadian All-round Championship in 1992. He is one of the few, if not only, cowboys to win all-round titles in Australia, Canada and the USA.

Then came the bullriders, led by the formidable Troy Dunn. Born in Mackay, he grew up in various places around north Queensland. 'Always had cattle about', he said — which is the main thing. Troy has three brothers, who also rode bulls. He started with the Bushies in north Queensland and was APRA Australian Bull Riding and All-Round Champion in 1989 and the Bareback and All-round Champion in 1991. He became the first Australian to qualify for the PRCA NFR (world titles) in bullriding in 1991. That year he also won the famous Calgary bonus round in the bullriding, which had a winner-takes-all purse of US$50 000. On and up he went, coming third in the PRCA NFR in 1995 and qualifying five times for the fledgling American Professional Bull Riders (PBR) finals. In 1997 Troy was the highest money-winner in their Bud Light Cup series and in 1998 he won the series itself, making him the number one bullrider in the world.

In the amateur stakes Australians have also been extremely successful. Saddle bronc rider Steve Gibson won the North American Rodeo Commission World Finals Rodeo in 1983, Bob Slim won it in 1986, Adam Newman in 1994, Jason

Newman in 1996 and Peter Kelly in 1997. Greg Gibson won the bareback in 1988 and Greg Leys in 1991.

There have been numerous Australian roughstock riders coming and going across the Pacific in the last few years. Bullriders: Eddie Fisher, Darren Brandenburg, Lance and Mike Kelly, Scott Maynes, Ben Jones, Henry O'Dell, Scott Fraser, Dean Pace, Scott Doyle, Robert Whalen, Brenden Barlow, Mark Flanigan and Gavin Woodall. Bareback riders: Tony Hecksher and Troy Thomson, and our latest whizz, Darren Clarke. Saddle bronc riders: Rick Galloway, Tom Christensen and Mark Thatcher and Shane 'Spud' Parker, who like Glen O'Neill is now a Canadian citizen.

Another PRCA World Titles qualifier, bullrider Rodney 'Hubcap' Lidgard, now lives permanently in the US, as does Troy's brother, Owen Dunn. Brendon Clarke, Dan Keliher, Ben Buckley, Chris Burke, Casey Lowick, Nicholas Birch, Jamie Manning and Jason O'Hearn, Duncan Steele-Park, Glen Mansfield and Anthony Bello and a whole stack more have been trying their luck, as has our number one time event champion, Shane Kenny.

Saddle bronc rider Glen O'Neill is currently one of our best ambassadors. In 1994 he won the PRCA Rookie of the Year and has qualified for the PRCA NFR on several occasions. In 1995 he, too, won the Calgary Stampede bonus round in saddle bronc — another $50 000 for eight seconds and in 1998 he won the average for the bronc ride at Calgary. Scott Johnson is up there with O'Neill, winning the saddle bronc riding average at the PRCA World Titles in 1996. As of October 1999, Glen O'Neill and Scott Johnson were placed third and fifth respectively in the PRCA world saddle bronc standings gearing up for the world titles and another Australian bullrider, Greg Potter, was leading the PRCA standings in the bullriding.

For all the progress and development towards international professionalism not every cowboy or cowgirl is imbued with the fanatic dedication and determination that it takes to be a champion. As with any sport many get involved as a pastime and for a social life. Rodeo is a sport the whole family can enjoy and a healthy, positive environment for children and teenagers. An outdoor sport for physical types, for horse lovers as well as the testosterone-driven. But as the song goes, 'Mummas, don't let your babies grow up to be cowboys'. It's a lifestyle made in heaven for the fiercely independent, the drifters and dreamers, those with a fire in the belly, or wanderlust, or lust and wander — the commitment-shy of this world.

Australian to the core

Whereas a large percentage of Americans live in big cities dotted throughout the American West, Australia's 'West', the towns and regions where our pioneer frontier cattle and stockmen work and worked, is completely underpopulated. As one old roughrider put it, 'once upon a time everyone wanted to go out west, now they just want to get the hell out of it'.

Yet, just like the American West, where cowboys, cattle drives, ranches and rodeos are part of a well-publicised pioneering frontier history and have become part of the popular imagination, Australia's Western heritage is alive and well, despite this being something of a well-kept secret. Regional centres and cities that have a historical link with the cattle and horse industries still have plenty of rodeos with plenty of fans. Rockhampton, Townsville, Mt Isa, Alice Springs, Darwin, Brisbane, Charters Towers, Mareeba, Warwick and Tamworth are all good examples.

Where Australia differs from America is that our urban public is mostly unfamiliar with the heritage behind our rodeo. Neither do they relate to contemporary bush life. Horses and horsemanship in Australian cities barely exist — just at pony clubs or in exclusive sports like polo and dressage or horse trials. Horses are about as accessible to the general public as Kerry Packer's polo ponies. Racehorses are also isolated from society. You can watch from afar or see them on television. You can gamble on the outcome, but you can't take your children over and give the horses a pat.

The big Australian cities do host plenty of great rodeos. Sydney has staged rodeos at various showgrounds in the city and suburbs and at the Entertainment Centre and Darling Harbour. The Sydney RAS continues to run a rodeo every year. Bullrides are held in clubs and pubs and indoor horse arenas on the fringes of the city, such as Windsor. Melbourne also ran rodeos at their RAS, albeit more spasmodically, they have also run excellent rodeos at the Moombah Festival, the Melbourne Tennis Centre and Festival Hall. Adelaide has its annual Invitational Rodeo and Brisbane and surrounds have rodeos every weekend.

The fabulous paradox of rodeo in this country is that despite the overt Americanisation of the sport, it remains quintessentially Australian. No matter how 'international' in style and content rodeo becomes and how quickly most of our best roughstock riders hot-foot it overseas, the spirit and ethos of the Australian rodeo community hasn't really changed at all. Perhaps because there are fewer contestants and there's less money at stake than overseas we have retained our sense of fun and friendship and a 'whatever will be will be' attitude. Strangers can still turn up and sign on for the day, have a go for the hell of it and someone will lend them the gear and throw them a line of advice. We have learned a lot from the Americans in terms of professionalism and showmanship, but the Australian public is casual, no matter how flash our cowboys and cowgirls might look. American rodeos are slick, fast, star-spangled entertainment and the competition is full on. Here our independent promoters go for that sort of pomp and pagentry, but the spirit at our average rodeo is nothing if not laid-back.

There are plenty of families who have been involved in Australian rodeo for several generations. And you can't really change Australian people. Our cowboys and cowgirls retain most of the attitudes and characteristics of their forebears — wry, laconic humour, self-deprecation and modesty, reticence and independence, an easy-going 'go with the flow' nature, a strong sense of fair play and a fair go for all — sportsmanship, mateship, and a collectivist, looking-out-for-each-other attitude.

Stock contractors remain salt of the earth individuals who work hard, travel harder and play the sport the hardest. The communities who run the shows are much the same as ever. Volunteers race around behind the teeming bar or slave behind the smoky haze of the BBQ; Country Women's Association types chat beside their table of sandwiches; hordes of children race around on various missions; the odd, ancient mangy-looking mongrel dog will be lolling in the shade — near the BBQ. And, of course, the Australian landscape hasn't changed either. The backdrop of gumtrees, sunlight, blue skies and buzzing flies is as much a part of rodeo as the people who play and watch it.

At heart Australian rodeo is a country sport, a bush sport, and every rural town in Australia has run or does run an annual rodeo. But as these towns have small populations, apart from independent promoters and producers, who come and go all the time, volunteers generally run the sport for charity. The Lions, Rotary, Apex or RSL club, or even the local footy club will work with the rodeo committee and hustle-up sponsorship from local businesses to cover running costs and prize money. Committee members work feverishly for weeks leading up to a rodeo, knock themselves out on the day and are tying up loose ends for weeks afterwards. Inside the ring the announcers, judges, time-keepers, clowns, bullfighters, pick-up men, stock contractors and ambulance officers are paid but the rest, the yard-workers, bar workers, lunch and tea-makers, secretaries, gate ticket-collectors, and sundry helpers — generally do it for love. The beneficiaries are likely to be the School of the Air, bush fire brigades, the flying doctor service, local hospital and ambulance funds and broader charities, such as cancer research.

The tiny town of Bourketown in the Gulf of Carpentaria has a population of 150, yet by 1994 their annual rodeo had raised $36 000 for the Royal Flying Doctor Service, a mighty effort. On a much larger scale, the annual Mt Isa Rotary Rodeo is owned and run by three local Rotary clubs. Over the last 40 years they've raised more than $2.5 million for local charities and community projects — not bad for a town of around 23 000. Bourketown is a port and Mt Isa is a mining town but both are slap-bang in the middle of cattle country. These rodeos are still an annual social occasion for the people who live on remote outback stations — in 1998 the bar at Mt Isa rodeo made $84 000 in three days.

In the last 30 years, with many graziers, stockmen, drovers and horsemen gone, their skills, relevance and romance have slipped from popular memory. The new breed of rodeo contestant came in, with a more professional but impersonal rodeo scene. Professional rodeo dropped a lot of time-consuming but home-grown community-involving events and replaced them with American rodeo contests like roping.

Some suggest that our cowboys and cowgirls got caught up with the professionalisation and 'yankification' of Australian rodeo and lost touch with the Australian people. The fact that Australian rodeo became derivative, that our heritage was sidelined for the sake of American showmanship and sporting professionalism certainly alienated some of the bushies and traditionalists. The Australian campdrafters, of course, never wavered for a second.

The changes were driven by economics and ambition. Away from the bush or the outback, the mainstream public wanted razzamatazz, spectacle and action-packed entertainment. And the cowboys wanted to be the best in the world. Professional rodeo has come a long way from being grassroots entertainment.

Since the 70s rodeos are increasingly being produced as sports–entertainment spectaculars by independent promoters. But standard committee-run rodeos are still drawing good crowds. The average attendance at the top 50 APRA rodeos is about 6000 spectators — pretty good considering that 90 per cent of them are held far from the sprawling metropolises where most Australians live.[3] The different kinds of rodeo in Australia are as varied as the country is vast. 'Performance rodeos', three-hour action-packed shows with professional stock prevail along the eastern seaboard and in the towns and cities. Large entertainment centres feature elite professionals, Australia versus America contests, laser lights, smoke machines and booming music. The crowds are boosted with Country and Western aficionados and boot-scooters. But head west or north to cattle country, 'the outback', where stockmen's skills are still part of life and you'll find all-day community events in the heat and dust, generally followed by an all-night party in the heat and dust. The audience are watching their friends and family and the local ringers in the arena; there are novelty events like mutton busters, and calf-rides for the kids and plenty of ribbons and trophies to go around. It's an annual pilgrimage; people come from hundreds of miles around, and there'd be a riot if the rodeo was over in three hours.

Revival

In the past few years Australians have shown a renewed interest in our heritage. Heading into the year 2000 Australia is going through an identity crisis. Facing the new millennium, the Centenary of Federation and the Republic debate, Australians are thinking more about their country. We search anew through our history, looking for meaning, references, common themes — cultural, spiritual and ethical — things to help unite and make us strong for the future. We're still arguing about it, but we'll get there.

There's also been a small but significant return to traditional methods of handling livestock — on horseback rather than by motorbike or helicopter. Now that the scrubbers and TB have been dealt with, using men and women on horseback for both mustering and droving proves economical in the long run. Outrageous rural fuel prices have pushed up truck transport costs and at $200 per hour, keeping helicopters in the air isn't always affordable. Most big stations still use planes or choppers but in conjunction with men and women on the ground on horses and bikes.

Horses also keep cattle calmer than helicopters and motorbikes. Quiet, well-behaved cattle are preferable when you've got a lot of them. Drovers are also making a bit of a comeback, nothing like the old days of course, but if you've got the time, it's pleasant enough and the beef's not bruised at the other end.

Because of their depleted numbers and renewed appreciation, the horse industry is now booming. Horsebreeders are smiling once again, Australian stockhorses, American quarter horses and mixtures of the two are in big demand. A good campdraft horse can sell for $30 000 yet 20 years ago you practically couldn't give them away. Horsemen, breakers and trainers are also back in demand. It seems that as horse traditions on cattle stations are revived, Western horse sports are enjoying a surge in popularity. There are plenty of other sports and competitions involving horse and stockmanship skills besides rodeo — campdrafting, Western pleasure, cutting and reining, the stockmen's challenges, the Man from Snowy River contest, and the most recent invention, bronco branding, which is a contest of traditional Australian roping and tying skills.

Australian traditions are also returning to rodeo arenas. There's a resurgence in old-time events at which locals can 'have a go'. Mount Isa has always had a station buckjump where hundreds of local ringers nominate to ride in stock saddles on local horses. In an effort to reinvolve the community, even APRA rodeos have recently been running station buckjumps, wild horse races, old-time bronc rides in poley saddles and poddy rides for the kids.

Omeo Rodeo started the trend in 1997 with the $15 000 Lance Skuthorpe Challenge; it's now $20 000 and Australia's most lucrative bronc ride. The catch is that contestants have to ride in the old Davidson-Smith poley saddle over two rounds with pre–1960s rules. This means they have to spur to the judges' satisfaction and the judges are old-time cowboys, Neil Hulm and Norm Bradly. In the first year around 40 top contemporary bronc riders saddled up, but the poley and the different style of riding got the better of them. Much to the glee of all the old-timers, most of them bucked off.

If rodeo, as with the case of the APRA, has grown away from its grassroots beginnings, it has been a journey towards professional showmanship and higher standards in every aspect. The sport has been cleaned-up, regulated, made humane to animals and safer for contestants. It is accountable to numerous government and animal welfare bodies and provides insurance policies for riders and spectators. Shows are faster and more dynamic and rules are fairer and safer. The level of talent, both two-legged and four, has gone through the roof and our cowboys and cowgirls are now world class.

Rodeo has ridden the ups and downs of economic booms and busts, disastrous floods and droughts, and internal dissension. Its has survived the invention of silent pictures, talking pictures, television, cable TV, mass entertainment, mass communication and information technology. It's also survived the revolution of transportation, the automobile, tram, train, road train, helicopter, motorbike and aeroplane. Its history encompasses the evolution of a consumer society with its resultant popular culture explosion and distractions. Australians have moved from the attitude of 'she'll be right' to 'I'll sue your butt off', which of course has made insurance costs hair-raising. Despite the occasional war cry of radical animal liberationists and the constant hawklike scrutiny of recognised animal welfare bodies, rodeo has prevailed. Throughout the vicissitudes of modern life, cowgirls and cowboys have always competed at rodeos and audiences have always loved them. But it is easy to see how our roughriding heroes have become lost in contemporary culture. Television has taken over our imaginations, and if we like the idea of cowboys, American ones are much more obvious and accessible.

But the biggest thing the sport has survived is the slow erosion — economically and socially — of the bush and with it the loss of much outback culture. The bush and its people are the life and soul behind the sport.

Over time Australian roughriders became Australian rodeo cowboys and cowgirls; bushmen's carnivals and paddock shows became rodeos, and the buckjump showmen have all but disappeared. Methods and techniques and styles and language have changed immensely. Rodeo has travelled a long, dusty, potholed and mostly corrugated road over the last hundred years, a road littered with hilarious incidents, high dramas and adventures. Its stories abound with heroes and villains, both two-legged and four, mateship, larrikinism, 'a lot of lovin' and a lot of fightin'', as Chilla Seeney would say, mighty victories as well as dreadful injuries and death. There has been poetry, music, danger, quite a few tears, fear, lots of beer and rum, dreams, humility, hopefulness, lots more laughs and plenty of hard work. Above all there've been innumerable gifted horsemen and women and many, many legendary horses.

The road shimmers hazy with legends, myths and apocryphal tales. And putting aside the buckles and glory, every one of those millions of bumpy miles was dedicated to chasing that perfect moment. Striving for that classic feeling when man or woman and beast come together in work, play or contest and everything goes ... just right.

Appendix 1: Description of modern rodeo events

There are nine standard events in contemporary rodeo, six for men and three for women, plus assorted rookie and junior events. Of the cowboy events, three are roughstock riding events — saddle bronc riding, bareback bronc riding and (bareback) bullriding — and three are timed events — steer wrestling, roping and team roping. The three cowgirl events are also all time events — barrel racing, breakaway roping and steer undecorating.

All events are contested by an individual or an individual and a horse, except team roping, which of course requires two riders. Team roping is also the only event where men and women compete together or against each other. In all events the contestants do not get to choose their stock. They rely on the luck of the draw. Any abuse of any animal incurs disqualification, heavy fines and a contestant can be banned from competing for a substantial period of time.

ROUGHSTOCK RIDING

In all three events, there are two appointed judges, who each award between one and 25 points for how well the horse or bull bucks and the same again for how well the cowboy rides it. The combined scores give a total out of 100 (highest score wins). All three events are one-handed contests. A rider who touches anything with his free hand is disqualified. If the beast bucks the rider off in less than 8 seconds, there's no score. In the bronc riding events, if the rider fails to have his heels in the break between the horse's neck and shoulder when its front feet hit the dirt coming out of the chute — called a 'mark out' — they are also disqualified. If the horse or bull doesn't perform to the judges' satisfaction, it doesn't buck, or slams the cowboy into the chute gate on the way out, the cowboy may be awarded a re-ride.

Saddle bronc
'Never was a horse that couldn't be rode, never was a man that couldn't be throwed' is an old showman's saying, and the contest between the two is the essence of the saddle bronc ride, formerly called buckjumping in Australia. It is the original rodeo contest and is still viewed by the traditionalists as the premier event of rodeo. It is considered to be the most technically difficult of the three roughstock events. Contested in a saddle, the horse wears a head stall with a single rope rein. Cowboys are judged on the style and panache of their designated spurring motions.

Bareback
Bareback riding is generally considered to be the most physically punishing of all rodeo events. The cowboys take enormous strain in the arm, shoulder and neck. Most of them strap or bind their riding arm to stop muscles and cartilage literally ripping away from the bones. For this reason it has the fewest competitors of all the rodeo events. Cowboys wear a heavily resined leather glove, which they jam into a wooden and leather 'bareback rigging' tied around the horse below the wither. The horse's head is free. It is the cowboy's control and far more free-form spurring motions which the judges watch.

Bullriding
Bullriding is the ultimate test of courage, strength, reflexes and craziness. Bulls buck differently to horses — they can spin and chop and lunge about as well as give high-kicking bucks, which are the point scorers. Special spurring motions are not as important for bullriders — they simply have to survive the G-force and stay on — preferably making it look easy. The cowboy ties himself onto the bull with a bull rope, which he winds around a resined leather glove and grip locks closed. The bell on the rope acts as a weight to help release the rope when the eight seconds is up. If a cowboy is thrown from a bull before he has a chance to release his hand from the rope, it results in the horrifying but spectacular predicament of being 'hung up' and flung about until he can free his hand.

TIME EVENTS

There are two common elements to all timed events. The beast is given a head start into the arena entering from the end of a 'race'(fenced runway) that is next to a time-event 'box'. The box is a three-sided enclosure at least 12 feet in length with a rope 'barrier' as the fourth side. The mounted contestant waits inside the box behind the rope barrier, which is automatically tripped by the beast as it reaches a certain point. The horse and rider give chase. If the horse and rider 'break the barrier', i.e. hit the rope before the beast has released it, they incur a 10-second time penalty. The second common factor is that they are all won on fastest time and are subject to time penalties for faults. There are two timers with flags to signal when the contestant has completed their task — a barrier judge and a field flag judge. All time events have a 30-second limit. All are won and lost on hundredths of seconds.

Steer wrestling

Steer wrestling used to be called bulldogging, and the mounted contestant has an offsider called a hazer. The hazer gallops alongside the opposite side of the steer to the contestant to keep the steer running straight. The steer wrestler rides up alongside the steer and leaps out of his saddle beside the steer, grabbing it by the horns. His horse carries his heels forwards past the steer, then he digs into the dirt using them as brakes. The steer wrestler then throws himself back and sideways, twisting the steer off balance and they land together in a heap, steer on top. Winning times are usually under five seconds.

Roping

The key to rope and tie, or calf roping — it's called both — is the teamwork between the cowboy and his roping horse. The contestant ropes the beast's head or horns from horseback. As soon as the rope has found its mark, the horse stops as the cowboy simultaneously jumps off, runs to the beast, lifts it onto its side and ties three of its legs together with his 'pigging string'. His rope is already dallied to the saddle horn and the horse keeps the tension between it and the beast. When the beast is tied the contestant throws up his arms up to signal 'time', then remounts and moves his horse forwards to loosen the rope and show that the 'tie' on the beast will hold for five seconds. You only get one shot with the rope. Roping times are around 8–10 seconds. Cowgirls are allowed to compete in the rope and tie but not many bother because they'd basically be throwing their entry money away. The cowboy's advantage is not in the chase and the roping but on the ground. It takes brute strength as well as technique to throw a beast and tie it. To compensate, some associations are starting to run ladies calf-roping competitions instead.

In Victoria they run steer roping instead of rope and tie. The contestant ropes the beast, leaps off their horse and instead of tying it up; they simply touch it forward of the shoulder to receive time. The horse must keep the tension on the rope for five seconds. As long as the contestants have two ropes they can have two attempts. As with rope and tie, bad roping — roping which jerks the beast, or where the horse drags the beast — means disqualification.

Team roping

Two mounted ropers, a 'header' and a 'heeler', work together to catch and immobilise a beast. The header ropes the steer's head or horns, then turns at a right angle to the fence, bringing the steer around in a smooth arc. As the beast resists, it hops rather than trots — meaning its two hind legs move together. The heeler then ropes its hind heels. This looks impossible but it's done by throwing the rope in under the beast so that the loop lands strategically in front of its hind hooves, which should then hop into it, and the rope is then pulled tight. Time is recorded when both catches have been made and the horses are facing the steer with both ropes taut. The ropes for team roping are not pre-tied to the saddle but are 'dallied' — wrapped quickly around the saddle horn — after each catch is made. If this isn't done properly, fingers get lopped. There are penalty points for incorrect roping, such as catching one hind foot only. Each team is allowed two attempts per rider. Times range between five and 10 seconds.

WOMEN'S EVENTS

All three cowgirls' events are time events, depending heavily — and in the case of barrel racing, exclusively — on their horse's skill and speed. Barrel racing is the premier women's event in rodeo. Steer undecorating is dangerous and is therefore not actively promoted by the WPRA but it is not banned either. It is most popular in Tasmania and Queensland. Steer undecorating and breakaway roping are similar to men's steer wrestling and roping and both incur a 10-second penalty if horse and rider break the barrier before it is released by the beast. Committees are free to run one or all three events for the cowgirls, but must run at least the standard two if holding a National Finals Rodeo.

Barrel racing

More than any other event in rodeo, barrel racing is a contest between horses. A barrel horse needs flexibility and agility to turn sharply around the barrels and it has to be fast. As with all time event horses, they need short spurts of speed and a calm disposition in between. For this reason American quarter horses are preferred. Horse and rider compete against the clock, galloping in a cloverleaf pattern around a course marked by three barrels (44-gallon drums). Knocking over a barrel incurs a five-second penalty; penalties also apply if a cowgirl overuses her whip. The fastest time wins, and in a full-sized arena winning times are between 16 and 17 seconds

Breakaway roping

The mounted contestant starts in the time-event box, behind the barrier. The beast (calf or steer) has a head start. The cowgirl chases and lassos its head or horns and the horse slides to a stop. The difference to the cowboys' roping starts here. Cowgirls stay astride and the roped beast keeps running until a string attaching the rope to her saddle horn 'breaks away', at which point time is taken. A coloured scarf is attached to the string so that the judges can see it drop. Winning breakaway roping times range around three and four seconds.

Steer undecorating

The mounted cowgirl has a hazer, who keeps the steer running straight. Instead of leaping off and wrestling the steer, the cowgirl gallops up beside it, leans down and plucks a ribbon from between its shoulders. It is dangerous because, like steer wrestling and campdrafting, there is always the risk that the beast will duck in front of or underneath the galloping horse and cause a bad accident. To be in the money as a steer undecorator, a cowgirl has to hold the ribbon up within three or four seconds.

Appendix II: List of Australian champions

AUSTRALIAN BUSHMEN'S CARNIVAL AND RODEO ASSOCIATION CHAMPIONS

All-Round Cowboy

1951 Stumpy Timmins; 1952 Alan Brambley; 1953–1958 No award given; 1959 Stumpy Timmins; 1960 Aubrey Tribe; 1961 Aubrey Tribe; 1962 Aubrey Tribe; 1963 G Capararo; 1964 J Purcell; 1965 L Bates; 1966 Bob Palmer; 1967 Terry Marshall; 1968 Lionel Caban; 1969 Lionel Caban; 1970 Les Buckingham; 1971 John Caban; 1972 John Caban; 1973 John Caban; 1974 Dudley Kearney; 1975 Dudley Kearney; 1976 Joe Pace; 1977 Danny Ward; 1978 Ron Raynor; 1979 Glenn Morgan; 1980 Glenn Morgan; 1981 Glenn Morgan; 1982 Ron Raynor; 1983 Glenn Morgan; 1984 Glenn Morgan; 1985 Bob Sim; 1986 Glenn Morgan; 1987 Steve Parkinson; 1988 Glenn Jones; 1989 Mark Gibb; 1990 Steve Parkinson; 1991 Kevin Cooper; 1992 Steve Parkinson; 1993 Steve Parkinson; 1994 Greg Frewin; 1995 Kevin Cooper; 1996 Kevin Cooper; 1997 Ron Finch; 1998 Lance Kelly.

Saddle Bronc

1972 John Caban; 1973 Kelly Rowsell; 1977 Danny Ward; 1978 Glenn Morgan; 1979 Glenn Morgan; 1980 Glenn Morgan; 1981 Glenn Morgan; 1982 Lindsay Clarke; 1983 Glenn Morgan; 1984 Glenn Morgan; 1985 Jack Gallagher; 1986 Glenn Morgan; 1987 Geoff Bullen; 1988 Kevin Cooper; 1989 Kevin Cooper;

~ APPENDIX II ~

1990 Kevin Cooper; 1991 Kevin Cooper; 1992 Glen O'Neill; 1993 Kevin Cooper; 1994 Scott Johnston; 1995 Kevin Cooper; 1996 Kevin Cooper; 1997 Ron Finch; 1998 Kevin Cooper.

Bareback Bronc
1972 Les Buckingham; 1973 Dudley Kearney; 1975 Ron Raynor; 1977 Danny Ward; 1978 Ron Raynor; 1979 Glenn Morgan; 1980 Glenn Morgan; 1981 Glenn Morgan; 1982 Ron Raynor; 1983 Glenn Morgan; 1984 Glenn Morgan; 1985 Greg Gibson; 1986 Glenn Morgan; 1987 Greg Gibson; 1988 Kevin Parkins; 1989 Greg Gibson; 1990 Steve Parkinson; 1991 Greg Gibson; 1992 Greg Gibson; 1993 Greg Gibson; 1994 Greg Gibson; 1995 Dale Carter; 1996 Greg Gibson; 1997 Darren Clarke; 1998 Lance Kelly.

Bullride
1972 John Caban; 1973 John Caban; 1977 Paul Farley; 1978 Paul Farley; 1979 Paul Farley; 1980 Phillip Mainey; 1981 Paul Farley; 1982 Paul Farley; 1983 Steve Thorn; 1984 Steve Parkinson; 1985 Maurice Bogie; 1986 Maurice Bogie; 1987 Steve Parkinson; 1988 Peter Lawler; 1989 Scott Maynes; 1990 Steve Parkinson; 1991 Mick Gray; 1992 Steve Parkinson; 1993 Matthew Bogie; 1994 Matthew Bogie; 1995 Matthew Bogie; 1996 Shane Griffiths; 1997 Brendon Allen; 1998 Lance Kelly.

Bulldogging/Steer Wrestling
1972 Les Buckingham; 1973 John Caban; 1977 John Kempton; 1978 Kelly Rowsell; 1979 Glen Jones; 1980 Alec Kallus; 1981 Cliff Lyons; 1982 Alec Kallus; 1983 Colin Gardner; 1984 Cameron Glass; 1985 Alec Kallus; 1986 Alec Kallus; 1987 Stephen Pereira; 1988 Peter Mills; 1989 Mark Gibb; 1990 Cameron Glass; 1991 Greg Frewin; 1992 Jim Bushell; 1993 Greg Frewin; 1994 Greg Frewin; 1995 Greg Frewin; 1996 Greg Frewin; 1997 Vern McVicar; 1998 Peter Mills.

Roping
1972 John Caban; 1973 J Pearce; 1977 Ron Raynor; 1978 Ron Raynor; 1979 Rick Norris; 1980 Ron Raynor; 1981 Steve Baker; 1982 Ron Raynor; 1983 Jeff Miller; 1984 Jeff Miller; 1985 Gordon Rossiter; 1986 Jeff Miller; 1987 Ron Raynor; 1988 Jeff Miller; 1989 Jeff Miller; 1990 Alex Campbell; 1991 Wayne Slater; 1992 Greg Frewin; 1993 Malcolm Fishenden; 1994 Greg Frewin; 1995 Shane Kenny; 1996 Greg Frewin; 1997 Gary Zilverberg; 1998 David Hallam.

Team Roping
1990 Malcolm Fishenden; 1991 Greg Frewin; 1992 Malcolm Fishenden; 1993 Malcolm Fishenden; 1994 Roger York; 1995 Kevin Cooper; 1996 Kevin Cooper; 1997 Kevin Cooper; 1998 Craig Mearns.

All-Round Cowgirl
1980 Lulu Lundholm; 1981 Mandy Cracknell; 1982 Mandy Cracknell; 1983 Mandy Cracknell; 1984 Mary Morgan; 1985 Mandy Cracknell; 1986 Jeanette Murray; 1987 Anne Stanborough; 1988 Marie Edwards; 1989 Marie Edwards; 1990 Marie Edwards; 1991 Marie Edwards; 1992 Kelly Holden; 1993 Fay Murray; 1994 Marie Edwards; 1995 Diane Parkinson; 1996 Julie Campbell; 1997 Helen McVicar; 1998 Sue Ellen Parkinson.

Barrel Race
1980 Gina Toparis; 1981 Mandy Cracknell; 1983 Mandy Cracknell; 1984 Mary Morgan; 1985 Jeanette Murray; 1986 Jeanette Murray; 1987 Anne Stanborough; 1988 Marie Edwards; 1989 Marie Edwards; 1990 Marie Edwards; 1991 Marie Edwards; 1992 Katrina Merrett; 1993 Fay Murray; 1994 Marie Edwards; 1995 Tracey Macey; 1996 Pam Patterson; 1997 Julie Campbell; 1998 Shona Tribe.

Goat Tying
1980 Rosie Farley; 1981 Rosie Farley; 1982 Mary Morgan; 1983 Mary Morgan; 1984 Mary Maorgan; 1985 Sally Major.

Steer Undecorating
1980 Lulu Lundholm; 1982 Mandy Cracknell; 1983 Karen Wellar; 1984 Mary Morgan; 1985 Mandy Cracknell; 1986 Julie Parkinson; 1987 Anne Stanborough; 1988 Baids McIntyre; 1989 Cherie Dolan;

1990 Jannette Jeffrey; 1991 Adele Goodear; 1992 Sandra Martin; 1993 Kim Thorn; 1994 Christine Bushell; 1995 Eileen Sheehan; 1996 Adele Edwards; 1997 Adele Edwards; 1998 Katryna Angus.

Breakaway Roping
1986 Anne Stanborough; 1987 Angela Paliskis; 1988 Angela Paliskis; 1989 Sally Major; 1990 April Hanby; 1991 April Hanby; 1992 Kelly Holden; 1993 Dianne Parkinson; 1994 Marie Edwards; 1995 April Hanby; 1996 Dianne Parkinson; 1997 Michelle Russell; 1998 Dianne Parkinson.

AUSTRALIAN PROFESSIONAL RODEO ASSOCIATION CHAMPIONS

All-Round Cowboy
1945 Tex Mooney; 1946 Johnny Pierce; 1947 Tom Willoughby; 1948 Bernie Smyth; 1949 Noel Bottom; 1950 Noel Bottom; 1951 Tom Willoughby; 1952 Allan Bennett; 1953 Allan Woods; 1954 Wally Woods; 1955 Wally Woods; 1956 Ray Crawford; 1957 Colin McTaggart; 1958 Wally Woods; 1959 Norm Woods; 1960 Wally Woods; 1961 Ray Crawford; 1962 Bonny Young; 1963 Bonny Young; 1964 Barry Gravener; 1965 Bonny Young; 1966 Bonny Young; 1967 Jim McGuire; 1968 Maurice Height; 1969 Jim McGuire; 1970 Jim McGuire; 1971 Garry McPhee; 1972 Garry McPhee; 1973 Garry McPhee; 1974 Garry McPhee; 1975 Jim McGuire; 1976 Jim McGuire; 1977 Scott Bloxsome; 1978 Neville McCarthy; 1979 Dudley Kearney; 1980 Neville McCarthy; 1981 Neville McCarthy; 1982 Bernie Smyth Jnr; 1983 Bernie Smyth Jnr; 1984 Bernie Smyth Jnr; 1985 Bernie Smyth Jnr; 1986 Bernie Smyth Jnr; 1987 Frank Green; 1988 Robert McPhee; 1989 Troy Dunn; 1990 Garry Longney; 1991 Troy Dunn; 1992 Shane Kenny; 1993 Owen Dunn; 1994 Shane Kenny; 1995 Shane Kenny; 1996 Shane Kenny; 1997 Shane Kenny; 1998 Jeff Miller.

Saddle Bronc
1945 Greg Canavan; 1946 Angus Frame; 1947 Allan Bennett; 1948 Basil Gollan; 1949 Dally Holden; 1950 Dally Holden; 1951 Tom Willoughby; 1952 Allan Bennett; 1953 Allan Woods; 1954 Ray Crawford; 1955 Allan Woods; 1956 Wally Woods; 1957 John Huey; 1958 Alwin Torenbeeck; 1959 Wally Woods; 1960 Wally Woods; 1961 Bonny Young; 1962 Colin McTaggart; 1963 Bob Hocking; 1964 Barry Gravener; 1965 Bonny Young; 1966 Bonny Young; 1967 Chilla Seeney;1968 Jim McGuire; 1969 Ken Coleman; 1970 Ken Coleman; 1971 Errol Lather; 1972 Scott Bloxsome; 1973 Errol Lather; 1974 Scott Bloxsome; 1975 Garney Beresford; 1976 Ken Coleman; 1977 Scott Bloxsome; 1978 Ken Coleman; 1979 Ken Coleman; 1980 Ray Hermann; 1981 Ray Hermann; 1982 Ray Hermann; 1983 Ray Hermann; 1984 Ray Hermann; 1985 Ray Hermann; 1986 Bernie Smyth Jnr; 1987 Ray Hermann; 1988 Rick Galloway; 1989 Jim Pierce; 1990 Mark Thatcher; 1991 Troy Dunn; 1992 Glen O'Neill; 1993 David Hoad; 1994 Jeff Baker; 1995 David Hoad; 1996 Mark Thatcher; 1997 Murray Douglas; 1998 Adam Newman.

Bareback Ride
1947 Johnny Pierce; 1948 Bernie Smyth; 1949 Tom Weeding; 1950 Kevin McTaggart; 1951 Chilla Seeney; 1952 Tom Willoughby; 1953 Allan Woods; 1954 Kevin McTaggart; 1955 Dally Holden; 1956 Ray Crawford; 1957 Lindsay Black; 1958 Wally Woods; 1959 Wally Woods; 1960 Wally Woods; 1961 Doug Flanagan; 1962 Colin McTaggart; 1963 Allan Hicks; 1964 Bonny Young; 1965 Allan Hicks; 1966 Don Hafemeisler; 1967 Peter Gill; 1968 Des Steffersen; 1969 Jim McGuire; 1970 Ross Piper; 1971 Allan Hicks; 1972 Allan Hicks; 1973 Ross Piper; 1974 Ross Piper; 1975 John Brearley; 1976 Ross Piper; 1977 John Brearley; 1978 Kevin Stockdale; 1979 Jim Dix; 1980 Les Bell; 1981 Mark Rowe; 1982 Mark Rowe; 1983 Brett Edwards; 1984 Eddie Fisher; 1985 Eddie Fisher; 1986 Dave Johnston; 1987 Frank Green; 1988 Steve Hilton; 1989 Dave Johnston; 1990 Tony Hecksher; 1991 Troy Dunn; 1992 Greg Gibson; 1993 Steve Hilton; 1994 Greg Leys; 1995 Tony Hecksher; 1996 Steve Hilton; 1997 Greg Leys; 1998 Darren Clarke.

Bullock/Bullride
1945 Greg Canavan; 1946 Allan Woods; 1947 Noel Hargreaves; 1948 Norm Dawson; 1949 Tom Willoughby; 1950 Ron Richards; 1951 Bob Weick; 1952 Tom Willoughby; 1953 Dally Holden; 1954 Tom Willoughby; 1955 Wally Woods; 1956 Tom Willoughby; 1957 Vic Gough; 1958 Wally Woods; 1959 Wally

Woods; 1960 Barry Gravener; 1961 Peter Gill; 1962 Barry Gravener; 1963 Allan Hicks; 1964 Barry Gravener; 1965 Barry Gravener; 1966 Maurice Height; 1967 Barry Gravener; 1968 Maurice Height; 1969 Bill Nichols; 1970 Allan Hicks; 1971 Garry McPhee; 1972 Garry McPhee; 1973 Doug Spann; 1974 Garry McPhee; 1975 Bill Nichols; 1976 Peter Wallis; 1977 Tom Kenny; 1978 Tom Kenny; 1979 Steve Hodge; 1980 Steve Thorn; 1981 Dave Johnston; 1982 Shane Connelly; 1983 Brett Larkin; 1984 Norm Hilton; 1985 Eddie Fisher; 1986 Eddie Fisher; 1987 Shane Connelly; 1988 Steve Hilton; 1989 Troy Dunn; 1990 Garry Longney; 1991 Steve Thorn; 1992 Darren Brandenburg; 1993 Owen Dunn; 1994 Danny Fraser; 1995 Scott Fraser; 1996 Scott Fraser; 1997 Gavin Woodall; 1998 Matt Wojcicki.

Bulldogging/Steer Wrestling

1945 Frank Maynard; 1946 Dan Mahon; 1947 Tom Willoughby; 1948 Noel Bottom; 1949 Tom Willoughby; 1950 Noel Bottom; 1951 Dally Holden; 1952 Ray Crawford; 1953 Allan Bennett; 1954 Allan Bennett; 1955 Allan Bennett; 1956 Vic Gough; 1957 Peter Poole; 1958 Vic Gough; 1959 Dick White; 1960 Dick White; 1961 Doug Flanagan; 1962 Barry Gravener; 1963 Trevor Christensen; 1964 Barry Gravener; 1965 Barry Gravener; 1966 Bonny Young; 1967 Barry Gravener; 1968 Jim McGuire; 1969 Jim McGuire; 1970 Jim McGuire; 1971 Garry McPhee; 1972 Jim McGuire; 1973 Des Dessaix; 1974 Jim McGuire; 1975 John Brearley; 1976 Neville McCarthy; 1977 Scott Bloxsome; 1978 Allan Simpkin; 1979 Dudley Kearney; 1980 Neville McCarthy; 1981 Danny McGuire; 1982 Neville McCarthy; 1983 Terry Noonan; 1984 Terry Noonan; 1985 Neville McCarthy; 1986 Neville McCarthy; 1987 Neville McCarthy; 1988 Robert McPhee; 1989 Alan Simpkin; 1990 William Day; 1991 Terry Noonan; 1992 Chris Gravener; 1993 John Day; 1994 John Day; 1995 Robert McPhee; 1996 Robert MCPhee; 1997 Shane Kenny; 1998 Hugh Steggal.

Roping

1946 Tom Willoughby; 1947 Dan Crotty; 1948 Noel Bottom; 1949 Dan Crotty; 1950 Dan Crotty; 1951 Buddy Crotty; 1954 Ray Crawford; 1957 Ray Crawford; 1958 Vic Gough; 1959 Dan Crotty; 1960 Vic Gough; 1961 Ray Crawford; 1962 Ray Crawford; 1963 Bonny Young; 1964 Bonny Young; 1965 Chilla Seeney; 1966 Bonny Young; 1967 Chilla Seeney; 1968 Reg Gale; 1969 Reg Gale; 1970 Bill Hughes; 1971 Boony Young; 1972 Garry McPhee; 1973 Garry McPhee; 1974 Garry McPhee; 1975 Garry McPhee; 1976 Neville McCarthy; 1977 Scott Bloxsome; 1978 Neville McCarthy; 1979 Dudley Kearney; 1980 Neville McCarthy; 1981 Neville McCarthy; 1982 Danny McGuire; 1983 Bernie Smyth Jnr; 1984 Danny McGuire; 1985 Bernie Smyth Jnr; 1986 Neville McCarthy; 1987 Neville McCarthy; 1988 Robert McPhee; 1989 Robert McPhee; 1990 Wayne Slater; 1991 Shane Kenny; 1992 Shane Kenny; 1993 Shane Kenny; 1994 Heath Litchfield; 1995 Shane Kenny; 1996 Shane Kenny; 1997 Shane Kenny; 1998 Mark Knox.

Team Roping

1969 Aub Chadwick; 1970 Bill Hughes; 1980 Bill Hughes; 1981 Bill Hughes; 1982 Stuart McPhee; 1983 Robert McPhee; 1984 Stuart McPhee; 1985 Stuart McPhee; 1986 Stuart McPhee; 1987 John Osborne Jnr; 1988 Robert McPhee; 1989 John Osborne Jnr; 1990 Robert McPhee; 1991 Garry McPhee and David Hallam; 1992 Garry McPhee and Robert McPhee; 1993 Heath Litchfield and Alan Woodley; 1994 Garry McPhee and Robert McPhee; 1995 Heath Kimber and Wayne Slater; 1996 Garry McPhee and Robert McPhee; 1997 John Osborne Jnr and Jeff Miller; 1998 John Osborne Jnr and Jeff Miller.

Wild Cow Milking

1945 Tex Mooney; 1952 Stumpy Timmins; 1953 Allan Woods; 1954 Ray Crawford; 1955 Allan Bennett; 1956 Lindsay Black; 1957 Ray Crawford.

NATIONAL RODEO ASSOCIATION CHAMPIONS

All-Round Cowboy

1970 Barry Brandenburg; 1971 Darryl Doyle; 1972 Trevor Voll; 1973 Terry O'Neill; 1974 Norm Hilton; 1975 Norm Hilton; 1976 Doug Reid; 1977 Doug Reid; 1978 Doug Reid; 1979 Tim Kelly; 1980 Rick Seeds; 1981 John King; 1982 David Collins; 1983 Frank Green; 1984 Frank Green; 1985 Frank Green;

1986 Frank Green; 1987 Bevan Eastwell; 1988 Frank Green; 1989 Frank Green; 1990 Rick Seeds; 1991 Kevin Kasper; 1992 Mark Stevenson; 1993 Kevin Kasper; 1994 Tony McIntyre; 1995 Mark Knox; 1996 Allan Flood; 1997 Brad Cavanagh; 1998 Heath Kimber.

Saddle Bronc
1970 Barry Brandenburg; 1971 Terry O'Neill; 1972 Terry O'Neill; 1973 Terry O'Neill; 1974 Lance Slack; 1975 Norm Hilton; 1976 John Friskie; 1977 Rod Tinney; 1978 Doug Reid; 1979 Ron Beasley; 1980 Rick Seeds; 1981 Rod Tinney; 1982 David Collins; 1983 Frank Green; 1984 Frank Green; 1985 Frank Green; 1986 Frank Green; 1987 Stuart Grayson; 1988 Frank Green; 1989 Frank Green; 1990 Jason Mendez; 1991 Stuart Grayson; 1992 Ken Reid; 1993 Robert Toole; 1994 Graham Browne; 1995 Troy Welsh; 1996 Clayton Hodgetts; 1997 Ken Reid; 1998 Clint Harm.

Bareback Bronc
1970 Des Gilbey; 1971 Darryl Doyle; 1972 Trevor Voll; 1973 Trevor Voll; 1974 Graham Tanner; 1975 Doug Reid; 1976 John Friskie; 1977 John Friskie; 1978 Doug Reid; 1979 Mark Dalzeil; 1980 Rick Seeds; 1981 David Sutton; 1982 Ian Rideout; 1983 Frank Green; 1984 Frank Green; 1985 Frank Green; 1986 Frank Green; 1987 G Learoyd; 1988 Frank Green; 1989 Frank Green; 1990 Col Clem; 1991 Kevin Kasper; 1992 Mark Stevenson; 1993 Mark Stevenson; 1994 Mark Stevenson; 1995 Brett Townsend; 1996 Dene Barram; 1997 Dene Barram; 1998 Mark Stevenson.

Bullride
1970 Ted Martin; 1971 Terry O'Neill; 1972 Trevor Voll; 1973 Terry O'Neill; 1974 Norm Hilton; 1975 Norm Hilton; 1976 Mark Morgan; 1977 Ian Jorgensen; 1978 Warren Jorgensen; 1979 Mark Morgan; 1980 Stephen Wraight; 1981 Victor Beazley; 1982 Ross Weiden; 1983 Chicken Wales; 1984 Kevin Kasper; 1985 Ross Weiden; 1986 Chicken Wales; 1987 Bevan Eastwell; 1988 Darren Jenkins; 1989 Mark Kasper; 1990 Mark Brennan; 1991 Mark Brennan; 1992 Gary Johnson; 1993 Robert Kennedy; 1994 Dale Jones; 1995 Dale Jones; 1996 Jeff Johnson; 1997 Wayne Darr; 1998 Jason McKinnon.

Bulldogging/Steer Wrestling
1970 Ron Kettleton; 1971 Kerry Hall; 1972 Dave Tucker; 1973 Dave Tucker; 1974 Graham Burton; 1975 Graham Burton; 1976 Graham Burton; 1977 John Turnbull; 1978 Alan Knox; 1979 Graham Burton; 1980 Daryl Cavanagh; 1981 John Wallace; 1982 John Wallace; 1983 Daryl Cavanagh; 1984 Doc Cavanagh; 1985 Peter Gesler; 1986 Ian Allen; 1987 Brian Elliott; 1988 Brian Elliott; 1989 Michael McPhee; 1990 Michael McPhee; 1991 Alan Flood; 1992 Mark Kasper; 1993 Wayne Rougham; 1994 Tony McIntyre; 1995 Mark Kasper; 1996 Kevin Kasper; 1997 Brad Cavanagh; 1998 Mark Kasper.

Roping
1970 Ron Kettleton; 1971 Kerry Hall; 1972 Dave Tucker; 1973 Kerry Hall; 1974 Kerry Hall; 1975 Peter Oberle; 1976 Peter Oberle; 1977 Alan Knox; 1978 Bruce Ryan; 1979 Peter Oberle; 1980 Greg Gall; 1981 Wayne Ashe; 1982 Mick Duffy; 1983 Frank Green; 1984 Frank Green; 1985 Frank Green; 1986 Tony McIntyre; 1987 Bevan Eastwell; 1988 Frank Green; 1989 Frank Green; 1990 Mick Duffy; 1991 Mick Duffy; 1992 Tony McIntyre; 1993 Alan Flood; 1994 Tony McIntyre; 1995 Mark Knox; 1996 Mark Knox, 1997 Mick Duffy; 1998 Heath Kimber.

All-Round Cowgirl
1976 Yvonne Wallace; 1977 Yvonne Wallace; 1978 Cathy Kimber; 1979 Kim Setvenson; 1980 Gaye Svensson; 1981 Kim Stevenson; 1982 Yvonne Wallace; 1984 Yvonne Wallace; 1985 Yvonne Wallace; 1986 Yvonne Wallace; 1987 Lisa Jeffries; 1988 Sharon Learoyd; 1989 Vicki Gough; 1990 Vicki Gough; 1991 Debbie Armitage; 1992 Debbie Armitage; 1993 Robyn Donoghue; 1994 Brooke Frahm; 1995 Brooke Frahm; 1996 Brooke Frahm; 1997 Brooke Frahm; 1998 Brooke Frahm.

Barrel Race
1976 Yvonne Wallace; 1977 Yvonne Wallace; 1978 Yvonne Wallace; 1979 Yvonne Wallace; 1980 Gaye Svensson; 1981 Gaye Svensson; 1982 Yvonne Wallace; 1983 Yvonne Wallace; 1984 Yvonne Wallace;

1985 Yvonne Wallace; 1986 Lisa Jeffries; 1987 Lisa Jeffries; 1988 Sharon Learoyd; 1989 Sharon Learoyd; 1990 Glenys Bate; 1991 Robyn Donoghue; 1992 Robyn Donoghue; 1993 Brooke Frahm; 1994 Brooke Frahm; 1995 Brooke Frahm; 1996 Brooke Frahm; 1997 Brooke Frahm; 1998 Brooke Frahm.

Steer Undecorating
1976 Georgina Oberle; 1977 Yvonne Wallace; 1978 Yvonne Wallace; 1979 Kim Stevenson; 1980 Shelly Robertson; 1981 Kim Stevenson; 1982 Yvonne Wallace; 1984 Yvonne Wallace; 1985 Chale Stevenson; 1986 Yvonne Wallace; 1987 Jo Bate; 1988 Roxanne Beasley; 1989 Judy Gough; 1990 Roxanne Beasley; 1991 Judy Gough; 1992 Judy Gough; 1993 A.M. Hasselbach; 1994 A.M. Hasselbach; 1995 A.M. Hasselbach; 1996 A.M. Hasselbach; 1997 A.M. Hasselbach; 1998 W. Eisentrager.

Breakaway Roping
1984 Debbie Armitage; 1985 Judy Gough; 1986 Vicki Gough; 1987 Jackie Bate; 1988 Dawn Tamini; 1989 Vicki Gough; 1990 Vicki Gough; 1991 Vicki Gough; 1992 Vicki Gough; 1993 Judy Gough; 1994 Judy Gough; 1995 Lisa Dibetta; 1996 Joanne Bate; 1997 Judy Gough; 1998 Lisa Sutherland.

WOMEN'S PROFESSIONAL RODEO ASSOCIATION CHAMPIONS

All-Round Cowgirl
1973 Cheryl McPhee; 1974 Margaret Gill; 1975 Delma Sutton; 1976 Cheryl McPhee; 1977 Tracey McMartin; 1978 Tracey McMartin; 1979 Yasmin McCarthy; 1980 Yasmin McCarthy; 1981 Sharon McCarthy; 1982 Roslyn Mangan; 1983 Kim Stevenson; 1984 Kim Stevenson; 1985 Kim Clarke; 1986 Helena Pritchard; 1987 Helena Pritchard; 1988 Vicki Schiller; 1989 Vicki Schiller; 1990 Vicki Schiller; 1991 Terri Lillyman; 1992 Terri Lillyman; 1993 Terri Lillyman; 1994 Vicki Schiller; 1995 Leanne Ryder; 1996 Tania Schiller; 1997 Tania Schiller; 1998 Tania Schiller.

Barrel Race
1968 Pam Schiller; 1969 Pam Schiller; 1970 Cheryl McPhee; 1971 Cheryl McPhee; 1972 Cheryl McPhee; 1973 Cheryl McPhee; 1974 Margaret Gill; 1975 Delma Sutton; 1976 Donna Gay; 1977 Tracey McMartin; 1978 Kay Markworth; 1979 Yasmin McCarthy; 1980 Cathy Kimber; 1981 Sharon McCarthy; 1982 Roslyn Mangan; 1983 Kim Stevenson; 1984 Ruth Berg; 1985 Joanne Fisher; 1986 Helena Pritchard; 1987 Helena Pritchard; 1988 Vicki Schiller; 1989 Vicki Schiller; 1990 Vicki Schiller; 1991 Tania Schiller; 1992 Tania Schiller; 1993 Terri Lillyman; 1994 Vicki Schiller; 1995 Tania Schiller; 1996 Tania Schiller; 1997 Tania Schiller; 1998 Tania Schiller.

Steer Undecorating
1973 Rhonda Jurgens; 1974 Emma Wilson; 1975 Emma Wilson; 1976 Emma Wilson; 1977 Helena Pritchard; 1978 Emma Wilson; 1979 Helena Pritchard; 1980 Helena Pritchard; 1981 Cathy Kimber; 1982 Jacki Quince; 1983 Helena Pritchard; 1984 Kim Stevenson; 1985 Kim Clarke; 1986 Cathy Hunkin; 1987 Cathy Hunkin; 1988 Jennifer Williams; 1989 Clare Remfrey; 1990 Zoe Stork; 1991 Netta Wharton; 1992 Netta Wharton; 1993 Kerry Johnson; 1994 Jan Snelling; 1995 Jenny Jamieson; 1996 Sharon Fayers (Hi-Point); 1997 Kerry Johnson (Hi-Point); 1998 Kerry Johnson (Hi-Point).

Goat Tying
1975 Emma Wilson; 1976 Margaret McGuire; 1977 Emma Wilson; 1978 Tracey McMartin; 1979 Peta Holden; 1980 Peta Holden; 1981 Ali Smith; 1982 Ali Smith; 1983 Ali Smith; 1984 Sharon McGuire; 1985 Casey Earl.

Breakaway Roping
1981 Cathy Kimber; 1982 Gayle Devenish; 1983 Kim Stevenson; 1984 Kim Stevenson; 1985 Sharon McGuire; 1986 Netta Wharton; 1987 Netta Wharton; 1988 Vicki Gough; 1989 Helena Simpkin; 1990 Jenny Heath; 1991 Dianne Breed; 1992 Terri Lillyman; 1993 Vicki Gough; 1994 Rachel Day; 1995 Leanne Ryder; 1996 Leticia McPhee; 1997 Jo Ann Bate; 1998 Kerry Johnson.

Endnotes

Note: Most quotes in the text from interviews with the author are not given an endnote.

Foreword
1 *Australian Campdraft and Rodeo Magazine*, October 1999
2 Malouf, David, *Boyer Lecture Series*, ABC, 1999
3 Cunningham-Graham, R.B., *El Rodeo*, London, 1925, p.12

Chapter 1, Early Days
1 *The Romance of the Stockman*, Viking O'Neil, Ringwood, Victoria, 1993. (Although no author is credited, the well-known historian, R.M. Younger, provided the original material.)
2 *Macquarie Dictionary of Events*
3 *The Romance of the Stockman*, (Op. Cit.)
4 Sawrey, H., *The Stockman*
5 *Australian Rodeo and Country Music Magazine*, October 1983
6 *Hoofs and Horns Magazine*, Rural Press Magazines, Brisbane, 1945–2000

Chapter 2, Travelling Buckjump Shows
1 Ward, Russel, *The Australian Legend*, Oxford University Press, London, 1958, p.12
2 Ibid., p.178
3 St Leon, Mark V., *Index of Australian Show Movements Principally of Circus and Allied Arts, 1833–1956*, Pilot Edition, Self-Published, 1992, p. 3
4 Cannon, Judy and St Leon, Mark, *Take a Drum and Beat It: The Story of the Astonishing Ashtons 1848–1990s*, Tytherleigh Press, New South Wales, 1997
5 Slatta, Richard W., *The Cowboy Encyclopedia*, W. W. Norton and Co., New York, 1996
6 Ridgway, Jim and Lowden, Jim, *Rodeo at Lang Lang*, Lowden Publishing Co., Kilmore, Victoria, 1976, p. 8–9
7 Wirth, Philip, *The Life of Philip Wirth*, Self Published, Melbourne, Victoria, 1933, p. 49–50
8 St Leon, Mark, (Op. Cit.)
9 There were at least two individuals who took the show name 'Broncho George'
10 St Leon, Mark, (Op. Cit.)
11 Cannon, Judy and St Leon, Mark, (Op. Cit.)
12 Pollard, Jack, *The Horse Tamer*, Rigby Ltd., Melbourne, Victoria, 1978, p. 11
13 Ibid., p. 12
14 Ibid., p. 25
15 Ibid
16 Ibid., p. 26
17 *The Referee* — correspondence between Skuthorpe and Mrs Martini
18 McConville, Ray, *Thorpe McConville's Wild Australia*, Specialty Press, Albury, New South Wales
19 Pollard, Jack, (Op. Cit.) p. 99
20 Various sources, including Jack Pollard and the Skuthorpes
21 St Leon, Mark V., (Op. Cit.)
22 McConville, Ray, (Op. Cit.) p. 4
23 Pollard, Jack, (Op. Cit.) p. 23
24 Ibid., p. 42
25 McConville, Ray, (Op. Cit.)
26 Fogarty, James, 'Chronology of Circus in Australia 1847–1997' in 150th Anniversary Edition of *Pro Circus*, Underwood, Queensland, 1997
27 Pollard, Jack, (Op. Cit.) p. 97
28 Ibid., p. 106–107
29 *The Referee*

~ ENDNOTES ~

30 Sources conflict about the location
31 *Sydney Evening News*, as quoted in Pollard, Jack, *The Rough Rider*, Landsdown Press, Melbourne, 1962
32 Pollard, Jack, *The Horse Tamer*, p. 61
33 *The Referee*
34 Ibid., 14 August, 1907
35 Ibid., 1 October, 1924
36 McConville, Ray, (Op. Cit.) p. 8
37 *London Morning Leader*, May 1911
38 McConville, Ray, (Op. Cit.)
39 Ibid.; *The Sporting Globe*, 21 January 1933; Manera, Brad, (source unknown)
40 *The Sporting Globe*, 21 January, 1933
41 Hayden Murray, Australian Stockmen's Hall of Fame newsletter, December 1998
42 Ian Moffitt, Australian Stockmen's Hall of Fame newsletter, December 1998

Chapter 3, The Rope Ring and the Tent Shows

1 Pollard, Jack, *The Rough Rider*, Landsdown Press, Melbourne, 1962, p. 81–82
2 Cannon, Judy and St Leon, Mark, *Take a Drum and Beat It: The Story of the Astonishing Ashtons 1848–1900s*, Tytherleigh Press New South Wales, 1997
3 *The Hawklet*, 17 September 1925
4 *The Referee*, October 1924
5 Grills, Ivan, *The Jack Stanton Story*, Self Published, Tamworth, New South Wales, 1994
6 Slatta, Richard W., *The Cowboy Encyclopedia*, W.W. Norton and Co., New York, 1996
7 Athearn, Robert G., *The Fictional West*, University of Kansas Press, 1986, p. 177
8 Pollard Jack, *The Horse Tamer*, Rigby Ltd., Melbourne, Victoria, 1978, p. 135
9 *The Daily Mirror*, 'Historical Feature', June 6 1979
10 Bowen, Jill, *Kidman The Forgotten King* (Revised edition), Angus&Robertson, Sydney, 1995, p. 200.

Chapter 4, Bushmen's Carnivals

1 *Queensland Farmer and Grazier*, July 1989 (reprint of article originally published in *The Sunday Mail*, 1938)
2 Haydon, Haydon, *Souvenir Program of the Murrurundi Bushmen's Carnival Association Golden Jubilee Bushman's Carnival*, October 1982
3 Ibid
4 Poole, Peter, historical notes for the Stockmen's Hall of Fame
5 Townsend, Jack, *History of Quirindi*; Haydon, Hilton, (Op. Cit.)
6 Slatta, Richard W., *The Cowboy Encyclopedia*, W.W. Norton and Co., New York, 1996
7 Unidentified article lent to the author by Dan Edwards. It is a retrospective piece and gives no indication whether the word 'rodeo' was used at the time, only that it was part of the annual agricultural show
8 Ibid
9 Taken from an interview with Dan Edwards, February 1999
10 Poole, Peter, *Fifty Years of Rodeo: a Pictorial History of the Warwick Rodeo*, The Warwick District Tourist Association, 1979
11 Pollard Jack, *The Horse Tamer*, Rigby Ltd., Melbourne, Victoria, 1978, p. 63–65
12 Unidentified Queensland newspaper clipping, 6 October 1930
13 *The Townsville Daily Bulletin*, 4 July 1932
14 Ibid., 28 July 1932
15 *Rockhampton Morning Bulletin*, 16 July 1932
16 *The Townsville Daily Bulletin*, 4 July 1932
17 Ibid., 2 May 1933; oral information from Larry Dulhunty
18 'Cestus', *The Townsville Daily Bulletin*, 8 May 1934
19 Ibid

20 *Maryborough Chronicle*, 14 September 1934
21 'Cestus', *The Townsville Daily Bulletin*, 8 May 1934
22 Ibid
23 *Quirindi Advocate, Murrurundi Times* and *Werris Creek Express*, on the Murrurundi Bushmen's Carnival, 16 November 1934
24 Ibid
25 *The Townsville Daily Bulletin*, 8 May 1934
26 *The Sydney Mail*, Royal Show Number, 31 March 1937, p. 9
27 Unidentified newspaper clipping from RAS Sydney Show, circa 1935
28 Scott, Jack, *Fair Crack of the Whip*, Misosa Press, Charters Towers, Queensland, 1984
29 Information supplied by the Heritage Centre of the Royal Agricultural Society, Sydney
30 *The Sydney Mail*, Royal Show Number, 31 March 1937, p. 9
31 Bowen, Jill, *Kidman The Forgotten King* (revised edition), Angus&Robertson, Sydney, 1995
32 *Western Mail*, 28 May 1936, material provided by Hesperian Press
33 Pollard, Jack, *The Rough Rider*, Landsdown Press, Melbourne, 1962, p. 154

Chapter 5, The Dawn of Professionalism

1 In 1945 the Turtles changes their names to Rodeo Cowboys Association of America and later the Professional Rodeo Cowboys Association
2 Williams, R.M. and Ruhen, Olaf, *Beneath Whose Hand*, Pan Macmillan, Sydney, New South Wales, 1986
3 Ibid
4 Johnson, Donald Hambleton, *Horseman Bold*, Glen Rowan Cobb and Co Pty Ltd, Glenrowan, Victoria, 1995
5 Lemon, Andrea, *Rodeo Girls Go Round the Outside*, McPhee Gribble Publishing, Penguin Books, Ringwood, Victoria, 1996
6 Ibid., p. 29
7 Slatta, Richard W., *The Cowboy Encyclopaedia*, W.W. Norton and Co., New York, 1996
8 APRA *News Sheet*, September 1994
9 Statistics from 1994 APRA Fiftieth Anniversary Program

Chapter 6, The Swinging 60s

1 Poole, Peter, *Rodeo News Sheet*, September 1994
2 *Hoofs and Horns*, January 1964, p. 12
3 Ampol and Canadian-Pacific Airways World Series

Chapter 7, Rodeo Today

1 This information provided by Kendall's Birricannia Station, Western Queensland
2 Steven Keeva, article in *New Woman*, June 1994, p. 124
3 Statistics from 1994 APRA Fiftieth Anniversary Program

~ INDEX ~

Index of people's names

A
Agnew, Jack 77, 79, 126, 133
Amos, Graham 183, 199
Anderson, Ron 88, 133, 172, 173, 185
Appleton, Dave 215, 216
Arkansas Kid (George Mellor) 30, 124
Armitage, Joan 79
Armstrong, Charley 42
Armstrong, Rosemary 142
Ashton, Doug 33
Ashton, James Henry 28–29
Atkins, Jack 42, 51
Atkinson, Bud 43
Atkinson, Joe 72, 77, 84, 109, 140
Atkinson, Margaret see Gill, Margaret
Atkinson, Sis 140
Attwater, Gordon 64
Autrey, Gene 74, 147

B
Back, Dave 214
Bailey, Jim 199
Baker, Jack 'Snowy' 72, 88
Baker, Snowy 72
Baldwin, Danny 158
Baldwin, Snowy 42, 43, 48, 49
Bamblett, Neville 79, 87
Baretta 37
Bargo, Billy 79, 83, 107, 109, 124, 133, 146
Barlow, Brendon 217
Barrett, Tom 104
Beetham, Gordon 19
Beeston, H. 104
Bell, Colin 73, 84, 100, 116
Bell, Curley 63, 66, 72, 85, 88, 139
Bell, P. 126
Bello, Anthony 217
Bennett, Allan 89, 133, 157, 165, 177, 183, 213
Bennett, Enid 142, 153
Beresford, Garney 186, 194
Berry, Ross 104
Biddle, Frank 184
'Bill Bowyang' 106, 107
Birch, Nicholas 217
Birrell, 'Snowy' 104
Bischoff, Stan 175
Black, A. 109
Black, Gordon 133, 146, 158
Black, Lindsay 133, 138, 139, 145, 146, 149, 150, 151, 153, 155, 156, 158, 159, 166, 167, 170, 172, 176, 184,
Black, Frank 146, 158, 171
Blackall, Peter 196, 214
Blair, Dave 77
Blaxland, Gregory 14

Blaxland, John 14
Bloxsome, Gib 117, 123, 124, 133, 136, 194
Bloxsome, Scott 194, 197, 199, 202, 207, 210, 215
Blundell, Bessie 141
Boake, Barcroft 26, 35
Boardman, Ron 124, 126, 133, 185
Boldrewood, Rolf 26
Borghero, Graham 213
Borghero, Lance 213
Bostock, Bluey 213
Bottom, Noel 124, 126, 133, 138, 150, 177
Bougoure, Eunice 141
Bourke, Keith 'Doogie' 150, 185
Bowd, Arthur 100, 126
Bowen, Jill 84, 118
Bower, Governor 109
Boyd, William 147
Brabon, J. 107
Brady, Johnny 86, 87
Bradly, Norm
Brandenburg, Barry 195
Brandenburg, Bridgett, 207
Brandenburg, Darren 208, 217
Brando, Marlon 150
Bratby, Marge, 124, 125, 141
Brearley, John 186
Breheny, Martin see 'Martini'
Brereton, Phyllis 142
Brewster, Bob 63, 66
Bridge, Ben 42
'Broncho George' 30, 31, 43, 118, 124
Brooks, Garth 9
Buckingham, Les 183, 198
Buckley, Ben 217
'Buffalo Bill' see Cody, William F.
Bullock, Jim 21, 133
Burke, Chris 217
Burrows, John 87
'Bushman Bill' 73
Buttson 62

C
Caban, John 183, 198
Caban, Leanne 207
Caban, Lionel 183, 198
Cadell, Johnny 133, 146
Cain, Lester 156, 205
Cakebread, Graham 133, 185
Cakebread, Norm 133, 172, 185
Cakebread, Norm Jnr 185
Callinan, Jim 100
Campbell, 'Bonshaw' Bob 117, 171
Campbell, Ken 100
Canavan, Brian 133
Canavan, Greg 117, 126, 133, 134
Canavan, Terry 133

Cannon, Judy 28, 33
Cannon, Tom 158, 186
Canutt, Yakima 78
Carey, Rick 75
Carey, Thel 75
Carlton, Jack 79
Carr, Clay 78
Carr, Snowy 67
Carruthers, Margaret 87
Carter, Kid 63
Carver, Billy 42
Carver, William Frank 'Doc Carver' 29–30, 31
Cassells (Mr) 46
Castles (Mr) 48
'Cestus' 109, 110
Chalkley, Jack 83
Charlton, Jack 99
Cherokee Kid 43
Chick, Beryl see Riley, Beryl
Christensen, Charlie 133
Christensen, Tom 185, 217
Christensen, Trevor 185
Clark, R. (Mr) 46
Clarke, Brendon 217
Clarke, Darren 217
Clarke, Pat 158, 176
Clarke, Sep 100
Clarke, Marcus 26
Cleeland, Gordon 61
Clemento, Steve 78
Clollard, Harry 77
Cocking, Tommy 118
Cody, William F. 'Buffalo Bill' 29, 31, 52, 74
Coleman, Ken 'Coley' 91, 171, 182, 186, 199, 215
Collins, Beryl 142
Collins, H. 77
Conder, Charles 26
Condon, John 208
Connors, Harry 118
Cook, Alan 79, 87
Cook, Harry 61
Cooper, Gary 74
Cooper, Kevin 198
Costa, Sam 75
Cottam, Ossie 186
Cotter, Billy 87
Cowan, Les 133, 158
Cowan, Mick 63
Cowan, Les 158
Cowan, Vic 63, 66, 67, 77
'Cowboy George' 30
Crawford (Mrs) 108
Crawford, Anne 181
Crawford, Barry 'Bo' 157, 177, 178, 186, 184
Crawford, June 154, 179

★

235

Crawford, Ray 123, 138, 142, 154, 157, 165, 166, 177, 178, 179, 187, 199
Crawfords, the 186
Creasy, Art 80, 87, 164
Crisp, Mick 79
Croasdale, Audrey 87, 139, 143
Cronin, Donald, 118
Cross, K. (Mrs) 144
Crotty, Buddy 138
Crotty, Dan 86, 112, 123, 126, 133, 138, 157, 165
Crottys, the 176
Cull, Freddy 87
Cummings, Bart 1

D
Dalton, Wally 185
Daly, J.P. see Kemp, Professor
Dargin, Arthur 37
Darwin, Jim 77
Daunt, S. (Mrs) 142
Davidson, Tommy 118
Davis, Arthur 100
Dawson, Norm 185
Dawson, Smoky 75, 148
Dean, James 150
Delahunt, Jack 61, 79, 87
Delroy, Ossie 79
Dempsey, Arthur 42, 60
Dempsey, Jack 42, 46, 60, 84
Denner, Violet see Gill, Violet Snr
Denner, Jack 62
Dessaix, Des 186
Diefenbach, Darrel 213
Dix, Jim 'Digger' 139, 183, 185, 194
Dodd, Billy 61, 67
Dodge, Bob 133
Dolan, Clint 'Wombles' 213
Dollard, Mary 133 see also Young, Mick (Mrs)
Douglas, Roy 79
Doyle, Scott 217
Draper, Alec 133
Dreshler, Bonita 43, 52
Dreshler, Cleo 43, 52
Dulhunty, Larry 88, 105, 117
Duncan, Gwen see Winter, Gwen
Dunn, Owen 217
Dunn, Troy 1, 196, 205, 207, 209, 216, 217
Dusty, Slim 2, 9, 75

E
Eastwood, Clint 5
Ebzert, Frank 104
Edmunds, Charlie 77, 109, 117
Edwards, Dan 50, 62, 63, 64, 65–66, 71, 85, 100, 104, 119, 120, 122, 124, 125, 130, 131, 132, 133, 205, 212
Edwards, Ettie 44, 63
Edwards, Tommy 87

Egan, Ted 75
Elder, Pat 140, 142, 143, 144, 150, 151, 153
Evans (Mr) 46
Evans, Harry 100
Evans, Jack 118
Everett, Andy 118

F
Fahey, Buddy 75
Farber, Harry 63, 118
Farley, Paul 199
Fenton, Mick 32, 63
Fetherstonhaugh, Cuthbert 21
Fish, Brian 184
Fisher, Eddie 217
Fisher, Jim 63
Flanagan, Doug 175, 183, 186
Flanigan, Mark 217
Fletcher, Bert 42, 118
Forbes, 'Bub' 124
Foster, 'Jumbo' 77
Frame, Angus 133, 139, 213
Frame, Bob 133
Frame, Campbell 184, 206
Frame, Jack 133, 175, 176
Frame, Russel 'Rusty' 213
Francis, Bill see 'Bushman Bill'
Fraser, Donald 'Ducko' 146, 155
Fraser, Noel 184
Fraser, Richie 146, 155, 185
Fraser, Scott 217
Fuller, Fred 158
Fuller, Sam 62, 171, 172
Furphy, Joseph 26

G
Gale, Reg 178
Galloway, Rick 217
Gardner, Frank 52
George, L. 107
George, Noel 72, 85, 87
George V (King) 36, 50–51
Gibb, Mark 199
Gibson, Greg 1217
Gibson, Hoot 60, 74
Gibson, Steve 75, 216
Gilbarto 37
Gilbey, Des 195
Gill, Alice 62, 77
Gill, Brian 89–90, 157, 173, 184, 186, 213
Gill, Brian Jnr 90
Gill, Clay 184
Gill, Denna 184
Gill, Doyle 62, 75, 77, 80, 88–89, 133, 158
Gill, Eddie 90, 184
Gill, Gladys 82, 89, 90, 133, 139, 142, 150
Gill, Jack 62, 75, 77, 80, 88, 89, 90, 125, 126, 133, 135, 140, 173, 177, 184

Gill, Jackie 90
Gill, Jane 184
Gill, Jarrad 184
Gill, Jason 184
Gill, John 'Happy' 80, 89–90, 140, 173, 184, 213
Gill, Justin 90
Gill, Kitty 75, 77, 82, 89, 125, 133, 139, 142, 143, 145, 148, 150
Gill, Malcolm 90, 184
Gill, Margaret 140, 144, 145, 181
Gill, Patricia 89
Gill, Pearl 62, 77
Gill, Peter 89–90, 172, 173, 184, 185, 194, 208
Gill, Peter Jnr 184
Gill, Stan Jnr 57–58, 59, 62, 75, 77, 80, 82, 88, 89, 125, 126, 133
Gill, Stan Jnr Jnr 89
Gill, Stan Snr 57–58, 62, 64, 77, 79, 89
Gill, Sylvia 90
Gill, Vicky 89
Gill, Victor 62, 75, 77
Gill, Violet Jnr 'Tibby' 62, 77
Gill, Violet Snr 62, 64, 77, 89
Glennon (Constable) 38
Glover, Bob 87, 158
Godfrey, Dolly 'Ma Baker' see 'Ma Baker'
Gordon, Adam Lindsay 1, 26, 35, 52
Gollan, Basil 117, 126, 131, 132, 133
Gollan, Justine 139
Good, Betty see Urquhart, Betty
Gorry, Jack 109
Gottfried, Allan 133
Gough, Frances 154
Gough, Judy 207
Gough, Vic 110, 153, 154, 157, 165, 175, 176, 177, 183, 207
Gough, Vicki 207
Gough, William 'Bill' 110
Grace, Tommy 87
Graham, Ted 118
Gravener, Barry 91, 158, 174, 177, 182, 184, 186, 209, 210
Gravener, Brian 158
Gravener, Buddy 158, 184
Gray, Joe 165
Green, Frank 195
Green, Harry 99
Greenaway, Jim 195
Greenough, Alice 78
Griffith, Jo 181
Guest, Phil 185
Gunn, Wally 176

H
Hafemeister, Don 185
Haley, R.C. 20
Hall, Bert 176
Hall, Kerry 184, 195
Hammond, Constance 125

236

~ INDEX ~

Hanby, April 199
Handley, George 105
Handley, Tom 50, 62, 63–64, 65–66, 67, 71, 77, 78, 104, 109, 172
Hargreaves, Edward 25
Hargreaves, Kenny 185
Hargreaves, Noel 133
Harmston, P.G. 37
Harris, A.W. 109
Harris, 'Bushman Bill' 77, 117
Harris, Laurie 100
Harris, Timmy 86
Harrison, E. 104
Hart, William S. 74
Hassett, Charlie 48
Hawkins, Dick 133, 158
Hawkins, Jack 'Jimbo' 51, 77, 158
Hay, Jack 72, 77, 100, 109
Haydon, Alec, 116, 133, 145
Haydon, B.B. 125
Haydon, Barney 98, 100
Haydon, Fred 100
Haydon, Hilton 100
Haydon, Jim 100
Hazlett, Vic 77
Healy, Ken 91, 142, 158
Healy, Max 158
Hecksher, Tony 217
Hehir, Jack 42, 58, 63
Height, Carol 181
Height, Maurie 185
Hempenstall, George 184, 208
Henderson, Alex, 99, 100
Henderson, W. 29
Hentschke, Alan 133
Hentschke, Ron 133
Hermann, Ray 91, 199, 204, 209
Hicks, Allan 88, 184, 185
Hill, Dick 109
Hill, Sam 109
Hilton, Bill 77, 117
Hilton, Steve 201, 215
Hock, W. 67
Hocking, Bob 91, 186
Holden, Dally 133, 142, 144, 153, 154, 156, 157, 183
Holden, Norah 142, 143, 144, 153, 154, 156
Holder, Bob 165, 166
Hong, George 72, 98, 99, 100
Hoskins, George 42
Huey, John 158
Hughes, Billy 199
Hughes, Kim 201
Hulm, Neil 222
Hunt, Aub 100
Hunt, Les 100
Hunt, Terry 100, 126
Huntley, George 72, 77
Huntley, Ken 72, 75, 77, 85, 86, 88, 124, 139

Hyland, Agnes (Miss) 51, 52
Hyland, Darcy (Professor) 31, 34
J
Jack, 'Jacky Jacky' 42
Jacobsen, Kerry 185
James, Buddy 143
Jamiesons, the 133
Jamieson, Geoff 87
Jamieson, Jack 124
Jamieson, Wally 87
Jansen, Roy, 107, 109
Jansen, Vic 109
'Jasbo' (clown) 212
Jeffreys, Gina 9
Jenkins, Jessie 142
Jensen, Sam 77
Johnson, Billy 196
Johnson, Claude 79
Johnson, Dave 'Johno' 199
Johnson, Denis 214
Johnson, Don 139
Johnson, Kerry 207
Johnson, Scott 199, 217
Johnson, W.J. (Colonel) 66, 131
Johnson brothers 184
Johnston, George 14
Jonas, Billy 42, 51
Jones, Barry 178, 185
Jones, Ben 217
Jones, Beryl 143
Jones, Buck 74
Jones, Galloping 42, 62
Jones, Toby 133
Jory, Norma 139, 142
Jupp, Jimmy 135, 164
K
Kasper, Kevin 184
Kearney, Dudley 199
Keliher, Dan 217
Kelly, John 212
Kelly, Kate 44
Kelly, Lance 217
Kelly, Mike 217
Kelly, Ned 44, 52
Kelly, Peter 217
Kelly, Tommy 73, 100, 104
Kemp, 'Miss' 39, 42, 44, 48, 58, 139 see also Martini, Jane
Kemp, 'Professor' 34, 38–39, 42, 43, 46, 48, 52, 58, 59, 64, 67
Kendall, Henry 26
Kennard, Lofty 172
Kenneally, Pat 142
Kennedy, Jim 77
Kenny, Shane 177, 216, 217
Kenny, Ted 66
Kenny, Tom 186, 199
Kenyon, Mike 185, 197
Kidman, Sidney (Sir) 35, 69, 102, 118
Kimber, Heath 198
King, Charlie 109

King, Norm 77
Kirkham, Frank 102, 133
Kirkham, Harry 102, 133
Kirkham, Jack 102, 133
Knight, Kinga 135
Knight, Pete 78
Knox, Jamie 177, 204
Kong, Darryl 183, 194
L
Lacey, Ron 186
Laird, Steve 117
Lane, Ted 79
Lather, Errol 91, 140, 182, 184, 199
Lather, Kevin 91, 135, 140
Lawson, Henry 26, 52
Lawton, Fred 116, 145
Lavell, 'Jigger' 42, 46
Lax, Johnny 185
Lea, Billy 51
Lear, Stuart 173, 175, 185, 213
Lee, Bruce 100
Le Garde Twins 140
Lemon, Andrea 140, 141, 145, 181
Lennon, Dolly 63, 73–74, 79, 83, 85, 86
Lennon, Mick 73, 79, 85, 86
Leslie, George 20
Leys, Greg 217
Lidgard, Rodney 217
Lillyman, Terri see Brandenburg, Bridgett
Lincoln, Jock 176
Lindsay, Reg 2, 75, 124
Lindley, Keith 158, 174
Lloyd, Ken 186
Lloyd, Leo 73, 77
Lloyd, Ned 42, 51, 52, 66
Lloyd, Tom Snr 21, 42, 73, 77
Lock, Emily 141, 144, 145
Lockwood, Harold 61
Long, Sid 165
Lowick, Casey 217
Lucas, Frank 118
Lundholm, Lulu see Parkinson, Dianne
Lytton, Phillip 51
M
'Ma Baker' 88
MacArthur, Douglas (General) 123
Macarthur, John (Lieutenant) 13
Macfarlane, T.B. 125
Mackay, Ken 100, 131, 134, 176
Macquarie, Lachlan (Governor) 13
McAdam, Margaret see McGuire, Margaret
McAuliffe, C. 105
McAulay, Penny see Perrett, Penny
McCann, Bill 176
McCarthy, Neville 199, 200, 215
McCarthy, Sharon 199
McCarthy, Yasmin 199, 200
McColl, Stuart 77–78, 111

McConville, Alice 60
McConville, Charlie 87
McConville, Douglas 'Thorpe Jnr' 60, 77, 79, 85
McConville, John 59
McConville, Noel 87, 88
McConville, Ray 87
McConville, Stella 87
McConville, Thorpe 42, 51, 52, 57, 59–61, 62, 66, 67, 68, 70–71, 73, 77, 78–79, 85, 86, 87, 100, 101, 103, 111, 118, 139, 164, 172
McConville, Violet 70, 77
McCoy, Tim (Colonel) 74, 80
McDonald, Billy 142
McDonald, Grosvenor 116, 117, 172
McFarlane, Eileen 143
McFarlane, Frank 43, 73, 88, 140, 172
McFarlane, Iris 143
McGhee, Jim 171
McGrath, Paddy 77, 79
McGuire, Danny 178
McGuire, Jim 112, 177, 178, 179, 184, 185, 187, 199, 209, 210, 216
McGuire, Margaret 112, 179, 180, 181
McInnes, Arch 100
McInnes, Neil 100
McIvor, Tom 75
McLaughlin, Buddy 195
McLaughlin, Colleen 142
McLeod, Colin 63, 117
McLeod, Rory 20
McLeod, Tex 43, 60, 66
McMartin, Darby 185
McMartin, Elsa 181
McMartin, Tracey 181, 199
McNair, Reg 185
McNamara, Les 117, 138
McPhee, Allan 60, 63, 67, 77, 164
McPhee, Cheryl 199
McPhee, Gary 172, 184, 186, 196, 199, 208, 215, 216
McPhee, Guy 177
McPhee, Harry 64, 73, 100, 103, 116
McPhee, Jack 100
McPhee, Robert 203, 204, 205, 210
McPhee, Ron 73, 80, 100, 116
McPhee, Stuart 91, 196
McPherson, Brian 185
McTaggart, Bruce 158, 183, 186
McTaggart, Cheryl 181
McTaggart, Colin 142, 155, 158, 159, 164, 183, 186, 196, 206
McTaggart, Hilton 63, 64, 100, 104, 105, 120
McTaggart, Kevin 91, 133, 138, 139, 157, 158, 165, 176, 183, 186
McTaggart, Lou 181
McTaggart, Malcolm 158, 186
McTaggart, Max 158, 186
McTaggart, Norma 181

Mahon, Dan 123
Mahoney, Kim 142
Mailman, Lenny 146
Mailman, Wally 133, 146
Maloney, Ernie 77
Malouf, David 3
Manning, Jamie 217
Mansfield, Glen 217
Marciel, George 78
'Martini' 34, 36–37, 38, 40, 42–43, 45, 46–49, 50, 52, 60, 156
Martini, Jane 43, 49, 51, 58
see also Kemp, 'Miss'
Mary (Queen) 51
Mathrick, Graham 185
Mattei, Ray see Texas Lil
Maynard, Frank 109, 112, 124, 133, 134
Maynard, Ken 74
Mayne, Phyllis 142
Maynes, Scott 217
Meadows, 'Arizona Charlie' 31, 37
Meek, Colin 158
Melba, Nellie (Dame) 42
Mellor, George see Arkansas Kid and Broncho George
Mendis, Bill 'Queensland Bill' 73
Menzies, Robert (Sir) 84
Mexican Bill 37
Middleton, Andy 52
Miller, Harry 98
Miller, Jeff 196, 199
Miller, Joe (Colonel) 60
Miller, Max 87
Miller, Micky 87
Mills, Peter 199
Mitchell, Carl 100
Mix, Tom 60, 62, 74, 110
Montgomery (Professor) 34, 38
Mooney, Tex 86, 124, 126, 133, 134
Moore, Jimmy 109
Moore, Piebald 72
Morant, Harry 'the Breaker' 1, 26
Morgan, Glenn 199
Morgan, Mary 199
Morlan, Johnny 164
Morrissey, Jack 42, 43, 51, 52, 61, 62, 164
Morton, Dorrie 75
Morton, Tex 2, 59, 70, 75, 76, 79, 81, 82, 85, 86, 88, 89, 148, 172
Mossiter, June 142
Mottershead, Arthur 172
Moyland, Johnny 135
Mulga Bill 76
Mulga Fred 63, 77
Mulga Jack 42, 58, 63, 77
Munro, R. F. 'Roly' 98, 125
Murdoch, Keith (Sir) 132
Murray, Alf 79
Murray, Bez 87
Myers, Harry 126

N
Napier, Joe 158, 180
Naylor, Teddy 109
Neave, Alf 36, 51, 60
Neave (Miss) 51
Nelson, Kevin 88, 91
Newman, Adam 216, 217
Newman, Jason, 216
Newton, Charlie 180
Nichols, Billy 186
Noack, Margaret 143, 144
Noble, Jack 42
Noble, Milton 124, 133
Nolan, Jack 100
Norman, Greg 209
O
Oakley, Annie 29, 74, 148
O'Brian, Mick 98
O'Dell, Henry 217
Ogilvie, Will 26
O'Hearn, Jason, 217
O'Neill, Glen 199, 207, 217
Oram, Bill 109
Oram, Roy 77, 107, 109, 116
Osborne, John Jnr 196
Osborne, John Snr 195
P
Pace, Dean 217
Packer, Kerry 218
Palmer, Jack 99, 100, 116, 117
Parker, Shane 217
Parkinson, Steve 199
Parkinson, Dianne 199, 207
Parter, Cecil 155
Parter, Headly 155, 185, 209
Partridge, Colin 69
Partridge, Lem 36, 69
Paterson, A.B. 'Banjo' 26, 171
Payne, Lindsay 175
Payne, Merv 175
Pearce, Cecil 77, 84, 99, 109, 112, 116, 124
Pendergast, Jack 42, 46
Perrett, Ken 158
Perrett, Owen 77–78, 111, 112, 116, 119
Perrett, Penny 77–78, 111, 112, 116, 121, 123
Peters, Pat see Elder, Pat
Peters, Vernon 79
Phillip, Arthur (Governor) 13
Phillips, Dorrie 61, 68, 139
Phillips, Fred 61
Phillips, Harry 104
Pickett, Bill 60, 111
Pierce, Johnny 124, 126, 133, 141
Pigeon, Roy 72, 85
Pilbeam, Rex 107
Piper, Ross 185, 186, 199
Pollard, Jack 35, 37, 38, 44–45, 58, 125
Poole, Peter 151, 165, 166, 199

~ INDEX ~

Poole, Reg 75
Portley, E.J. 'Ned' 99, 143
Potter, Greg 217
Potter, Violet *see* McConville, Violet
Potts, Bluey 158
Powell, Dallas 186
Powell, Dick 29
Powell, Gus 29–30
Powell, Jack 158, 171
Purcell, J. 126
Purcell, Jim 100
Purcell, Joe 100
Purcell, Johnny 136
Purcell, Tony 100
Purcells, the 136
Purdie, Fred 175
Q
Quale, Brenda 142
Queensland Harry 42, 88
Quinlivan, Martin 165
Quinlan, Zella 135
R
Raaen, Johnny 186
Radford, Robert 27
Ralph the Mexican 30
Ramsay, Doug 82–83, 84, 85, 113, 124
Rank, Russell 87
Rawson, Henry (Sir) 47
Raynor, Joe 185
Raynor, Ron 199
Reichstein, Leo 133
Reilly, Jack (Sergeant) 124, 125, 126
Reilly, Virgil 132
Remfrey, Allan 205
Remfrey (Mrs) 181, 184
Remfrey family 184
Reynolds, Billy 77, 105
Richards, Ron 124, 133, 158
Richardson, Rupe 133
Ridgeway, Jim 102
Riley, Beryl 81, 88, 124, 125, 139, 140, 141, 142
Riley, J. 105
Ritter, Tex 75
Roberts, Johnny, 133, 135, 138, 164
Roberts, Tom 26
Robertson, Barbara 143
Robertson, St John 106, 108, 109
Rogers, John 52
Rogers, Roy 74, 147
Rogers, Will 43
Rolly Doctor 42
Russell, Colin 72
Rudd, Steele 26
Ryan, R.S. 'Dick' (Lieutenant Colonel) 123, 124
Ryder, Lian *see* Caban, Lian
S
Salman, Matt 133
Saltbush Bill 45, 60
Sawrey, Hugh 19

Sawtell (Mr) 45
Schiller, Des 181
Schiller, Pam 181
Schiller, Paul 181
Schiller, Tania 181, 198, 204, 207
Schiller, Vicki 181, 204, 207
Schmidt, R. 125
Schneider, Johnnie 78, 111, 112
Schneider, Johnnie (Mrs) 78
Scott, Bessie 112
Scott, Jack 113
Scriven, Bill 100
Seeney, Chilla 142, 149, 150, 151, 153, 157, 158, 165, 166, 167, 170, 177, 180, 184, 187, 223
Selman, Allan 29
Seymour, Harry 43
Sharpe, Vivian 182
Shield, Johnny 72
Shields, Neville 158, 165
Shirmer, Dawn 141
Shutes, Col 105
Simmes, Harry 66
Singleton, Ben 64, 100, 105
Singleton, John 199
'Sister Dorrie' 75
Skinner, Billy 118
Skinner, Dick 81, 85–86
Skinner, John 185
Skuthorpe, Jim 34, 77
Skuthorpe, Lance Jnr 69, 75–76, 77, 80–82, 83, 85–87, 124, 125, 126, 132, 133, 164
Skuthorpe, Lance Snr 'Skuey' 21, 34–36, 37, 39–40, 42–43, 44–45, 46–48, 49–50, 52, 57–59, 60, 62, 67, 68–70, 72, 73, 75–76, 77, 79, 81, 83, 84, 85–86, 89, 105, 111, 118, 124, 125, 156, 169, 172, 222
Skuthorpe, Madge 69, 77, 80
Skuthorpe, Violet Jnr 69, 75, 77, 80–82, 83, 86, 87, 125, 133, 139, 150, 164
Skuthorpe, Violet Snr 44, 69, 75, 77, 83, 89, 105, 139
Slim, Bob 216
Smith, Bert 66
Smith, Eva 109
Smith, Ruben 99, 100
Smith, Tommy 'T.J.' 1
Smyth, Bernie Snr 91, 133, 216
Smyth, Bernie Jnr 199, 216
Smyth, Tom 124, 133, 135, 164
Smythe, Jim 124
Snyder, Smoky 78
Somerville, G.C. (Colonel) 103, 105
Spann, Doug 186
Speedy, Pat 213
Stanborough, Anne 199
Stanton, Les 100
Stanton, Jack 63, 64, 72, 76, 80, 84–85, 99, 100, 133, 136, 169

Stanton, John 135, 182, 183
Stanton, Tom 199
Steele-Park, Duncan 217
Steffensen, Des 'Yogi' 178, 186
Steffenson, Lyn 178
Stevens, Keith 132
Stockdale, Lance 100
Stockholm, Frank 158
Streeton, Arthur 26
Stuart, Jim 199
Sullivan, Jack 'Coolibah' 149, 165
Sutherland (Duke of) 69
Sutton, Jack (Captain) 30
Sutton, John 212
Swift, Brian 185
T
Terry, Mick 51
Texas Jack 31, 37
Texas Lil 143, 150
Thatcher, Mark 217
Thompson, 'Snowy' 61, 66, 67
Thomson, Troy 217
Thorogood, George 9
Thorn, Steve 196
Tibbs, Casey 173
Timmins, Billy 64, 100
Timmins, Stumpy 100, 117, 123, 133, 135, 136, 157
Toohey, Bram 142, 158
Toomey, Noel 158, 186
Torenbeeck, Alwyn 158
Townsend, Ray 176
Tracey, Jack 77
Travers, Billy 79
Tribe, Aubrey 182, 183
Tribe, Shona 207
Trindall, Gerbie 100
Trott, Archie 104, 117
Tullipan, Harry 72, 109
Turner, Doug 79
Turner, Les 185
Twohill, Darcy 177, 185
U
Urquhart, Mr 38
Urquhart, Betty 140, 141, 142
V
Val, Mena (Miss) 43
Vater, Allan 133
Vickers, Norah *see* Holden, Norah
W
Wain, Joseph 89
Waite, Billy 37, 42, 46–47, 48, 51, 52
Waite, Marion (Miss) 52
Wakeman, Jack 135
Wall, Alec 72
Ward, Mick 183, 199
Ward, Russel 25
Watson, Jack 'Queensland Jack' 67, 80, 124, 164
Watson, Sam 109
Wayne, John 5, 74

Webster, Dick 133
Weekly, David 183
Weick, Bob 158
West, Jack 58
West, Johnny 82
West, Kitty *see* Gill, Kitty
West, Phillip 82
Whalen, Robert 214
Wharton, Herb 19, 146, 169
White, Deane 139
White, Dick 158, 184
White, Eileen 139, 140
White, James 108
White, Joe 42, 49
White, Les 186
Whyte, Les 158
Wiles, Reg 91, 186
Williams, Buddy 2, 75, 79, 85, 88, 148
Williams, Frank 124
Williams, Jack 43, 62, 107
Williams, Jim 116
Williams. R.M. 'Reg' or 'R.M.' 132, 137, 149, 150, 157, 165, 199
Williamson, Doug 75
Williamson, Walker 75
Willie and Waylon 9
Willoughby, Eileen 154
Willoughby, Eric 124
Willoughby, Tom 123, 124, 126, 133, 154, 157, 187
Wilson, Bill 133
Wilson, Brett 214
Wilson, Leslie Orme (Sir) 110
Winneger, Ned 78
Winning, Ernest 51
Winter, Arthur 84, 99, 100, 116, 142, 182
Winter, Gwen 100, 124, 142
Wirth, George 30
Wirth, Harry 30, 37
Wirth, Johannes 30
Wirth, John 30
Wirth, Philip 30, 63
Wiseman, Alec 100
Woodall, Gavin 217
Woodall, Ron 184
Woodbridge, Ron 117, 133
Woodhouse, Brian 186
Woods, Allan 133, 139, 144, 149, 150, 154, 156, 157, 177
Woods, Barbara 154
Woods, Bill 72, 91
Woods, Dave 79, 87, 91
Woods, Kay 154
Woods, Lexie, 154
Woods, Norm 158, 177
Woods, Robert, 154
Woods, Tommy 'Stirrup Iron Mick' 72, 91
Woods, Wally 133, 139, 153, 154, 157, 165, 173, 175, 177, 179, 182, 187, 216
Woods brothers, the 183
Wordsworth, C. 109

Y

Yates, Robin 137, 158, 165, 166, 184
Young, Bonny 175, 176, 177, 178, 184, 185, 186, 216
Young, Brian 75, 175
Young, Fred 61
Young, Mick (Mrs) 133

Picture credits

In many cases the identity of the photographer is unknown. It may be assumed that the pictures taken in the late 1940s, 50s and 60s in Queensland were the work of either John Harrison (dec) and his associates, Gordon Brown and Ray Weiden or by Fred Lang (dec).

Cover picture
Dick White rides the always spectacular 'Cloudbuster' at Carrieton, SA, 1959 — Keith Stevens/courtesy of Keith Stevens.

Section 1
Page 1 'A Buckjumper' — *Town and Country Journal* 7 July 1873, p. 728, courtesy of The State Library of Victoria; 'The Buckjumper Collared' — *The Graphic*, 1 August 1880, p. 147, courtesy of The State Library of Victoria; **Page 2** (Top) 'A Straight A-head buck' — Christmas supplement of *The Weekly Times* 18 December 1897, courtesy of The State Library of Victoria; (Bottom) 'Buckjumping Displays in Melbourne' — *Weekly Times* (Melbourne) 18 June 1904, courtesy of The State Library of Victoria; **Page 3** Ashton's circus — *Town and Country Journal* 3 May 1873, p. 56, courtesy of The Oxley Library, The State Library of Queensland; Cowboys from Wirth's Circus — Wirth family collection, courtesy of Margaret Wright and Gregory Wirth; 'Wild Australia' — McConville family collection, courtesy of John McConville; Lance Skuthorpe Snr — *The Hawklet* 13 October 1925, courtesy of The State Library of Victoria; Miss Kemp (1906) at 15 years of age — courtesy of The Oxley Library, The State Library of Queensland; Mr Martini — *The Referee* (Sydney) January 1906, courtesy of The Image Library, The State Library of New South Wales; Professor Kemp — courtesy of The Oxley Library, The State Library of Queensland; **Page 4** (clockwise from top left) Harry Farber — courtesy of Ms Imogen Fletcher, via Peter Bridge, Hesperian Press; Jack Morrissey* — courtesy of Mrs Joy Baines, via Peter Bridge, Hesperian Press; Billy Waite* — courtesy of Mrs Joy Baines, via Peter Bridge, Hesperian Press; Thorpe McConville* — courtesy of Mrs Joy Baines, via Peter Bridge, Hesperian Press; Joe Atkinson postcard — courtesy of Doug Underwood (ex-Atkinson roughrider); Cleopatra* — courtesy of Mrs Joy Baines, via Peter Bridge, Hesperian Press; Cleo and Bonita — courtesy of Mrs Joy Baines, via Peter Bridge, Hesperian Press; **Page 5** (clockwise from top left) Wild Australia programme — courtesy of Mrs Joy Baines, via Peter Bridge, Hesperian Press; Two horses and two men — the McConville family collection, courtesy of Ray McConville; 'Bobs' — courtesy of Mrs Joy Baines, via Peter Bridge, Hesperian Press; Group shot, 'On their way to the USA to work for Col Tim McCoy's "Roughriders of the World"' — photographed by Sam Hood at his Sydney studio, courtesy of The Image Library, The State Library of New South Wales; Billy Jonas in London in 1911 with 'Wild Australia' — courtesy of Mrs Joy Baines, via Peter Bridge, Hesperian Press; **Page 6** (top to bottom) Thorpe McConville — courtesy of Mrs Lola Rowe; Jack Hay's and Co — courtesy of The Image Library, The State Library of New South Wales; Ken Huntley's show — courtesy of Mrs Ellen Johnson; **Page 7** (top to bottom) Thorpe McConville's Roughriders — courtesy of Mrs Lola Rowe; Lance and Tex — courtesy of Mrs Ellen Johnson; Jack Clarris riding in his father's buckjump show — courtesy of Jack Clarris; **Page 8** (top to bottom) Flank rope at Bill Clarris's show — courtesy of Jack Clarris; Violet Skuthorpe — Fred Lang/courtesy of The Stockmen's Hall of Fame

*NB: Publicity shots for Alf Neave's 'Wild Australia', which went to England for the Coronation of King George V in 1911. (The owner, Joy Baines, is a relative of Alf Neaves.)

Section 2
Page 1 *The Sydney Mail* cover page, 8 April 1931 — courtesy of the Fairfax Photo Library and The Heritage Centre of the RAS, Sydney; **Page 2** (top to bottom) Parade at the Sydney Easter Show, 1939 — courtesy of the Fairfax Photo Library and The Heritage Centre of the RAS, Sydney (from Steve Laird's collection, donated by Mrs Leslie Bellden); Cecil Pearce — courtesy of The Heritage Centre of the RAS, Sydney (from Steve Laird's collection, donated by Mrs Leslie Bellden)

Mount St John Rodeo — *The North Queensland Register* and The Oxley Library, The State Library of Queensland; **Page 3** (top to bottom) Alec Haydon winning the 1938 Australian buckjumping championships on Arrawidgee — courtesy of John Stanton; Sydney Royal Roughriders — courtesy of John Stanton, compliments of *The Land* newspaper; Mount St John — *The North Queensland Register* and The Oxley Library, The State Library of Queensland; **Page 4** (top to bottom) Group shot, Maryborough 1934 — courtesy of Penny McAulay (nee Perrett); Stumpy Timmins, Warwick 1954 — courtesy of Colin McTaggart; Dan Crotty — courtesy of The Australian Stockmen's Hall of Fame; Three shot — courtesy of The Australian Stockmen's Hall of Fame; **Page 5** (clockwise from top left) Kitty Gill — courtesy of The Australian Stockmen's Hall of Fame; Buddy Gravener — Keith Stevens/courtesy of Buddy Gravener; Gwen Winter — courtesy of The Australian Stockmen's Hall of Fame; Enid Bennett at the Rocky Roundup 1951 — courtesy of Pat Peters (nee Elder); Pat Elder, early 1950s — courtesy of Chilla Seeney and Jan Seeney; **Page 6** (clockwise from left) Gals group shot, early 1950s — courtesy of Pat Peters (nee Elder); Wally Woods — courtesy of The Stockmen's Hall of Fame; Allan Woods rides Curio, Marrabel Rodeo, 1953 — Keith Stevens/courtesy of Keith Stevens; Vic Gough and Chilla, 1950s — courtesy of Colin McTaggart; Group shot — courtesy of Chilla Seeney and Jan Seeney; **Page 7** (clockwise from top left); Group shot — courtesy of Colin McTaggart; Lindsay Black — courtesy of The Australian Professional Rodeo Association; Group shot — John Harrison/courtesy of *The Warwick Daily News,* from the collection of Colin McTaggart; Barry Gravener on McPhee's 'Whirley Gig', Rockhampton's International Rodeo 1981 — Mike Kenyon/courtesy of the Australian Stockmen's Hall of Fame; **Page 8** (clockwise from top left) Ray Crawford — Keith Stevens/courtesy of Pat Peters; Bernie Smyth Jnr — Mike Kenyon/courtesy of the APRA collection; Neville McCarthy roping — Mike Kenyon/courtesy of the APRA collection; ARRA board of directors 1965 (L–R: Chilla Seeney (Saddle bronc), Des Steffensen (Bulldogging), Darcy Twohill (Roping), Wally Woods (President) Peter Poole (Secretary/Treasurer) Monica Mulkerin (stenographer) Robin Yates (Bullriding), Happy Gill (Vice-President), Barry Crawford (Bareback broncs), Dally Holden (Vice-President)) — John Harrison/courtesy of *The Warwick Daily News,* from the collection of the late Rex Phillot; Bullfighters at Kooralbyn Rodeo 1976 — Mike Kenyon/courtesy of Kenyon Sports Photos

Section 3
Page 1 Jim and Margaret McGuire — photographer unknown/courtesy of Margaret McAdam (nee McGuire nee Clariss); Gill Brother's poster — courtesy of Jim Fogarty (circus historian); **Page 3** Allan and Mavryn Remfrey — Jenny Hicks; **Page 4** Brian Fish — John Skinner/courtesy of the APRA. All other the photographs in this section are by official APRA photographer, Mike Kenyon (courtesy of Kenyon Sports Photos – Brisbane)

Additional illustrations
Wild Australia program X2 — courtesy of Mrs Joy Baines, via Peter Bridge, Hesperian Press; rodeo carnival advertisement from *Townsville Daily Bulletin* May 1932 — courtesy of *Townsville Daily Bulletin;* Robin Yates illustration — from the John Stanton collection, courtesy of Robin Yates; Rodeo Western belts advertisement — *Hoofs and Horns* magazine, courtesy of Rural Press; R.M. Williams Slim Fits — courtesy of R.M Williams Pty Ltd and *Hoofs and Horns* magazine (by courtesy of Rural Press); Dan Crotty saddles — *Hoofs and Horns* magazine, courtesy of Rural Press

Additional quotes
Page 11 A.B. (Banjo) Paterson, 'The Man from Snowy River', *A Tribute to The Man from Snowy River*, Angus&Robertson, Sydney, 1982; **Pages 23 and 189** Will Ogilvie, 'An 'Orsetralian Alphabet', Meredith, J. (ed.), *Breaker's Mate: Will Ogilvie in Australia*, Kangaroo Press, Kenthurst, NSW, 1996; **Page 55** Henry Lawson, 'A Word to Texas Jack', Roderick, Colin (ed.), *Henry Lawson Collected Verse Vol 1: 1885–1900*, Angus&Robertson, 1967; **Page 93** Will Ogilvie, 'The Riding of the Rebel', Meredith, J. (ed.), (Op. Cit.); **Page 127** Harry 'The Breaker' Morant, 'Who's Riding Old Harlequin Now?', Stewart D. and Keesing, N., *Australian Bush Ballads*, Angus&Robertson, 1986; **Page 161** Will Ogilvie, 'The Stockyard Liar', Meredith, J. (ed.), (Op. Cit.).